THE TANNING
OF AMERICA

THE TANNING
OF AMERICA

How Hip-hop Created a Culture That
Rewrote the Rules of the New Economy

STEVE STOUTE
with
MIM EICHLER RIVAS

GOTHAM
BOOKS

GOTHAM BOOKS
Published by Penguin Group (USA) Inc., 375 Hudson Street, New York, New York 10014, U.S.A.
Penguin Group (Canada), 90 Eglinton Avenue East, Suite 700, Toronto, Ontario M4P 2Y3, Canada
(a division of Pearson Penguin Canada Inc.); Penguin Books Ltd, 80 Strand, London WC2R 0RL,
England; Penguin Ireland, 25 St Stephen's Green, Dublin 2, Ireland (a division of Penguin Books
Ltd); Penguin Group (Australia), 250 Camberwell Road, Camberwell, Victoria 3124, Australia
(a division of Pearson Australia Group Pty Ltd); Penguin Books India Pvt Ltd, 11 Community
Centre, Panchsheel Park, New Delhi—110 017, India; Penguin Group (NZ), 67 Apollo Drive, Rose-
dale, Auckland 0632, New Zealand (a division of Pearson New Zealand Ltd); Penguin Books
(South Africa) (Pty) Ltd, 24 Sturdee Avenue, Rosebank, Johannesburg 2196, South Africa

Penguin Books Ltd, Registered Offices: 80 Strand, London WC2R 0RL, England

Published by Gotham Books, a member of Penguin Group (USA) Inc.

First printing, September 2011

10 9 8 7 6 5 4 3

LIBRARY OF CONGRESS CATALOGING-IN-PUBLICATION DATA
Stoute, Steve, 1970–
    The tanning of America : how hip-hop created a culture that rewrote the rules of the new
economy / Steve Stoute with Mim Eichler Rivas.
      p. cm.
    ISBN 978-1-59240-481-0 (hardback)
    1. Marketing—United States.   2. Hip-hop—United States.   3. Consumers—United States.
4. Rap (Music) 5. Hip-hop—Economic aspects.   6. Hip-hop—Social aspects.   I. Rivas, Mim
Eichler.   II. Title.
    HF5415.1.S76 2011
    306.1—dc22   2011004316

Printed in the United States of America

Set in Cheltenham Book

Designed by Sabrina Bowers

While the author has made every effort to provide accurate telephone numbers and Internet
addresses at the time of publication, neither the publisher nor the author assumes any responsibility for errors, or for changes that occur after publication. Further, the publisher does not
have any control over and does not assume any responsibility for author or third-party Web
sites or their content.

TO MY DAUGHTER SOPHIA . . .
May you grow up in a world without divisions
that are based on color or ethnicity, a place
where aspirations become shared realities.

CONTENTS

AUTHOR'S NOTE:
ON DEFINING UR·BAN

adj \'ər-bən\

From *Webster's*

- of, relating to, characteristic of, or constituting a city

- Latin *urbanus,* from *urbs* city. First known use: 1619

Notes for *The Tanning of America*

Prior to the 2000 census, the term ***urban*** referred to all territory, population, and housing units located in places with a population of 2,500 or more. After the 2000 census, the definition changed to incorporate a population density of at least 1,000 people per square mile.

However, in marketing speak and with everyday dialogue, the word ***urban*** has come to refer to inner city youths and is loosely associated with minorities.

As we use ***urban*** in this book, our aim is to speak to density and not to make reference to race or creed.

INTRODUCTION

Graydon Carter

It could be fair to say that Steve Stoute is one of the more noticeable figures in the recent flurry of Madison Avenue ad talismans. That's partly because he is African-American. But it's also because he still has the unfazed complexion of a baby—a baby with a mustache, mind you. He doesn't look much older than he did when I first met him almost twenty years ago. Back then, Peter Arnell, who was on his way to becoming a certifiable ad legend, used to frequent the same Italian restaurant in Greenwich Village that I did. Peter was a big fellow in those days and he would often share a table with a lot of main courses and a good-looking young kid named Steve. Steve had the sort of winning way that indicated he might be going places, and I just assumed he was Peter's assistant. A few years later, I was surprised to discover that not only was Steve not Peter's assistant, he was *his partner*. Not only that: They had just sold their marketing company for a good many millions of dollars.

In a way, if you were there, you could see it all happening in front of you. Steve was like a sponge. He wanted to know about everything and everyone. He trimmed down, got a great tailor, and even figured out how to show up for lunch on time. Beyond that, he had the passion, the curiosity, and a willingness to try anything that all successful people have. And he had enough moxie to fuel the long journey from Queens across the East River to Manhattan. For the son of hardworking immigrants from Trinidad, that is about as tough and as far a distance as you're ever going to travel in this country.

Steve founded Translation Consulting & Brand Imaging in 2004. I'm never quite sure what branding people do exactly, but I know that Steve is broadly admired for his lucrative pairings of the well known and the well made. He's fashioned himself into the host of a kind of commercial cocktail party where some of the world's biggest stars and some of the world's biggest companies couple up at just the right moment. And in advertising, as with show business or the hospitality industry, timing is everything. Steve is the architect behind Gwen Stefani and Hewlett-Packard, Justin Timberlake and McDonald's, Jay-Z and Reebok, Lady Gaga and MAC Cosmetics. The list goes on.

The Tanning of America chronicles the economics, politics, and poetry of hip-hop culture and how it propelled the rise of brands as diverse as Tommy Hilfiger, Cristal champagne, Versace, Timberland, Nordica, and Woolrich. Insofar as I have come to understand him over the years—both as a friend and as someone I just generally admire—Steve's success comes from being a master observer. He has the great adman's ability to pick up on imperceptible ripples in the culture—ripples that will in time become waves. And then he just gets on top of them and rides the big ones to glory.

\tran(t)s-'lā-shən, tranz-\

an act, process, or instance of translating: as
(a) a rendering from one language into another; also :
the product of such a rendering (b): a change to a different
substance, form, or appearance

OVERTURE:
TANNING IN TRANS·LĀ·TION

O ur story begins on a sweltering summer night in New York City—Friday, July 19, 1986, to be exact—during a sold-out show at the legendary Madison Square Garden, which some twenty thousand exuberant fans, mostly in their teens and early twenties, mainly African-American and Hispanic, had traveled from near and far to attend. For most observers of popular culture at the time, little significance would be attributed to the events of the evening, despite its being one of the first rap concerts to command the Garden. But for those fortunate enough to have been there—and those like me, then a sixteen-year-old growing up in Queens, already obsessed with hip-hop yet sadly unable to score a ticket—this night was about to take on biblical relevance in our generation's cultural DNA.

Across the five boroughs and beyond, the streets had been humming with anticipation for weeks. The Garden's promoters, however, along with the rest of the mainstream media, were apparently so disinterested in whatever this ghetto-born musical oddity was, the only advance published mention of the show appeared the day before in *The New York Times*. In a brief attempt to characterize the concert's lineup of Run-DMC, LL Cool J, and newcomer Whodini, the *Times* asserted:

> Rap music—syncopated rhymes atop electronic funk—has become a long-running rock style, in no small part due to the popularity of Joey Simmons and Darryl McDaniels, better known as Run-D.M.C. Shouting in unison or filling in each other's lines over the funk drumbeats and hard-rock guitar chords supplied by the disk jockey Jam-Master Jay, Run-D.M.C. boast about their exploits and put down others' follies. Some of their rhymes were once supplied by James Todd Smith, alias L. L. Cool J. (which stands for Ladies Love Cool James), now becoming a rap star in his own right—a cocky word-slinger who is fond of polysyllables and unexpected pauses. . . . While recent rap concerts . . . have been marred by incidents, the security force inside and outside the arena will be, a Garden spokesman said, "beefed up a lot" for the concert. Tomorrow at 8 P.M.; tickets are $17.50.

Even if the writing seems quaint by most standards, the *Times* got one thing right: The threesome—Joseph "Run" Simmons, Darryl "DMC" McDaniels, and Jason "Jam Master Jay" Mizell—were already considered titans of the small but expanding kingdom of rap. After first appearing on the scene in the spring of 1983, the trio from Hollis, Queens—not far from my neighborhood of Queens Village—had been blazing trails across urban America, gathering momentum. Three years later, Run-DMC were on their way to becoming the first true superstars of hip-hop. In terms of record sales, they were riding a meaningful wave with *Raising Hell,* their aptly named third album, released earlier that year. Dropping hit singles one after the other, the album would go on to be certified multiplatinum and, in time, would be critically hailed as a genre-defining masterpiece.

But the tale I'm here to tell is less about the music itself and more about the atomic reaction it created, a catalytic force majeure that went beyond musical boundaries and into the psyche of young America—blurring cultural and demographic

lines so permanently that it laid the foundation for a transformation I have dubbed "tanning." Hip-hop had come about in a time,
in places, and through multiple, innovative means that enabled
it to level the playing field like no other movement of pop culture,
allowing for a cultural exchange between all comers, groups of
kids who were black, white, Hispanic, Asian, you name it. Somehow this homegrown music resonated across racial and socio-
economic lines and provided a cultural connection based on
common experiences and values, and in turn it revealed a generationally shared mental complexion.

Granted, the journey of tanning—as we'll be exploring it—
didn't begin or happen solely with the advent of hip-hop. But
without a doubt the trajectory was significantly altered on July
19, 1986, at Madison Square Garden during one of the final numbers performed by Run-DMC. Unlikely? Yes. Even more unlikely,
tanning history was made that night, all because of a sneaker.

And not just any sneaker. Of course, I'm referring to that
most coveted, finest of German imports, the white shell-toed
Adidas athletic shoe with the iconic three black stripes, worn
with either no laces or, later, with fat laces and a popped tongue.
This was not only the sneaker that was part of Run-DMC's early
signature style—along with track suits, big-ass gold chains, and
black-brim fedoras—but a shoe that the trio had immortalized
in a single they proudly entitled "My Adidas."

So what exactly possessed the threesome to rap about their
love for a sneaker? A logical question with a logical answer. No,
it wasn't just how cool the shoes were or how even more f**kin'
cool it was to wear them without laces, at the same time that you
kept them blindingly white, spit-polished, tissue paper stuffed
inside when you weren't wearing them to make sure not a wrinkle or a blemish ever marred the virgin leather. But the coolness
of owning and wearing an elite brand that informed the owner's identity wasn't what inspired the song. As it turns out, the
idea had come from none other than Russell Simmons, hip-hop
impresario, founder of Rush Management and cofounder of Def
Jam Records—not to mention Run-DMC's manager and Run's big
brother. According to lore, Russell had glanced at Joey's sneakers

one day and had thrown the suggestion out to the group, saying something like, "You should make a record about all the places where your sneakers have been."

The concept, as I understand it, was to tell a story about their shoes as a metaphor for how far they'd traveled already, coming basically from nowhere along a path that was leading onto the largest, grandest stages of the world. Case in point: In 1985 Run-DMC was the only rap group invited to participate in Live Aid, the first-ever intercontinental telethon rock extravaganza, a fund-raiser to end starvation in Africa, starring marquee artists Sting, U2, Sir Paul McCartney, the Who, Madonna, Bob Dylan, and Led Zeppelin. Hence the lyrics: "*My Adidas walk through concert doors and roam all over coliseum floors / I stepped onstage, at Live Aid / All the people played and the POOR got paid . . .*"

Released as the B-side to the megahit "Peter Piper"—a medley of nursery rhymes in rap—"My Adidas" didn't do much out of the box. That is, at first. Then something happened and suddenly it began to appeal and sell to consumers from zip codes where rap wasn't even on the radio, much less being stocked in the record stores. Suburban, white zip codes. Where before black-bred music that went on to appeal to the masses was known to cross over, moving from R&B to pop charts, records like "My Adidas" were beginning to hint that hip-hop (a term intended to refer to the music and the urban youth culture surrounding it) was different. Instead of adapting to the mainstream, it was causing something along the lines of a reverse crossover. Hip-hop was an invitation to join in the cool it embodied. It often required the audience to come to it, to travel beyond borders just to buy the records, to walk in somebody else's shoes. And meanwhile, with those buying patterns changing, with concert-goers arriving at shows sporting their own Adidas sneakers, Russell and the rest of Rush Management recognized immediately that the modest hit had sparked a fashion trend.

A risky plan came together to take advantage of that trend at Madison Square Garden. Not knowing how it would play out, Russell and his team convinced Adidas executives to fly over from Germany for the show. What specifically was said to get them to make the trip—not to mention attend a rap concert populated by a constituency not aligned with their brand—I don't know. What I can report is that in the mid-eighties, after dominating the world's sports shoe market for decades, Adidas was struggling.

Adi Dassler, the company's founder—who had spent sixty years putting Adidas at the front of the pack and who, early on, was the first to sign an African-American, Jesse Owens, to an endorsement deal—had passed away some years earlier. Internationally, elite athletes and soccer enthusiasts could still be counted in the Adidas camp. But in the United States, at a time when Nike was making its first couple billion with Michael Jordan and when Reebok was still raking in sales (thanks to the aerobics craze), Adidas was facing extinction. In fact, together Nike and Reebok controlled half the North American athletic footwear market, while Adidas was down to 3 percent of U.S. sneaker sales. Given the landscape, the decision makers at Adidas apparently figured they had nothing to lose by attending the concert, and even opted to send Angelo Anastasio, their head of marketing, along with an entourage of company heavyweights, across the Atlantic to see what was going down.

Up until the moment of truth when Run began to chant the first line of "My Adidas," Russell and his people had to have been holding their breath. In other venues, the crowd reactions had been so ecstatic that there was no reason to expect this audience would be any different. But then again, this was Madison Square Garden, New York City, where concertgoers were unpredictable, even mercurial. So it was only when Run and DMC, backed by Jam Master Jay's spinning turntables, roared into the first verse and the crowd immediately chimed in, full-throated— twenty thousand strong—that they knew the Adidas guys would be wowed. Nothing could have prepared them, however, for what happened next.

As if driven by the fervor of the crowd, suddenly Run reached down and removed one of his shoes, rapping out its name in the singular—"My Adida!"—and held it high over his head, like a warrior holding up his blade for all to see. Egging the audience on, Run and the others dared them to respond. And they did. On cue, as hoped for, they all reached down to remove one of their sneakers and then held it in their hands above their heads, so that it looked like a pulsating sea of the black triple-striped Adidas emblem on white leather waving in unison over the heads of everyone at Madison Square Garden.

In the ensuing years, accounts of the events that followed took on mythical proportions. Though the details I'd hear as my career evolved would vary—what was said and by whom, when it was proposed, how much was offered—the central fact of the matter is that when the Adidas executives witnessed twenty thousand young urban fans jubilantly holding their brand aloft, they immediately saw the incredible economic potential that this new, raw form of entertainment possessed. Besides the vision of Russell Simmons and company in anticipating this reaction, I have to acknowledge how far ahead of his time Angelo Anastasio was. An Italian in his thirties, Anastasio would have been foolish to think Run-DMC in any way resembled the all-American mainstream images that global companies yearned to associate with their brands. But by all accounts, the cultural revelation that night at the Garden was as akin to a religious conversion as anything the Adidas brass had ever experienced.

According to Run (a.k.a. Reverend Run in later decades), the instant he walked offstage, one of the executives took him in hand and announced he was going to be given his own Adidas line. In a move that was completely unprecedented in the annals of marketing history, Adidas went on to negotiate an endorsement deal with Run-DMC to promote the company's sneakers, the threesome's own signature products, and an array of accessories. At upward of 1.5 million dollars, the deal made the rappers the first-ever nonathletes to become the international standard-bearers for what had theretofore been strictly marketed as an athletic shoe. The deal also transformed the fortunes of Adidas Group AG, bringing them back from the brink of marketplace irrelevance and infusing their brand with the unbridled energy and electromagnetic cool of urban youth, all of which translated into a quantum boost in revenue too.

This translation—a convergence between two entities from totally dissimilar, distinct cultural galaxies—was a foreshadowing of greater magic still to come. Not only did it school hip-hop artists and their promoters as to the opportunities to be seized in the cosmos of corporate marketing, but it was also an even bigger eye-opener for the corporate marketers. That said, I don't think anyone knew what the alignment of the two forces that had officially commenced that July of 1986 was going to do to accelerate the tanning effect and alter the landscape of America—racially, socially, politically, and especially economically. It's even more doubtful that anyone envisioned the extent to which hip-hop would take root—as a culture and a mind-set—for the younger generations it drew into its fold, becoming a way of life and, moreover, for all intents and purposes a religion.

As for me, it wasn't until November 2008—more than two decades after Run-DMC blasted off into pop culture history in their sneakers—that I grasped the personal significance of the momentous concert at Madison Square Garden. The relevance to my life and career finally dawned on me in the midst of a very memorable occasion—on November 18, 2008, to be precise—during a gala luncheon at Cipriani in midtown Manhattan where I was being inducted into the American Advertising Federation's Hall of Achievement. As I sat at a table surrounded by some of my most important influences—including my parents—it occurred to me that if not for the wheels set into motion by "My Adidas," I might not have been sitting there at all.

At thirty-eight years old, as a relative newcomer to the advertising business, I was more surprised by the honor than just about anyone—that is, maybe, except for my father. After watching me switch in and out of five different colleges (without graduating) and try my hand at a series of occupations, he had every reason to think that I was never going to settle into a career.

Nothing had really changed his mind during the 1990s. Those were the years of my twenties, when I was working my way up in the music business. After starting out as a roadie-turned-road-manager for the rap duo Kid 'n Play, I launched my own company as an artists' manager and producer, overseeing the careers of artists like Nas and Mary J. Blige, before going on to head up a record division at Sony Records and ultimately being made president of urban music at Interscope/Geffen/A&M Records. The universe of hip-hop was expanding exponentially in those days and for me it was like being at the forefront of the action when the wild, wild west was won—while being in the mix with everyone from Jay-Z to Sean "Puffy" Combs, from Mariah Carey and Will Smith to Dr. Dre and Eminem, to name a few.

For the Queens teenager in me who grew up taping rap music on pirate radio at two in the morning, to have risen to the heights of the music industry as an executive, not even thirty years old, with a Grammy and an American Music Award as icing on the cake, I was living a dream come true. Not that it was all glory. From without and within, obstacles abounded.

Even in these big boom years for hip-hop, most of the major record labels had no idea how to market the music, much less understand the culture. Many powerbrokers—like the head of the record label at Sony, Don Ienner, who was known to have dropped both Alicia Keys and 50 Cent from their first label—seemed to uphold the status quo that continued to view black music, in general, as appealing mainly to African-American audiences; rap continued to be seen by the industry as viable only with a subgroup of that niche demographic. As a result, for much of the nineties, getting radio play and music videos on TV had been a daily battle royale.

But against the odds and sometimes in spite of itself, rap and hip-hop culture couldn't and wouldn't be stopped. Incredibly, by the end of 1999 it was determined that rap music had outsold country music for the year. Crazy! The craziest part wasn't just the sales figures but where they were being generated: in those illogical zip codes in places like Orem, Utah, and Kennebunkport, Maine; in rural outposts and on Ivy League campuses; in suburbs and inner cities alike.

How was this possible? In short: It was the phenomenon that's at the center of this book, *The Tanning of America*. The cultural explosion occurring mainly under the radar made me wonder if there was some kind of millennial mind meld happening. Were younger generations disproving the conventional wisdom that was running corporate America and Madison Avenue? To unravel those questions and others, I decided to leave the music business at the top of my game and go in search of answers in a radically different direction—in the advertising world. As an outsider, this meant I would have to start at the bottom of the ladder in an industry that was driven by baby boomers, many stuck in mind-sets from yesteryear, none eager to give up the keys to the car. But there was also a new developing arena within the ad business, what has been called branded or entertainment marketing, that provided an opportunity for me to have a hand in its evolution. That's when the story of "My Adidas" and Run-DMC began to resonate.

Clearly, cultural tremors of the magnitude that were being generated in hip-hop's early glory days had caused changes in commerce—currents that had spread over time and were starting to cause seismic shifts in consciousness. So the convergence back in July 1986 wasn't a fluke or chance meeting. It was a mirror for what was happening on a broader scale in urban America and beyond, revealing how rap was a litmus test for where youth culture was going, and how a savvy marketer from Europe picked up on the cues—doing so in ways that much of Madison Avenue and corporate America hadn't yet figured out. (And many still haven't.)

That was the kind of mirror I wanted to hold up. Which, I should add, still didn't convince my father that I had a real job. Try telling your parents that you make your living by translating cultural cues to Fortune 500 companies and helping them communicate more effectively with consumers. After partnering with advertising veteran Peter Arnell for a couple of years before our company was sold, I went on to launch my own agency—with the collaboration of some of the most brilliant individuals I've ever met. Our team comes from not only a mix of business worlds (including marketing, music, and media) but also a multigenerational, multiethnic mix of backgrounds: a literal representation of global tanning.

From the start, I recognized that the countercultural nature of hip-hop didn't lend itself to being packaged or regimented in the way that advertising campaigns run by corporate America move. But I also knew that there was a natural meeting place for the two. Uncommon bedfellows? No question. But they also each have something the other needs. My role was to be the conduit—the bridge. And so that was the thinking behind the name, *Translation,* that I chose for my company and to describe what we do.

As a kind of pop culture anthropologist, what I also do is help clients find relevant ways to reinvigorate their brand—whether, as a few examples, it's McDonald's, Target, Estée Lauder, Hewlett-Packard, Wrigley, Tommy Hilfiger, Verizon, State Farm, Samsung, a shoe company or two, or a host of public and philanthropic organizations. In a time of economic upheaval the likes of which we've been living through in recent years, marketers' connecting meaningfully to the new young consumer—the single most powerful purchasing force ever measured, who is currently driving the global marketplace—is a life-and-death brand survival act. This too has to do with translating. No, not in sending messages to be crammed down the throats of consumers, but in extending an invitation, communicating it with nuance and cool.

Others have pointed out, and I agree, that marketing must evolve beyond the monologue, to dialogue and to megalogue. No longer can advertising lecture or dictate to customers; interaction and exchange are vital. Add to that the social networking media and technology that the millennials have understood since nursery school, and it means that marketing to the group conversation—the megalogue—must be seamlessly incorporated.

Translated, this has required a thorough housecleaning of the old demographic boxes—for example, the "black 18 to 24" box that you mark differently from the "white 18 to 24"—along with questioning worn-out assumptions about who *wants* what and why and, more importantly nowadays, who *needs* what and why. It requires an authentic, vibrant, hip, and, at times, reinvented means of storytelling—and a rejection of yesterday's rules. Why not, for instance, start with a hip-hop/pop superstar, produce a hit single by said artist, and invite millions of consumers to *pay* for it, to sing the words, and to dance to its beat in clubs and dance halls? With the stage thus set, why not then reveal in a similarly contagious upbeat commercial that it's a jingle—and blow everyone's mind? Translation has done it on more than a few occasions for blue-chip institutional brands, only as one element in multitiered campaign strategies. We employed the work of fashion's modern godfather, Valentino, to showcase Samsung products—marrying the timeless art of fashion with the immediate cool of cutting-edge technology, all in the middle of a New

York City street. We conceived and launched new brands for the likes of Reebok, attaching them to signature lines based on the tastes of global hip-hop icons, transforming images stuck back in the day into ones being given a street pass.

Reflecting the changes in attitudes influenced by tanning, we celebrate the clash of cultures and generations in mash-ups that bring together often the least likely pairings from the worlds of sports and pop culture. A musical remix for General Motors with artists that run the gamut from hip-hop to rock to country. A McDonald's Super Bowl spot putting together multigenerational basketball icons like Larry Bird and LeBron James. A campaign making Gwen Stefani/Hewlett-Packard relevant to mothers with cameras. Making a connection in values to black audiences and communities of color for Disney's film *The Princess and the Frog* by aligning it with the most genuinely natural beauty line on the market to lend credibility to their first African-American princess franchise!

What I do for a living also involves assisting clients, the public at large, and my own team to find comfort in the discomfort of going where we have feared to tread before. This has involved representing the core values of artists while grooming them as entrepreneurs and philanthropists, and on the flip side bringing the worldwide creative directors of brands such as Gucci and Crest toothpaste physically into the inner city. It has involved having a voice in diverse media and educational forums to promote the need for seeking the same fluency in the boardroom as on the street. Comfort in discomfort.

At Cipriani on November 18, 2008, it was with great pride that I accepted the induction honor and, standing at the podium, was able to confirm to Dad, "Yes, I really do have a job." No one present that day was any prouder than him, except maybe my mom.

Up until that moment, I had continued to feel like an outsider in the advertising world. That wasn't necessarily a bad thing either, if the goal is bringing fresh insights to the table. But that day there was no denying a new sense of belonging. And I realized then that it wasn't just about me or about the convergence of the worlds of hip-hop and mainstream marketing that had lit a spark with "My Adidas" and had been a magic charm for my career. It was about the positive, powerful potential of urban youth culture, which, when harnessed properly, managed to bring disparate groups of people together in ways that the combined energies of previous generations could not.

Lest there be any question about that proposition, I only had to think of how the planet had shifted on its axis a mere two weeks earlier with the 2008 presidential election. To my parents, their generation, and the generations before them who had marched for freedom and equality, this was crossing the river Jordan into the Promised Land—the end of the struggle. To us, generations raised post–baby boom and post–civil rights, it was the first true flexing of our political muscle—a beginning. The playing field had been leveled for everyone—black, white, brown, yellow, red, blue, green, rich, poor, educated or not, those with access and those without. For many who had never believed it possible, this was the first time they could honestly say, "Hey, you know what, maybe *I* can be president."

Here's how Jay-Z put it, calling out to the legions, asking first, "*Roc nation, what up?*" and then going on to answer:

My president is black
In fact he's half-white
So even in a racist mind
He's half right
If u have a racist mind, u be aight
My president is black
But his house is all white
Rosa Parks sat so Martin Luther could walk
Martin Luther walked so Barack Obama could run
Barack Obama ran so all the children could fly.

So there I was, twelve days after the election, at Cipriani, where I was celebrating a personal career highlight and a historical pinnacle for our country, when the dots connected for me that became the outline for this book. The premise was suddenly simple. If you stuck a pin in a place in time, not long after the dawn of the 1970s in the Bronx—where hip-hop would have its official birthplace in a rec room at 1520 Sedgwick Avenue—you could draw a direct line from that location to 1600 Pennsylvania Avenue, where President Barack Obama took up residence almost forty years later. It's a journey that would have never been completed without the adhesive of youth culture and its embrace of a mind-set inclusive of racial diversity—a phenomenon wrought by the tanning of America.

One of the complications in understanding how such a cultural revolution is propelled is that as it gathers individuals from different backgrounds into a more like-minded stratum, at the same time there is an equal and opposite reaction causing pushback and opposition to change. For that reason, I recognize that not everyone believes that what I have identified as tanning is actually happening or that there is this new mental melting pot that impacts all of us. And that is one of the main purposes I have in writing this book.

For anyone at any level of commerce, from corporate execs to aspiring entrepreneurs, from marketing directors to college students who will soon be entering the working world, this is therefore a cautionary tale: Ignore the globalization of popular culture at your own peril. Just as I believe passionately in pointing out there is such a thing as tanning that matters for marketing, I also think it is to the benefit of every sector of society to learn how we can better communicate with one another—which involves understanding code and learning to speak the language of tanning, which is not static and written in stone but is continually, rapidly evolving. From the point of view of sheer economics, this fluency is not only necessary for knowing and connecting to today's younger consumer (without losing existing, core consumers), it's all the more important for the generations who could be pulling the levers on the forces shaping the global marketplace.

My hope is that the audience for this book is as inclusive as the generation most influenced by the tanning process. You don't have to be a teen or tween or in your early twenties to take part in a culture that has gotten rid of segments ruled by color. Tan really has no age. And cool really is a state of mind. At the same time, *The Tanning of America* is more than a chronicle of how we arrived at where we are. I also want it to be a coming-out party for those of you in the generation stepping into adulthood in the new millennium who've grown up without the cultural stereotypes of the past. Putting myself in your shoes, I imagine that it would be empowering to have someone open the world's eyes to my generation's way of thinking, my generation's capacities that contrast with those of other generations—those dinosaurs who see society in columns and who hold on to beliefs bound by compartmentalized ways and behaviors.

Because I come out of the hip-hop generation and have the unique dual perspective of having worked in the music industry and in advertising, I have had a chance to both observe the cultural revolution of tanning and experience it. What I don't want to see happen is that we ignore its hybrid-power properties or that it goes by the wayside as disposable history or that credit isn't given to our generation and the next ones. We're the ones who will need to grapple with how to keep the American dream alive and well in our time—the dream that is still intrinsic to popular culture, our number one most profitable national export.

My ultimate goal in writing *The Tanning of America* is to put an end, once and for all, to the boxing of individuals based on color. From a marketing standpoint, yes, I understand why the interests of an age group like 25 to 34 might be different from those of the 62 to 75 group. But color is no longer a determining factor in how people think. Run DMC and "My Adidas" proved that. The fact that the music, the language, the style, and even the belief system of hip-hop culture have gone global, spurring the next wave of tanning around the world, also proves it.

Oh, and I want to add that, yes, by pointing out that there is a belief system I am arguing that hip-hop has taken on the attributes of a religion. Not a name-brand religion practiced as such or one that's rooted in existing religious orders. But I do want to argue that a mentality that embraces all colors is godly. I also will argue that hip-hop can be seen as having the same markers that occur with all major religions—among them a connection to community, a connection to spirit through personal experience (in the music itself), a coherent doctrine and morality, code, ritual, an organization and hierarchy, and a mythology featuring heroes and leaders. History matters too, especially in the telling of how hip-hop rose up from urban ashes to elevate and empower its adherents in much the same way that the most enduring religions throughout history have come about.

If this point seems incongruous with some of the more sensational, more destructive aspects of rap music, I would further argue that those characteristics are not representative of the core values of the movement. While it is true that religion is only one component of culture—along with other connectors that include ethnicity, geography, customs, arts, language, legends, and lifestyle—I believe that the essence of the culture is what it provides that is meaningful to people's lives. At its best, a religion does that. At its best, hip-hop can too. Tanning shows us the way.

Because there is a parallel in the chronology of my career path and the three stages of the journey of tanning, I've personalized my experience of the phenomenon with my own stories and anecdotes. Also included are insights from several leading pop culture influences and marketing thought leaders who were willing to come along for the ride. In part 1 (which covers the seventies to the nineties) we'll gain an understanding of how tanning happened and how economic rules began to be rewritten. In part 2 (the nineties to the early 2000s) I'll report the lessons learned in the field from harnessing the unruly power of urban culture and its iconic representatives (stars and consumers alike). And in part 3 (2008 on) we'll explore where we're headed next in terms of shifting political, cultural, and economic crosscurrents, given the globalization of tanning.

No matter how far I've traveled in miles and time away from where I came from, it's never failed to amaze me how the spread of urban youth culture has outpaced me. A few years ago I decided to go on a vacation that would let me leave modern civilization and the fast pace of daily life behind. So I booked a trip that would take me through the French countryside. In a tiny village outside of Aix that was built in the 1700s I stayed at a beautiful hotel, Le Columne d'Or, with a restaurant known for the famous artists—Picasso and Matisse—who used to frequent it and who left behind masterpieces they actually painted on the walls. Walking through the village the first morning there, I was enjoying the charming narrow cobblestone streets and the shops carved out of stone when I came around a bend and, lo and behold, arrived face-to-face with a jewelry store that had its name emblazoned on its awning: BLING.

I laughed out loud. As the saying goes, wherever you go, there you are. The world is smaller all the time. *Bling*. Universal. Timeless. That's how far hip-hop culture had infiltrated, through the process of codification, conveyed via a language and infrastructure built on the same pillars that create governments and religious institutions and global economies. Because Madison Avenue and others in corporate America were late to understand the code, youth culture got to call the shots and shape the game. We could then say to those who missed out: *You could get it, but you didn't want it. I couldn't get it, so I took it. We're in the same place. Tanning.*

PART ONE

HOW TANNING HAPPENED

(cod·i·fi·cā tion)
[*kod*-uh-fi-**kay**-shun]

(a) the act, process, or result of arranging in a systematic form or code (b) the act, process, or result of stating the rules and principles applicable in a given legal order to one or more broad areas of life in this form of a code.

CHAPTER 1

WALK THIS WAY

Most cultural movements that go on to have staying power begin in the grass roots. They may appear to come about by accident and more or less spontaneously. But more often than not there is an underlying need that summons the energy required to build a movement. As anyone who was around in hip-hop's formative years can tell you, it was born from the need to know how to rock a party. Plain and simple. That's how tanning really was propelled. And before the terms "hip-hop" or "rap" officially existed, that's what a handful of resourceful individuals understood and did to get the whole ball rolling.

We're talking generally about the year 1970—the same year, by the way, that I was born. But it wasn't until I was nine years old, late in 1979, that I even heard the words "hip" and "hop" strung together or was able to grasp the notion of what being a rapper actually meant. That was when, fatefully, I heard a record that changed my life (and pop culture) forever.

Like it's yesterday, I can still remember that moment over at my aunt's home in Brooklyn—where it seemed there was always a party under way with relatives and neighbors hanging out, a great spread of food, and new, hot music on the record player. Most stereo systems in those days could be adapted for the single two-sided records that were smaller and had the big hole in the middle (45 RPM) as well as the bigger records with the small holes (33⅓ RPM)—which were the full albums that had several songs on each side.

But as the intro plays to what I recognize as "Good Times" by the group Chic and I'm drawn into the living room because it's a familiar hit song from the previous summer, I encounter a record on the turntable that defies categorization. Instead of the sweet female lead vocals of that disco smash, I hear something totally different and spot a baby-blue label on the black vinyl record I've never seen before. Even though it's a twelve-inch disc, the size of an album, as I listen to the rhyming words being spoken— *"Singin' on 'n' 'n' on 'n' on / The beat don't stop until the break of dawn / Singin' on 'n' 'n' on 'n' on on 'n' on / Like a hot buttered a pop da pop da pop dibbie dibbie pop da pop pop / Ya don't dare stop"*—it hits me that this entire side is one long song.

Almost fifteen minutes long as it turns out. Or, to be exact, fourteen minutes and thirty-six seconds of pure fun laid over the thumping bass beat from the break of "Good Times" with sing-along words easy to remember and repeat. The record, I discover, is by an unknown group, the Sugarhill Gang, and is called "Rapper's Delight."

From then on, nobody ever has to tell me what rap is. It's whatever words are spoken, chanted, or talk-sung, or whatever philosophies, stories, or ideas are espoused, by the house party Master of Ceremonies (the emcee, also known as the MC). Halfway through this first hearing I'm hooked and start playing the song over and over again until I have it memorized, beginning with the invitation to the party that needs no translation: *"I said a hip hop the hippie the hippie to the hip hip hop / A you don't stop / The rock it to the bang bang boogie / Say up jumped the boogie to the rhythm of the boogie, the beat."*

Hip hop? There it was. For most of us this was the first general public outing of the hybrid word. People disagree about who exactly coined the term but most sources cite Lovebug Starski as the DJ/MC who, in the early seventies, started referring to the house party scene as cultivating a *hip-hop* culture. Kids would bring their boom boxes or a DJ would show up with his gear and the party could rock. "Rapper's Delight" used music that was already in the vernacular (the familiar "Good Times" by Chic) and added new ingredients in the form of spoken-word lyrics made out of fresh expressions. Code. Even if you didn't know what a "*sucka MC*" or a "*fly girl*" was, or how a rhyme could be "*vicious*," "Rapper's Delight" put the language into context and passed the expressions along.

What I loved at nine years old was how the lyrics were really funny nursery rhymes, easy to memorize and repeat. Phrases like "*Hotel, motel, Holiday Inn*" just stuck in your brain, as did the humor of rhyming "*hands in the air*" with "*shake your derriere*" or getting sick "*from food you ate*" and running to the store "*for a bottle of Kaopectate.*" There was no real social protest. Rap wasn't there yet. But there was already an authenticity in a brand being shouted out. And the situations were ones that even I at age nine had experienced: "*Have you ever went over to a friend's house to eat and the food just ain't no good? / I mean the macaroni's soggy the peas are mushed and the chicken tastes like wood . . .*" On top of all that, it was exciting to think that you could be part of a crew, have a record, just from making up poetry and chanting about stuff that happened all the time. That was fly, seriously fly.

Obviously, I wasn't the only one who thought so. Within a few weeks, it seemed like every kid in Queens had memorized the words to "Rapper's Delight"—no easy feat for a song that had no bridge or hook—and we would hold battles to see who could recite it from the top without messing up. We were extending our own breaks on the playground or after school, using a popular record to bring fun and meaning into our lives.

However, as I noticed at my aunt's house in Brooklyn, not everybody dug the free-form storytelling and irreverent rhyming. Made no sense. After all, if you listened to the words, you'd hear that the invite was to come one and come all: "*I like to say hello / To the black, to the white, the red, and the brown, the purple and yellow.*" If Sugarhill was shouting out all colors, it would follow that all generations were welcome too.

Maybe, I concluded, there was some frequency level coming from this record that could only be appreciated by the young and the hip and would otherwise fall on deaf older ears, the way a dog whistle can only be heard by canine ears. No doubt this must have been the same reaction older generations had when soul singers like Ray Charles and Sam Cooke started taking music out of the church, or earlier when Charlie Parker and Miles Davis broke from the standards of big-band jazz to bend notes and clash chords.

In the days and weeks and months that followed, with "Rapper's Delight" exploding onto the scene, blasting out of boom boxes, car radios, and record stores, pumping out of windows onto the streets, the generational gap showed itself in the marketplace. Before long, the dog-whistle effect had permeated barriers of color and geography and transformed one of the first-ever rap records from a word-of-mouth success to certified gold. After hitting number four on the R&B list and as high as number thirty-six on the pop list, "Rapper's Delight" became an anthem for a changing era. It was buoyed by the outdoor fitness craze starting up, including skate and surf culture, along with a growing market for cassette tapes instead of records, and the advent of the Sony Walkman and other personal listening devices. Soon folks of all backgrounds in the cities and suburbs of America were on the move like never before, rocking their own parties and heading into the uncharted waters of the 1980s. The Sugarhill Gang had lit a tanning spark.

Ironically—and this is not the only part of the story that is ironic—the three MCs were newcomers who had only performed together as a crew for the first time on the same day as the actual recording session. To explain how that turned out as well as it did, some background is in order.

Rules of Aspiration

Whenever we revisit history or examine the forces that launched a cultural movement, we naturally speak of the heroes who led the way. So the question of who invented hip-hop is in order. But the question to ask first should not be *who* so much as *what* invented this culture. And that answer, easily, bluntly, is the force of aspiration. It's the power that turns nothing into something, that creates worlds and paves destinies, and changes the have-nots into the have-somes and occasionally the have-it-alls. Without it, I should add, the field of marketing would become obsolete. Aspiration. It's a mix of desire, hope, imagination, creativity, fearlessness, and a few other ingredients, among which last but not least is belief—specifically, a belief that whatever it is that's the focus of the aspiration is obtainable.

In the late sixties and early seventies, when hip-hop was gestating in pockets of activity scattered around New York's inner city—with the Bronx at the epicenter—the house party scene had elements that were definitely aspirational. By that I mean if you were network-connected, hooked up to the right people who were at the forefront of seeing who could rock the best parties, that would set you apart, lend you stature, and give you a local calling card. With concerts, clubs, dance halls, and discos propelling existing musical genres into the mainstream, another function of the house parties was to create the newest counterculture. It had aspects of being an underground society, accessible to younger generations in communities of color who couldn't get into those other venues because of age or disinterest or racial barriers or inability to pay cover charges and afford the nicer clothes those venues required.

Youthful rebellion that had fueled movements of the sixties and earlier could have an outlet now as part of the house party counterculture—much like the punk rock scene that was starting up in European cities. Not surprisingly, this was the same steam being vented in the breakout days of ghetto graffiti—known as "writing" and sometimes "tagging"—that revealed another aspect of the aspiration to go against the grain, to gain credibility for having something to say, for saying it with bold lettering, pictures, symbols, and other abbreviated code, and even for breaking the law to say it. Without a doubt, it was vandalism. But it was also, without a doubt, art.

In the 1990s, when I started traveling to other cities in the U.S.

and abroad, graffiti on unfamiliar walls was a sight for sore eyes. It made me feel at home, regardless of the language, like somebody was there who understood my conversation, my experience and background, and I could understand theirs. Global tanning. And by then, graffiti had become inextricably woven into hip-hop culture, considered one of its four intrinsic elements right alongside DJing, MCing, and B-boying.

All of those elements, combined with the energy of youthful aspiration, were in the recipe back in the burgeoning house party era. Add to that the music and attitudes of newly arrived immigrant populations, bringing the strong island flavors of reggae and ska, mixing with the rest of hip-hop's musical melting pot inheritance. Who wouldn't want to be around for that? Plus, being part of something you needed a pass to attend gave you credibility, proved that you knew the code, that someone had given you the lowdown. Like most parties in most eras, your coolness quotient would be determined by whether or not you showed up in style, by your ability to hold court (especially with the opposite sex), and absolutely by whether you could hold your own on the dance floor. But to really be the man (or the woman) at any house or yard party, the ultimate aspiration was to control the turntables and/or the mic. The DJ/MC—often one and the same in the early days—was king.

In the South Bronx at the time that my generation and I were toddlers, three such kings—known forevermore as the holy trinity of hip-hop—were DJ Kool Herc, Afrika Bambaataa, and Grandmaster Flash. Historically, each played a distinct role in pioneering and expanding the musical/cultural field that grew out of the house party scene. Though they battled for supremacy in terms of local appeal—sometimes with literal DJ battles where sheer volume usually ruled the day—each needed the other two to push his own game forward.

True to his name, Flash took the basic elements of rap and turned up the wattage on performance and production values. As a DJ, he put himself front and center, over and above his playlist, inventing certain scratch-and-mix techniques almost singlehandedly—like the day when he accidentally dropped the needle on a record and had to hustle to move it in sync to the beat. Flash also increased the number of rappers onstage with him, making the inclusion of a crew of MCs with showmanship skills a rap mainstay.

Afrika Bambaataa was a mash-up maestro, playing everything from soul to salsa to disco, from rock, pop, funk, and reggae to TV theme songs. A former gangbanger, he also used his prominence as a DJ to convince some of the warring gangs to take their battles onto the mic or the dance floor. To create order for these functions, Bam went on to devise his own set of rules. As one of the first to codify a means for building the youth movement, Bambaataa would be credited with identifying the required elements that constitute hip-hop.

In 1970, the future DJ Kool Herc (fifteen-year-old Clive Campbell, who had recently come to the Bronx from Jamaica) started a house party business, spinning a funky collection of 45s on a rustic borrowed sound system wherever he could get hired. Probably the most daunting issue for him and most aspiring DJs in those days was a technical one—how to extend the break in the music, the most danceable section of the record. Extending the break, logically, was a matter of finding a way to repeat it, to keep the groove steady enough for the break dancers—the break boys and girls, also known as B-boys and B-girls—and hang on to the beat long enough to rap to it, using language, humor, and rhythm to fire up the crowd. Without sampling or the digital devices of future eras, to keep the break repeating on a continuous loop the pioneering DJs came up with the practice of setting up two turntables with the same record and extending the break by switching back and forth, jumping from one turntable to the other, playing the break over from the start, as seamlessly as possible.

While Clive refined his technology and style, honing his skills all across the Bronx, he ran track and lifted weights at school, where he earned the superhero nickname of Hercules. Meanwhile, a short-lived stint as a graffiti writer had led him to the sign-off that didn't totally reveal his identity to the authorities— "Clyde as Kool." Putting all three identities together, in 1973 he officially became DJ Kool Herc, taking just the Kool from his tagging name and shortening Hercules to Herc.

And then, finally, ready to put his learning to the test, in August 1973 Herc decided to join forces with his sister and become an entrepreneur. The two pooled their resources and rented the rec room of the apartment building to which they'd recently moved. The address? It was 1520 Sedgwick Avenue. With nothing more by way of advertising than handwritten invitations promoting the first party and charging a few coins to get in, there must have been the smell of history in the making, because after word got out, kids showed up in droves. The crowd was mixed, mostly African-American, some Hispanic who were mainly of Caribbean black descent, and some whose families had recently arrived to the increasingly poverty-stricken, institutionally abandoned neighborhood, along with a few outliers from other backgrounds. But when the makeshift strobe started to pulse—thanks to a friend flicking the light switch on and off—and DJ Kool Herc took to the mic and began to play the breaks, there was only one language being spoken: pure, unadulterated fun.

Hip-hop was born that night, even if it hadn't been named yet, and so had the legendary status of DJ Kool Herc, whose reputation preceded him far and wide almost overnight. Other masterful MCs and DJs would rise to equal and greater prominence, but because Herc helped to create the language and would therefore remain in a class of his own, nobody could truly take the throne from him. He would forever remain proof of the possibilities, that you could come from nothing, from the streets and even from the least likely circumstances, and make an indelible mark on the world.

The quest to leave a mark was not abstract—as could be heard in other voices contributing to the street code. There were the top graffiti writers, who spoke of "bombing" to describe their middle-of-the-night aerosol painting forays into the subway tunnels and onto tracks where the trains were locked down for the night. Battling individually or in crews, the objective was to see whose signature style could be most recognized and whose artwork could travel the farthest—literally, over the greatest stretch of tracks. B-boys and girls, many in their early teens, took existing dance moves out of the clubs, taped down cardboard on concrete, and invented new ways of twisting, flip-ping, and spinning to create their own signature moves, each one winding up in a gravity-defying "freeze" that if you could nail could make you a legend. The classic B-boy stance, arms folded over your chest, chin jutted, sideways lean, one foot extended, said everything without words—code in the form of gesture that was about defying the odds, about being proud of who you were, what crowd backed you, and inviting or challenging others to engage.

So the party kept on rocking throughout the 1970s. Fueled by aspiration, collaboration, and competition, it continued almost completely under the radar of the rest of the world—including most of the island of Manhattan. That is, until some visionary individuals started to bridge the divide for no other reason than that they could. Fab Five Freddy, a Renaissance man of tanning, was one of those people. From Brooklyn, Freddy Brathwaite dis-tinguished himself as a graffiti writer by tagging a particular train on the IRT line so often that he took the number—5—as part of his name. Also known as Freddy Love, a nickname that fits his outgoing energy and embrace of everyone and everything hip-hop, he had the crazy idea early in the game that graffiti artists were as important to popular culture as was, say, Andy Warhol. To make that statement, Fab Five Freddy began bombing trains by painting them with oversized Campbell's soup cans, Warhol pop art style. It was a shout-out to an icon most graffiti writ-ers didn't necessarily know, and at the same time it signaled to the downtown art world that subway art could stand alongside high-priced works in their galleries, all day, any day. In fact, that idea would be captured in the 1983 breakout movie *Wild Style,* in which graffiti artist Lee Quinones starred and Freddy played a supporting role, as well as contributing to the soundtrack. A fea-ture film with a fictional story line but shot like a documentary, *Wild Style* brought to life the roots of hip-hop culture. Writer/director Charlie Ahearn cast many of the actual leading figures from the scene to make the movie all the more authentic.

Whenever Freddy describes how the gaps between these seemingly disconnected worlds were bridged, he usually goes back to hip-hop's jazz underpinnings, particularly in bebop—one of his earliest influences. Freddy's godfather, jazz drummer and bebop pioneer Max Roach, was best friends with his dad, and in that mingling of black and Jewish and other immigrant sensibilities seeds were planted for cultural tanning and for the musical disobedience of conventional rules. Freddy told me, "My dad and Max and all the jazz guys believed that they were pushing music forward out of the underground to become the most important popular American art form. But then rock 'n' roll and the Beatles happened and jazz, more or less, was pushed to the sidelines." Miles Davis—and other musical rule-breakers—then rebelled against being segregated to a genre that spoke only to a narrow constituency. So Miles found the intersection between jazz and rock after going to the Fillmore and seeing Jimi Hendrix and Janis Joplin.

One day when Max Roach had come to the Bedford-Stuyvesant neighborhood of Brooklyn for a visit, a party was taking place with a DJ and Fab doing some of his own fun rhyming to the beat. After he had done his thing, Roach pulled him aside and told young Brathwaite, "This is some serious sh*t." Popular music had always balanced melody, rhythm, and harmony; but now, Max Roach observed, the rhythm was going to take center stage and it was as powerful a force, even in infancy, as he had ever heard.

To Fab Five Freddy, the baton really had been passed from bebop to rap pioneers with some help from R&B and rock 'n' roll—as early as the sixties—so that the next form of counterculture expression (hip-hop) could pick up where jazz had been sidelined in order to give musical/cultural sharing its popular due.

Freddy didn't stop there. Before long, amazingly, he was instrumental in helping bring the uptown house party sensibility downtown. Not only did Fab Five Freddy help connect rap with the artsy disco/punk rock scene, but he also convinced gallery owners to open their doors to the work of graffiti writers. The next thing everyone knew, the most notorious East Coast graffiti artists were being linked with the likes of Fab's downtown friends Jean-Michel Basquiat and Keith Haring. Suddenly gallery owners, art collectors, and critics were proclaiming the magnificence of graffiti on canvas as both serious and worth investing thousands of dollars in.

The aspirational message that you could leave your mark on the world—*and* make some real money doing it—was new to the practitioners who had been doing the graff writing and rapping, as Fab observed, "from the standpoint of teenage angst." And it was going to reverberate much more powerfully once rappers started to become recording artists. But that process, believe it or not, was not going to be so easy.

It Takes a Woman

The atmosphere of a house party, by its nature, never lent itself in any obvious way to recording or media technology. For radio programming and the sales of single records, the cut needed to last about three minutes. With most MCs rapping over the breaks of existing records, besides the fact that they could go on and on 'n' 'n' on for as long as an hour (or many more), they weren't exactly writing songs that could be copyrighted lyrically or melodically. Besides that, the raps were frequently improvisations—freestyles—and included input from the crowd.

What had been successful was the homemade mix tapes made and sold through word of mouth, not too differently from other street fare. Also, selling mix tapes at house parties—or at other performance settings where rap was becoming a viable offering—could be a lucrative business for local and celebrity DJs. That was enough to convince a new crop of independent producers to try to solve the puzzle of how to get rap onto records. For a while, nothing really worked and the consensus was that perhaps the elements were only suited for the live experience.

But as the decade flew by and disco ran its course while R&B and other black artists were signed to major corporate labels— making Michael Jackson's *Off the Wall* one of the biggest recording phenomena of 1979—there was a void in the marketplace.

Time for something different, something new. With the belief that rap's moment had come, enterprising African-American indie-label producers stepped up their game, now with better results from a rap record or two that had existing fans impressed. Still, the magic hadn't yet transferred to vinyl. While everyone was looking for the right mix, the resourceful producer who believed that such a translation was imminent and who wanted to be the one to do it first was former recording artist Sylvia Robinson of "Love Is Strange" and "Pillow Talk" hit fame.

In mid-1979, Sylvia and her husband had recently opened the doors of their new label, Sugar Hill Records, in Englewood, New Jersey, and needed product. And, as the story goes, after hearing MCs rhyming at a few different parties, she began scouring the town to identify the top talent and record them. But much to her surprise, no crew with name value or real credibility was interested. Why should they have been? After all, the motivation for rappers was to master the art form and win the love of the live and local audience. So any commercial recording enterprise might run the risk of being seen as inauthentic to the house party/performance art medium. Besides, if you were among the best MCs and wanted to put out a record, you would either produce it yourself (as with mix tapes) or go with an established label, not a start-up spearheaded by an outsider with ties to conventional R&B in suburban New Jersey.

But as I learned from my own mom, later from my daughter, and pretty much from every influential female in my life, there is no stopping a woman on a mission. Sylvia Robinson was relentless and resourceful. Instead of discovering a crew of leading rappers who had MC'd together and had an identity and a following, Sylvia ended up signing three guys on the fringes of the scene—if that—who had never performed together up until the day they went into the studio the first time. One was Wonder Mike, a friend of Sylvia's son, who theretofore had been employed in a pizza joint, where he practiced his rhymes on customers. Another was Master Gee, signed by Sugar Hill Records after he arranged for an audition. The third, Big Bank Hank, was allegedly discovered when Sylvia heard him rapping in the kitchen of a nightclub where he worked as a bouncer.

Now that the crew had been built to order, the real producing challenge was deciding what the track would be and how the
instrumentation would be laid down without a DJ. Here history
gets kind of murky, but as best as I can put it together, it seems
that the resourcefulness of another woman, Debbie Harry—lead
singer of the band Blondie and a key figure in tanning for a few
reasons—played an unwitting role in the selection process.

It was Harry, a sex symbol and seventies sensation, American but aligned with British punk rock and new wave, who
helped connect the megahit-making writer/producer Nile Rodgers of the band Chic to the house party rap scene then moving
into clubs and dance halls. Pulling the strings for that connection as well was none other than Fab Five Freddy, who had been
talking to Debbie and her boyfriend/musical collaborator Chris
Stein about pulling off a huge concert that would feature up-and-
coming MCs along with Blondie, Chic, and the Clash. Though the
big concert never took place, they were able to get Nile Rodgers
out to a rap show. And when he took to the stage and began to
play Chic's latest summer hit, "Good Times," all of a sudden Fab
and some of the top rappers in the audience leapt onto the stage,
grabbed mics, and began freestyling away.

Whether or not anyone from Sugar Hill Records was in the
audience, no one knows. But what is known is that from then
on, at shows around town, a mainstay of the entertainment
was often somebody getting up to rap to "Good Times." When
that was chosen as the basis for Sugar Hill's first rap record, it
showed how well the label was paying attention. When some of
those freestyle lyrics that got passed from party to party ended
up on the record, it was hard for anyone who may have come up
with the original lines to claim credit because they weren't copyrighted or published.

After "Rapper's Delight" came out, however, there was no
debate about the fact that Nile Rodgers and Bernard Edwards
were owed songwriting credit for the recognizable bass line that
had been borrowed, innocently or not, from "Good Times" and
they had no problem getting it. To this day, no one can believe
that the bass player hired for the session—before recording
techniques for sampling were around—was able to keep the

same line going perfectly for the entire fourteen minutes and thirty-seven seconds. Everyone assumed that they were playing the actual record and extending the break.

Some might say that Sylvia Robinson had gotten lucky, having gone out to find gold where everyone else was looking for it and then coming up with the first catch. But I think it was much more than luck or great timing when she made the strategic decision to record and release "Rapper's Delight" as an almost-fifteen-minute extended-play twelve-inch single. Even as a novelty record that only sold on the street by word of mouth, it would have been brilliant. Yet the real brilliance was following up the street success by enflaming consumer demand for radio play. How else do you get DJs to disrupt rotation rules to play a fifteen-minute single other than by flooding the station's request lines?

So the gauntlet had been thrown down. The proof was in. If you were aspirational, you now believed in the possibilities. If you had seen what Sugar Hill Records had accomplished, going from nothing to being the hottest indie label for a genre that had yet to be defined—with the serious profits to go with that— your conclusion would be that you might have a shot too. If you had heard a nearly fifteen-minute hip-hop record on the radio at prime time and you were paying attention to its broad-based appeal, you had to know there was a lot more gold in them thar hills.

You probably would have been thinking those things if you were a charismatic young man from Queens with incredible instincts and entrepreneurial blood in your veins, say, by the name of Russell Simmons, and were starting to try your hand at managing hip-hop artists and producing rap records—now that the field had broken wide-open. Or at least that's what I would assume by the fact that just in time for the winter holidays at the end of 1979, one of Russell's artists, Kurtis Blow, was signed to Mercury Records—the first rapper to go with a major label— and they released his "Christmas Rappin'," which promptly sold four hundred thousand copies. Following that up with "The Breaks," Kurtis soon went on to become the first rapper to have a gold record and to perform it on the popular music TV show *Soul Train.*

Of course, the increasingly corporate-run music industry and mainstream media should have now been on notice that hip-hop was more than a passing fancy, more than a disco afterthought tossing crumbs out to the ghetto kids. Even if it was conceivable that there was a hungry market behind the graffiti'd walls or on the other side of the tracks, the industry executives didn't speak that language—and, frankly, had no interest in learning to. As in any cultural disconnect, one could say that there was a degree of ethnocentricity in their lack of concern about urban blight and the fact that stretches of the inner city right in their backyards were beginning to look like war zones, with working-class families teetering on the edge. One could say that they saw but looked away, unable as they were to understand why it was that at the dawn of the 1980s, most of the symbols of aspiration, with a few exceptions, were turning out to be drug dealers and pimps.

The sociology of rap's future, however, wasn't really at issue. The music was simply not commercially enticing, nor was it justified to an industry really marketing to white kids in suburbia. The math told the story. With the sizable price tags for producing the music videos that were going to be mandatory for record promotion, given the advent of MTV, the costs of investing in an unproven genre like hip-hop, without superstars, made the discussion a nonstarter. Lest we forget, the MTV platform when it launched in 1981 was rock, mostly new wave and hard rock and later metal—with artists like David Bowie, Duran Duran, and, eventually, Bon Jovi. MTV flat-out refused to show the video of Rick James's smash "Super Freak," and it wasn't until 1983 that Michael Jackson videos were approved for rotation.

All of this is to say that if you were betting the odds, as is the case for most businesses most of the time, after "Rapper's Delight" and Kurtis Blow's appearance on *Soul Train,* the assumption might have been that the fun had by hip-hop and its fans was over. But not everybody was betting the odds, thankfully.

Enter Blondie and their 1981 single "Rapture," on the Chrys-alis label—with its accompanying music video that took every-one by surprise. With a song that followed a rock model, out of nowhere, after the first verse, here was a white girl, a punk/pop singer, suddenly doing a change-up—rapping over the break. Not just rhyming, Debbie Harry was also talking about the sexy world of rap, even going so far as to name two of its celebri-ties, Fab Five Freddy and Grandmaster Flash. In fact, they were both supposed to be in the video but Flash couldn't make it, so Fab Five Freddy showed up with Jean-Michel Basquiat; the two can be seen to this day in the video, graff-writing on the walls. This was not the last time that Freddy would play a role in hip-hop's migration into the world of music videos, as we'll see later on. And meanwhile, the door couldn't have been opened at a better time. True, "Rapture" didn't make Debbie Harry's career. But what it did for rap music was everything. When the record charted at number one on the Hot 100 *Billboard* list, it became the first rap-infused single to do so. Plus, the "Rapture" video made history as the first outing of rap on MTV. Coming from Blondie, it was a signal of how adaptive the genre was and how it would not be restricted to one kind of music over another. A creative liberation! What's more, by using her prominence at that time to shout out two hip-hop icons, Debbie Harry authen-ticated an art form.

The translation was that hip-hop proved that it was as akin to rock as it was to soul and funk. For those ready to push boundaries, it could be as full of protest and social relevance, and also as capable of creating a culture, a mind-set, a voice for the voiceless. The first record on which I heard a semblance of those properties was Melle Mel's "White Lines," released in 1983 on Sylvia Robinson's Sugar Hill Records. The production, to me, was memorable, laying Melle's rock-laced voice over an addic-tive track. Once again, Sylvia Robinson was paying attention to the competition, and keeping one step ahead.

Well, not quite. Apparently, Sylvia Robinson made the mis-take of turning down a video of "White Lines" starring a young Laurence Fishburne that was made on spec by an up-and-coming filmmaker. You might have heard of him: Spike Lee.

The Color of Confidence

Hip-hop came of age in the mid-1980s, in the same era that members of the generation who couldn't remember a time without it were coming of age. We weren't in the record business and weren't watching from the sidelines taking notes about how many units of this or that release had shipped or what the demographics were that turned "Christmas Rappin'" into a huge hit or that allowed "Rapture" to be shown on MTV or that pushed "White Lines" up to number seven on the UK pop charts—yes, pop. For us, in our lives and concerns, we would have been like, *Where the f**k is the UK?*

No exaggeration. Fab Five Freddy once told me a story about the early days when rap artists first started making money and then began touring overseas. Fab happened to run into a DJ he knew who was bragging about all the foreign places their crew had visited—"France, Italy, and London . . ." As if that wasn't the really big news, the guy quickly added, "And next year, we go to Europe!"

Encompassed in these anecdotes is one of the most important rewritten rules of the new economy that can be traced to hip-hop's formative years. For far too long the classic rags-to-riches stories had been told about dead guys with names like Ford, Rockefeller, and du Pont—all far removed from most people's reality. Now, suddenly, acts of wonder had come to pass and kids you knew personally or had heard about in your own neighborhood—who had come out of the projects or been born without wealth and stature—had become famous and were making money to go with that too. You could do that? Even if you couldn't shoot hoops or win the lottery? Suddenly, you could wipe away the stigma of poverty and lower-class status pinned on you by other forces because of color or immigrant background or all the other reasons for not making the grade. Now you could claim your unlikely beginnings as a badge of honor, of authenticity, as a way of saying, "I come from nothing and look where I am now." Actually, as the culture congregated further with the force of tanning, you had to have a badge to make you credible, to prove that you had come up through hard times that were real—possibly that you had even held your own with killers and gangsters and drug dealers. But wait. Better yet, you could wear a badge of authenticity with trend-setting style, and at the same time be a poet and speak about experiences that the rest of the world seemed to be ignoring.

That was Run-DMC. With cuts like "Hard Times" actually talking about real-world problems and "Sucker MC's," a record that compared the aspirational success of rappers authentically working on their skills to that of the wannabe "sad-faced clown" imitators and posers, the rhymes and stories echoed the feel of Sunday morning sermons. Those songs were transformational for me, especially "Sucker MC's." They came from where I did and were calling themselves rap royalty. Who did that? Who had that kind of nerve? But that was the point—that if hip-hop didn't shout itself out, nobody else would. The idea was planted then and there that would take root and would later drive me as an entrepreneur to dare to take on the Goliaths of the competition— and would convince me that I could win.

And to top all that, Run-DMC had the bold confidence not just to borrow elements from rock but also to cast themselves as the rightful purveyors of it, that they together were the "King of Rock" as the title of a 1985 single and album (their second) put it. The video of that single was their second that MTV agreed to air and its success suggested there was a niche for a hybrid rock-rap genre ready for prime time.

Then the game changed with "Walk This Way"—the tipping point for tanning. Everything that had happened going back to DJ Kool Herc and 1520 Sedgwick Avenue had helped put hip-hop over the top, even if it had been an uphill climb over unknown terrain. "Walk This Way" was going to send the next moves into fast downhill skiing. Released as a single on the same album as "My Adidas," it would also set the stage for history to unfold in August 1986 at Madison Square Garden.

When I talk about Run-DMC as being groundbreaking—for all kinds of reasons and especially for knowing that their art form was much bigger than two turntables and a mic—I am including the team that made their impact possible. Russell

Simmons was the individual who proved to one and all (and has continued to do so since) that the ceiling for rap and hip-hop that everyone else believed was there really wasn't. Three others in the Rush/Def Jam circle who should have special mention are Bill Adler, Lyor Cohen, and Rick Rubin. Besides the fact that I know them and have a kinship to them personally and professionally, the three all happen to be white—yet have soul in their veins and urban sensibilities from Jewish and/or immigrant backgrounds. As a publicist, Bill Adler was way ahead of the curve in recognizing the mainstream marketing potential for rap artists. Lyor Cohen—now a top record-industry executive and a former Rush partner who started as a promoter and road manager for Run-DMC—believed early on in the cultural melting pot that was being brewed for and by the younger generation. The genius producer Rick Rubin, who launched Def Jam before joining forces with Russell, was a key contributor to the DNA of hip-hop. What's more, Rick was the audio architect and sound engineer of tanning—a bridge between rock and rap that worked because he sonically knew what was authentic to the mix and what appealed to young audiences, regardless of background.

From the start through his present-day post at the helm of a major record label—after working with everyone from LL Cool J and the Beastie Boys in the early years to the Red Hot Chili Peppers, Metallica, U2, and the Dixie Chicks (to name a few)—Rick never had any use for the color/demographic boxes used in creating and marketing music. Someone who has always understood the beats and rhythms of culture because he observes it authentically rather than packaging it, Rick Rubin is to me the Norman Rockwell of popular music—an artist portraying Americana at its heart and providing insights into the culture in the process.

As reports have it, the irony of "Walk This Way" was that when the team at Rush Management first proposed the idea for Run-DMC to use Aerosmith's 1977 hit single and merge rock and hip-hop elements on the record, there was hesitation. The main pushback was that just rapping over the tracks would be inauthentic and not original enough. So Rick proposed that Run-DMC do a cover of the single, a reinvention, and then the rockers could come in and add flavor from their rock roots. It was a true mash-up. Anyone betting the odds would say that doing a musical clash is risky, resulting in neither fish nor fowl. Yet when it works, it's not a musical clash at all but actually a cultural clash. In fact, the word "clash" is wrong. When it works, it's tanning, a synergy of music and attitude that swirls everyone into the same vortex and connects them.

"Walk This Way" did that musically, culturally, rhythmically, and lyrically. And, oh yeah, visually. Even though it was assumed that Aerosmith would benefit somehow from having one of the group's biggest hits back in circulation in a new form, nobody could have predicted to what extent. Lo and behold, when Steven Tyler and Joe Perry agreed to be on the record and in the video, all of a sudden the new "Walk This Way" reinvigorated *their* career and launched *them* to unprecedented heights, giving them a street pass with a whole new following in communities of color. And there was more. After being lured out of the 1970s rock 'n' roll mausoleum, their collaboration with Run-DMC returned them so much to the game that Aerosmith soon entered their most prolific decades. To date, they are considered the all-time top-selling American rock band, with more gold and platinum records than any other group—over 150 million albums sold around the world.

And as for Run-DMC, when they appeared in their own video with rock legends as *their* guests, they made history in being instantaneously embraced by an audience that had never heard of hip-hop—let alone bought their records.

There was nothing earth-shattering in the song's story— about a loser who gets schooled in how to improve his odds with the opposite sex by changing his attitude and learning to "*Walk this way-ay-ay!*" and "*Talk this way-ay-ay!*" But in describing a situation that is universal in every neighborhood on the planet, it had a perfect message for bringing different audiences onto common ground. After all, beyond the things like having fame and money and being cool that were sought through aspiration, the super-objective was getting girls. Or appealing to guys if you were a girl. Maybe not for everyone. However, speaking for teenage males, as I was back then, and for young men too, in my experience, it was not just why you wanted to be successful but why you woke up every morning and why you even breathed in the first place. The translation was that everybody, regardless of color or background, wants to get some and to have the sexual confidence to get it. Who couldn't relate to that?

So "Walk This Way" was tanning at work at a primal level. On another deep, equally powerful level, the video spoke to cultural differences and similarities with a story that came down to a rock/rap battle. At the start, it had the two groups in two separate recording studios divided by a wall, each first annoyed at having their music co-opted by the other, and then in the end bashing through the wall to jam and dance together. Speaking now in one collective voice, even with different accents, Aerosmith and Run-DMC doubled down on the message to be who you are and not to be afraid to define yourself by your own style, authentically. It was all about having confidence in yourself and in how you walked and carried yourself, with individuality, pride, purpose, and insistence. The word popularized to describe this commodity and attitude, as we now know, is "*swagger.*"

The first strand of code in the cultural translation could now be identified. It combined within it the elements of aspiration, authenticity, relevance, cool, and confidence that were obtainable by association with the music. Oh yeah, and it came with a sexy, irresistible beat. For any smart marketing person, this concoction was made to order no matter what the product. Right?

Well, yes, if you cut to the future. Over the next two decades or so, as rap stars aligned themselves with status goods and services, they would indeed be a gold mine for marketing all manner of high-end consumer brands—as they voluntarily sang the praises of everything from Courvoisier cognac and Cristal champagne to Louis Vuitton and Versace to Range Rovers and Cadillac Escalades. Even the *Robb Report,* the magazine of conspicuous consumption for only the über-rich, would get a shout-out. And just like "My Adidas" back in 1986, because none of these endorsements were solicited or purchased, the marketing value was all the more meaningful. Expressions of brand loyalty, in short, were manifestly genuine—which, when embraced in culturally fluent ways, would make them incredibly effective.

Today, all of that is a foregone conclusion. But it would have read like a fairy tale if you had presented such a scenario to marketing people—even back in the go-go 1980s heyday of conspicuous consumption. Why? Frankly, because of two groups of haters who weren't interested in rap music or hip-hop culture or the demographics they represented.

Curiosity as Cultural, Economic Yeast

Haters are reactionary, hate anything new or different, and see danger in venturing off into the unknown. They are certainly not friendly to creative expansion or marketing risk. In the 1980s, a decade of conglomerate takeovers and corporate megamergers, one group of haters who stood in the way of hip-hop's mainstream success was populated by the marketing power players at leading brands.

That's why it was so unprecedented when Adidas marketing executive Angelo Anastasio came to Madison Square Garden and was wowed enough by what he saw to strike the endorsement deal for the trio of rappers. As it was pointed out to me by Lyor Cohen (there that night as Run-DMC's road manager), the mainstream market appeal wasn't the main selling point for Anastasio. The crowd that night was still mostly African-American, with a smaller percentage of Hispanic and Asian concertgoers and a sprinkling of white urban kids. But what made Anastasio different from other corporate representatives, according to Lyor, was his curiosity. He was simply open-minded enough to contemplate the possibilities of introducing hip-hop to the marketing machinery behind Adidas sneakers.

When Lyor described that night and how everything fell into place, it occurred to me how important curiosity is in general for tanning to occur. And as a marketing 101 lesson, one that I had to learn and one I have to remind corporate clients not to forget, advertising dollars don't mean a thing without genuine curiosity about what consumers want and need. In fact, as Lyor recalled, while the Adidas/Run-DMC alliance did well for all concerned—saving the company from extinction—it could have been much more successful. Unfortunately, instead of gaining consumer insights and bringing Run, DMC, or Jam Master Jay in on designing the footwear and in on how to promote their line of sneakers, the company took over for Angelo and ran a campaign with the old-school "father knows best" approach. They let the designers try to figure out the culture and design into it without a true understanding of the consumer. They marketed via the monologue that dictates cool rather than inviting consumers to partake in the cool.

That said, the Adidas missteps were going to be lessons learned for certain entrepreneurs who were paying attention and whose business wheels were starting to turn. For them, it was fortunate that there were mainstream corporate haters who even by the late 1980s weren't curious enough to even consider hip-hop's musical future. Why do I say that it was fortunate for these entrepreneurs? Because it allowed them and local economies to benefit and prime the pump for everyone else to follow suit.

Surprisingly, the second group of haters who slowed rap music's mainstream success—and who weren't curious about its potential—actually came from within the African-American community. Typically older, wealthier, assimilated generations who had come out of the era of protest and civil rights, they reacted with discomfort to the bravado of youthful aspiration and the booming bass of rap blasting out of car stereos and trekking down the streets. Their position, it seemed, was that they had worked too hard for too long, following paths into higher education and into positions of influence in politics, business, and media, to support the hip-hop phenomenon that might outshine them or disrupt their means of having stature. Black media, usually the first to back African-American entertainment, was especially resistant to embracing hip-hop. Until rap music proved itself worthy of mainstream consideration, most of the top black radio stations and video programmers just weren't interested. In fact, there were radio stations that specifically said on air, "We don't play rap music," in order to get more listeners. However, because of the mostly generational divide, it forced hip-hop to become bigger than just a genre of popular music with merchandise; it forced it to prove itself in mighty ways and to develop capacities for spreading into the worlds of fashion, beauty, art, dance, sports, gaming, language, lifestyle, and eventually politics.

And that's how the culture left behind its house party roots and really took on a life of its own to become bigger than the sum of its parts. It was like any other teenager, determined to grow up and become whoever it chose to be.

If you are a marketer hoping to attract new customers without losing your core consumers, this early phase of hip-hop still has relevance for how you appeal to aspiration and how you use code to do so. As we will see later on, consumers provide all the needed cues for how to do that—as long as attention is paid to them.

CHAPTER 2

HARD KNOCK LIFE

Not many years ago during a business-related trip to Monaco, at a time when I'd already left the music industry and had recently opened the doors of my own marketing/consulting firm, I had another one of those revelations about how small the world had become. Thanks to overlapping relationships, I found myself at dinner one night with a most distinguished gathering of individuals. We were from different places of origin, of different ethnicities and generations, and each of us worked in a different corner of the entertainment world. At Monte Carlo's Hôtel de Paris, at the top of this stunning one-hundred-fifty-year-old palace, there in the world-class restaurant with its retractable roof opened up to allow us to dine under the stars, I not only had one of the most delicious meals of my entire life but was in a state of amazement the entire time. The fact was, in spite of our differences, we could all understand great wine, all savor the experience, and all talk the same language.

It didn't mar my enjoyment in the least that I'd arrived without proper attire and had to put on a tie and blazer loaned to me by the restaurant management—even if it was a little snug. At the table with me were Jay-Z, Bono of U2, music mogul Jimmy Iovine of Interscope/Geffen/A&M Records, and Sir Roger Moore along with his very beautiful wife, Kristina. As men, our ages spanned the decades—starting with Jay-Z and me, then in our thirties, Bono in his forties, Jimmy almost fifty, and Roger Moore pushing eighty. And yet, much to the amusement of Mrs. Moore, the instant we finished our dinner, we all lit up cigars and started talking the same trash!

Dressed in white from head to toe, Roger Moore was as meticulous about his appearance as we used to be about our pristine white Adidas sneakers, and had every ounce of cool and finesse that had made him perfect to come in and take over the James Bond franchise from Sean Connery—reinventing the 007 mystique and owning it longer than anyone else. What I never knew until meeting him was that Sir Roger (he was knighted by the queen of England, as was Bono) debuted in the role at age forty-five and was fifty-eight when he made the last of seven 007 films. Absolutely unapologetic about owning his success, he radiated perpetual James Bond confidence. Moore had us on the edge of our seats, telling tales from the old days, describing what it was like to be one of the biggest stars on the international scene and be able to enter any room anywhere—into the finest, most rarefied air—and command total attention. And he still does! Of course, he was saying all this tongue-in-cheek—cigar lit up, eyes full of life. Next thing we knew, he went on to start discussing William Shatner, openly admitting there had been an unspoken battle for years over who was the biggest global superhero, 007 or Captain Kirk.

No one was taking sides. In reality each had accomplished a lot with his respective franchise, but Roger Moore was our guy. Jay and I were as hell-bent on winning the duel as he was! So what if *Star Trek* had gone around the universe on global television and had Trekkies showing up by many thousands at conventions scattered everywhere on Planet Earth? We weren't saying anything.

"You know what?" Moore said. "F**k William Shatner!" He described the luxury building where both he and Captain Kirk of the USS *Enterprise* (a.k.a. William Shatner) had lived. His point? "I had the penthouse. I lived *above* Shatner!" With that, Roger

Moore cast his eyes down in another direction and all of our glances followed as he nodded right toward his wife's crazy huge diamond ring. Like an ice cube sparkling under the stars, perfectly crystal clear. His expression said, *Need I say more?*

We were all falling out, laughing our asses off! Jay and I probably laughed harder, mainly because of how far hip-hop's language and its unspoken, unwritten rules had traveled. Besides that, not one of us at the table, to my knowledge, had come from privilege or any semblance of affluence. Roger Moore had grown up in a small working-class town in England before going off to fight in World War II, no auspicious destiny ahead of him whatsoever. There was Jimmy Iovine, Italian-American, from a rough-and-tumble Brooklyn neighborhood. Jay-Z, a.k.a. Shawn Corey Carter, also came from Brooklyn but from the Marcy Houses projects—a notorious war zone in the impoverished ghetto where he grew up without a father, raised by a single mother. And Bono had come from the outskirts of Dublin, an actual war zone at times, where bombings were familiar signs of the age-old bloody conflict between Catholics and Protestants. The son of a Catholic father, a taskmaster with a temper, and a Protestant mom who died when Bono was growing up, he experienced the Irish brand of lack and dysfunction in the streets and at home.

As for me, my three siblings and I were lucky to be raised in a household in Queens Village with two parents—something that was becoming less and less the norm. Both immigrants from Trinidad, my parents had a relentless work ethic that drove them to each work full-time jobs with second and sometimes third jobs to make ends meet. Still, we lived paycheck to paycheck and knew what it meant to go without—from our own situation and from watching what was happening around us.

So, yeah, my dinner companions and I recognized through code, without any biographical data necessarily being exchanged, that we'd all walked very different but rugged roads to get to the top of the Hôtel de Paris, where we could talk trash and smoke ridiculously expensive cigars. We could understand why it mattered to Roger Moore, because of where he had come from, to be able to sit there dressed like a prince all in white and say, "F**k Shatner, I lived above him!"

We could understand, because of the spirit of the whole hip-hop cultural platform that had now circled the globe far beyond anything *Star Trek* could ever attempt through fact or fiction, that Roger Moore's rap actually had nothing to do with William Shatner or the friendly rivalry of that relationship or the stuff he'd acquired that was superior to his rival's. He was saying in his own way, *Here I am, here we are, look at me, look at us, remember where we came from?* Of course you want to have someone else whose status you can one-up. That's how you win. And Roger Moore, with a totally unapologetic approach to life, spoke that language.

Yeah, I remember thinking, *the unapologetic approach, now that is the definition of cool!*

As I thought about it more, the realization helped me see how the unapologetic hip-hop mind-set—which had started to become much more vivid in the music and the culture in the mid-to late 1980s and early '90s—had given tanning a turbocharge. First of all, the artists gaining the most popularity came from diverse backgrounds with distinct points of view. We had Salt-n-Pepa, female rappers from Queens unapologetically taking on the guys, talking street and sexy with infectious hits like "Push It" on their first album release, *Hot, Cool and Vicious.* We had the Beastie Boys, white suburban Jewish kids from Long Island, unapologetically bringing their punk-rock roots along in their reverse crossover to rap and then telling like-minded youth that you have to "fight for your right to party" on the album *Licensed to Ill* (interestingly enough, the bestselling rap album of the entire 1980s). We had another Long Island group, Public Enemy, who unapologetically pushed the genre to address political and racial issues (not without controversy) with anthem songs like "Fight the Power"—which Spike Lee used as a setpiece in his unapologetic *Do the Right Thing.*

Lack of apology was nowhere more audible than in gangsta rap, a.k.a. reality rap, which was just warming up in the 1980s with West Coast rappers Ice-T and Ice Cube of NWA coming onto the scene. Nor was there anything apologetic about any of the new voices being heard in cities like Oakland, D.C., Baltimore, Philadelphia, Atlanta, Miami, Houston, and New Orleans, and in places least expected.

The other thing to consider was that even with diverse points of view appealing to an increasingly diverse audience, the common story line was no less than a remix and reinterpretation of the American dream. It was the most gangsta—as in bold and daring—thing that a movement could have dared to do at the time. The eighties, let's not forget, were disastrous for anyone growing up in the inner city. Reaganomics and the corporate free-for-all that were supposed to send some trickledown into the streets only exacerbated unlivable conditions. The crack epidemic in the midst of hard times opened the floodgates for cheap drugs, guns, and other illegal businesses to set up stands at every corner. As crack cut a swathe across inner cities of America—turning neighborhoods into third-world countries, dealers into glamorous high rollers, and loved ones into crackheads—the reality was so negative and so full of despair it couldn't help but alter the tenor of the poetry. In the process, the crack epidemic that created so much pain and destruction enriched the storytelling about how terrible it truly was— through the characters, villains, and even heroes it created. And so, to be a poet, to come out of that kind of poverty and violence and make it, was literally miraculous. Yet it was possible.

Hip-hop, in marketing a new brand of hope, was simply doing what it always did well by borrowing from the classics and adding its own twist. Once an updated version of rags to riches was in the code, part of America's DNA, the art form widened its audience exponentially. If you were generationally attuned, had an understanding or empathy toward impoverishment and/or dysfunction, and were aspirational, you were in. With no one even imagining the numbers that this marquee was going to attract, the cultural infrastructure had to quickly adapt to address the demand.

And one of the ways that it did, as it became clear to me that night in Monte Carlo, was by inventing the outlines of a creed or belief system or, yes, a religion for itself. Music, interestingly enough, developed originally to connect tribal members to one another and allow religious adherents to commune with a higher power. This is to say that music, by its nature, breeds culture. On top of that, hip-hop is a kind of confession, at times a soul-baring about stuff you're not even supposed to say in public, sometimes inappropriate, sometimes gut-wrenching—*My moth-er's on drugs, my father abandoned me, I'm broke, I'm f**ked up, what am I supposed to do?*

So, as the art form became a culture and began to fulfill the same functions that religious institutions have served throughout history, the most obvious thing it did was to provide governance. Religion has always been influential in governing people without hope and who are in despair, giving them a reason to believe, to go on. Incredibly, that's what hip-hop did, stepping into the void of meaninglessness to provide governance for people without any-thing, riddled with crack, dope, and hopelessness. Rap music, using language that was old and new, literal and metaphoric, was like scriptures, full of vivid, accurate depictions of life that gave people who were poor and powerless a way to feel better. As the poets were telling the real stories, speaking over beats that you loved, the impact happened at a cellular level, elevating your emo-tional/spiritual metabolism. Sports heroes were still larger than life, but now another class of hero, by the laws of this system, could come from nothing and find purpose with just their words that would lead toward redemption, with all their sins and bag-gage included. The fact that they had no resources made their journey to fame and fortune even more epic. Rappers—the street poets—now became legends, not just locally but everywhere, and gave the culture a winning history, a bible.

The impoverished-yet-unapologetic mind-set thus became the hip-hop religion's unifying concept. Who knew that way of thinking could turn a profit?

The Business of Culture: An Intro

One reason I believe hip-hop was able to grow from a small niche market (seen as a subgenre of black music at the record com-panies) to a full-blown dominant musical force and industry—a mainstay of popular culture capable of impacting the worldwide economy—is that it began in the bedrock of hard times. With that as a draw pulling in everyone, the color lines dropped, and there was a common language and attitude to share that created a sense of unity, of community.

To clarify, this new urban religion—which, after "Walk This Way," had begun to infiltrate most major cities and parts of their suburbs—was not a rallying cry for an almighty being, or for "the One." The rallying cry, at first, was just to tell and hear the truth—that being poor f**king sucks. It was a call to confront the other truth that in coping, the ways of the old institutions—the church, the schools, the government, the law, and the parents—had failed.

Then it became more than just a badge of credibility to be the rapper who could stand up and say, *I come from nothing and look at my success.* Technically, not all hip-hop artists were from abject poverty or gang-infested turf either. The cry accommodated that fact and it became enough to say, *Hey, I know the life, I know being poor, I know injustice, hypocrisy, I know the pain, the crack, the burned-out buildings, the terror of the hallways, the killings, the drive-bys.* Or, later on, if you're white and you're Eminem—*Hey, I know the drugs, the emptiness, the trailer parks, and I hate my mom.* That, by the way, was just crazy, especially in the African-American community, because, as you may know, *all* our mothers are saintly.

Plainly, the core experience of poverty, however it was described, had a dog-whistle effect in the frontal lobes of youth around the world. Ghetto and barrio kids would hear the stories of trailer parks and get it. Kids in affluent homes or in sleepy suburbs heard the call of generational despair and understood it. The commonality no longer had to be shared experience per se but was about the linkage of feelings—all kinds of emotions that could be conjured by a thumping beat, rhymes, wordplay, anger, humor, arousal, resentment, boredom, joy, excitement, curiosity, you name it.

All of this was a rallying cry that crossed so many color, class, and even age lines and drew in so many followers that by the time Jay-Z came along in 1998 with "Hard Knock Life"—in which he sampled none other than a song from the Broadway show *Annie* with little orphan voices singing "instead of kisses we get kicks"—coming from poverty was the status symbol that gave definition to all the other status symbols. Later, Jay-Z and Will Smith would team up to produce a remake of the movie musical.

The impoverished, unapologetic mentality was seductive. The

attitude became viral. Coming from nothing and having a reason to push, to grind, the "can't stop won't stop" part of the hip-hop creed, gave life meaning and light in dark times. And the attitude was f**king hot. It had a look, a language, gestures, a posture, a dance, such that kids who didn't come from nothing wanted to have the badge too, to dress like it and act like it. That was the mix that became contagious. Because of the music, and, as we will see, especially music videos, it caused contagion that would lead to consumption in order to have the badge. Mass consumption.

It was only natural that brands were destined to become the beneficiaries of aspiration when the common message was one of going from poverty to success. Brands, after all, were being used by hip-hop to chart growth and proclaim the possibilities. I can play a thousand rap songs from every era that all say the same thing—*I went from this to that.* Brand alignment was your proof: *See, I made it here, I have a BMW.* (Or fill in the blank.)

Your imagined or real rival for supremacy could then answer: *A BMW? Wow. Guess what? I got a Mercedes.*

The dialogue required you to top that: *Mercedes? Oh yeah, well, I have a Maybach.*

Next? *Look, you drink Moët & Chandon, but I'm drinking Dom Perignon.*

Here comes the opening for someone else to jump in—*Well, I'm drinking Cristal!*

And the chorus from the megalogue of everyone listening: *Wow!*

When you come from nothing, you have license to have this duel without being uncool—*Oh, your diamond's real? So's mine and I got a* VVS (Very, very slightly imperfect, almost flawless).

Oh? My whole sh*t is diamond.

Oh? I'm bling the f**k out.

Yeah? I got rims.

Well, I got 20-inch rims.

So? I got 22s.

Whatever. I got 24s!

Of course, this level of unapologetic jousting evolved over a period of time. Thanks to proximity, the code borrowed attitude from ballers on the court, along with rules of the game lifted from drug dealers, pimps, and gangsters, and especially the sense of style that the rappers came to epitomize.

Let me emphasize here that being brand-conscious was nothing new for African-Americans—or honestly any oppressed race as they notoriously use badges to show they have arrived. African-Americans, I contend, are the absolute best consumers in the world. How so? Because they buy products that aren't even marketed to them, over-indexing in commodities and brands that are aspirational. A scene in the TV series *Mad Men* dealt with this phenomenon in 1960s terms. In it, Pete, the ambitious junior ad executive, suggests to clients at Admiral, a popular television brand of the day, that they market to Negroes by buying ad space in black media such as *Ebony* and *Jet*. One of the Admiral executives acts surprised that Negroes even own TVs. Then the point is made that the reason blacks buy their brand is because Negroes think Admiral TVs are what whites want. That being the case, they conclude, advertising in black newspapers and magazines would hurt that dynamic and so the idea is rejected. Even though Pete gets nowhere with his pitch and is berated by his bosses for trying, the British character at the firm warns the team that they're not paying attention to cultural changes and ought to think again about capitalizing on the emergence of "Negroes."

Besides the power of brands as badges for minorities, in the increasingly diverse hip-hop mix you also had younger generations of consumers for whom brand awareness wasn't a new concept either. What was new was the market impact of a movement that embraced coming from poverty as part of its creed—a movement with a growing army poised to seriously influence the success of brands.

If really smart corporate executives had wanted to save money on all that market research about what the next new *new* thing was going to be, they would only have had to turn to the hip-hop community—who were doing the research anyway, selecting trends that looked promising, creating overnight word-of-mouth promotion, and even adding their own product development ideas. When I talked to Russell Simmons about how urban culture came to influence the mainstream economy, he noted, "If the hip-hop community decided that Ralph Lauren was cool, even if that company had become a little stale or those Polo jeans were cold, it was instantly trendsetting and Ralph Lauren got hotter than ever. The core hip-hop community is the best brand-building community in the world."

Being first to discover the new cool brand carries huge weight, Russell pointed out. The prime example of the brand-building power that would reverberate across the 1990s was the mutual love affair between hip-hop and Tommy Hilfiger. In spite of a lover's quarrel later on that arose from a rumor of a comment by Tommy that was seen as disparaging the hip-hop market (which he fervently denounced as not true), it could still be said that the hip-hop stamp of approval for all products Tommy Hilfiger helped build the brand from the ground up into a multibillion-dollar mainstream American company. (More on this later, along with the problem Cristal caused and didn't redeem.)

Then too, Russell reminded me, beyond discovering the new, the hip-hop tastemakers and thought leaders love to rediscover and rebuild brands like Versace, waving the wand of go-ahead coolness. Making something old new, vital, and relevant again— by putting an original spin on it—is a power of the hip-hop consumer too few companies recognize.

Putting on a different spin could take all forms and manifestations. For instance, there was the sudden craze for wearing eyeglasses without the lenses. Imagine that conversation at retail when hip-hop consumers showed up in droves and bought designer eyewear, and would insist, "Take out the lenses. Don't want 'em." Or then there was the shift from wearing sneakers without shoelaces to the even more popular fat shoelaces. Hip-hop design would take something popular like that and push the boundaries, like Ben Franklin using a kite to harness electricity, and puzzle over how to make one cool usage even cooler. Fat shoelaces; why not?

The repurposing was masterful. If faded, distressed jeans were the thing, then the new spin would be ironing in permanent creases, using so much starch you could wear your pants like armor. Or then there were the new urban usages for brands not intended to even sell in the inner city—hiking boots by Timberland that you'd wear to a party or out on a date. The illogic sometimes was the logic. How could a company like Nordica, which makes ski-wear, or Woolrich, known for heavy plaid woolens—or other makers of apparel for camping and rugged outdoor excursions, with materials that emphasize waterproofing and extremes in weather—get rejected for its intended purpose but be embraced as fashion? That was the point. If hip-hop consumers could co-opt and repurpose, the loyalty would be evergreen.

As Russell pointed out about hip-hop consumers' love for the classics, "They not only rebuilt Versace, they made him legitimate again." Taking the market power even further, Russell went on, "They decide if it's Pepsi or Coke. They decide on most of what's cool in American culture, whether it's luxury brands or everyday necessities."

In the choosing process, Russell observed, the culture is elevated all the more, especially by featuring language that is also new, cool, and fresh, or old language that might be stale but is being remixed with expressions and intonations from different voices being drawn into hip-hop. There is an internal exchange between blacks, whites, Hispanics, Asians, inner city residents, suburbans, athletes, skaters, surfers, college students, and young professionals, with everyone code-sharing in order to translate to the masses what is cool and how to speak about it. So in picking the obvious and less obvious necessities, like socks, brand identification is still a talking point. The legions of the hip-hop generation, it would turn out in time, would be "more brand conscious than any other group in America." Russell's awareness was backed up by studies done by Walmart's market research group, among others. That's why "hip-hop consumers always come up on top in terms of picking new American trends. And they also come up on top in terms of reaffirming old American trends."

When I asked about the unique relationship between hip-hop core consumers and older brands, Russell's view was that in addition to co-opting or reclaiming classics, they remain loyal. He also said, "They don't worry about things getting too big." Other youth culture groups tend to move on once a trend gets too big.

My experience of that arc would happen in the music business at the end of the 1990s, when most heavy metal acts, with a few exceptions, had become "hair bands" and could no longer excite their audience enough to sustain a following. Fans did move on.

Russell's reasoning for the consumer loyalty in the hip-hop community was, "When these consumers have branded something and it gets big, they are more and more proud of it. They like stable, lasting, strong brands. The core tastemakers in the hip-hop group come out of poverty, so they are on the lookout for big." Russell spoke about how marketing-savvy the hip-hop generation became early on. Whether they were poor, working-class, suburban, or affluent, they had grown up watching TV and deciding ahead of time what they were going to have when they got the money to spend.

So how did these core hip-hop consumers who grew up in the culture from the start originally become tastemakers? Basically, I believe, from being "live on the scene" when the music was being bred and from determining which acts were hot or not. It started as a marketplace unto itself, as I can well remember from when I became a paying consumer, back in my late teens. Coming home from a live performance, loaded up with gear I'd bought, I'd still be in the throes of having cheered the loudest for whoever won the battle or for some brilliant turn of phrase by Rakim or Big Daddy Kane—two of the most gifted pioneering rappers in those years.

Besides the feeling of empowerment from helping determine the winner, there was also the sense that business opportunity was attached to this scene. Definitely I was drawn to that possibility, but these were the years when I was supposed to be settling into an education and a real job. If I had thought there was a career for me attached somehow to hip-hop, I would have signed up. Nothing registered. Meanwhile, I figured, I'd remain a fan and just enjoy the total experience—the crowd roaring, the street entrepreneurs selling T-shirts and hats and mix tapes, everyone on the periphery hawking their stuff that you had to buy. And there was the glamour, the cars, the clothes, the fans, the magic, and, yeah, the endorsement deals that superstars like Run-DMC and LL Cool J were starting to attract.

LL was the hip-hop celebrity who gave the marketing world an early tutorial about the value of aligning their brand with the genre. Part of what made him effective as an arbiter of style—a guy who could wear something one day and the next day have it sell out in the stores—was that LL was always, as he would say, "at the front end of the bell curve." If everybody else was wearing it, LL was off to find something else—like the Kangol hat before it became part of the hip-hop uniform.

LL would later explain that, for him, trying to pick out trends wasn't the point. When he discovered Kangols, he said, "I just liked the way it looked on me. I didn't need anyone else to tell me whether it would work or not. One thing about me, everything that I've done with fashion has been my own natural thing, because I thought it was cool. Period."

In 1985, after LL wore his Kangol hat in the movie *Krush Groove*—a stroke of marketing genius to promote Def Jam artists by telling the fictionalized story of the company's rise to success—it unleashed an endless buying spree of this obscure English brand of hats. Before long, hip-hop haberdasheries began opening their doors everywhere—from Harlem's elite boutiques to major suburban shopping malls.

As for brands that nobody was touching until LL Cool J did, like Le Coq Sportif and Sergio Valente glasses, he would say, "I'm just an early adopter."

Clearly, being an early adopter of rap had put LL in the forefront of the field, both as a writer of some of the early Run-DMC records and then when he carved out an iconic role with R&B-tinged rap that, true to his name, the ladies loved. I'm just saying. They went nuts! In short order, LL Cool J became the first big hip-hop heartthrob, not to mention the guy whom every other male wanted to be. From the standpoint of tanning, his appeal definitely skewed rap's demographics in terms of color and geography. But he didn't blow up on charm, good looks, or talent alone. For years, LL toured out in the sticks, spending more time in Maine than in New York, gigging in basement bars and small nightclubs—where R&B artists on the bills wouldn't even talk to him.

As I would later point out to artists about paying their dues too, those are the hurdles you have to face, as much the requirements for building a loyal fan base as they are necessary for brands to earn consumer loyalty. If you've never "plowed through the drama, through mud, through the gauntlet" (as LL put it), how are you going to know what it means to ignore the naysayers and remain authentic?

By the late 1980s, the plowing was behind him and LL was

rocking arenas as a top draw, second only to the kings, Run-DMC. Both coming out of the Rush/Def Jam stable, they were proof of how visionary Russell Simmons and the rest of his management team were. By this stage, Russell and Rick Rubin had more or less parted ways as Rick heeded the call of the west and went out to L.A.—where most of the record business had headquartered and where he would continue to be more involved producing metal and alternative rock bands. Out of these events and upon the theme of heading west, Rick came to LL with an idea for a record that was as crazy as "Walk This Way" had been for Run-DMC. Let me revise: It was crazier because it was against LL Cool J's already successful brand.

The song that LL agreed to write and have Rick produce was called "Going Back to Cali," and the first time I heard it, I almost choked. Don't get me wrong. The record was hot (and the video was even hotter). But the music was stripped of LL's usual R&B groove and had a more sophisticated, sped-up tempo with a jazzy horn section playing atonal rock chords, almost with a Peter Gabriel feel, not what you'd expect of a rapper from Queens. Why was he even rapping about going back to the West Coast with the glitz and glamour and chicks in bikinis when he wasn't from there to start? Even if he did make the decision in the song not to go back and it did have the refrain "I don't think so."

Many years after the fact, when I asked LL how he was able to put his authenticity on the line, he said that because Rick believed in it, he went along but was actually terrified about doing something that wasn't in his artistic DNA. What was his concern? He told me, "That it was so different it would ruin me." Being aspirational was one thing. But as he put it, "I don't need to be fancy." Still, LL believed that sometimes you have to venture into the unknown, take the risk, and be different. He came from the school of finding comfort in discomfort. That said, "Going Back to Cali" ran the risk of being too different and ending his career.

Instead, as I remember watching with amazement, its 1989 super-success sealed the deal with mainstream consumption that "Walk This Way" had primed. Like a one-two punch! If Run-DMC doing an Aerosmith song in 1986 had been the bridge to making hip-hop a legitimate force in the music industry, with "Going Back to Cali" LL Cool J walked over the bridge for himself and every other hip-hop artist to follow. The genre was presenting to the mainstream a group and a soloist, both musically versatile, widening the bandwidth to include rock and R&B flavorings without losing its essence. The *MTV* video was so brilliant because even though the music had evolved—so it could hoover up new audiences like those who went crazy for Peter Gabriel's "Sledgehammer"—LL's image stayed exactly as authentic and rooted in Hollis, Queens, as possible. The lesson to be noted and never forgotten for anyone in the entertainment industry or in corporate marketing is that in advancing the genre musically to gain greater popularity, Run-DMC and LL Cool J *never had to mortgage their image or the unapologetic values inherent in the culture.*

No one had a measure yet of how this moment in entertainment commerce was going to alter the mental complexion of the country. But they would soon.

Tales of Proximity

None of these advances of tanning happened in a vacuum or without precedent. The commingling of commerce and pop culture to produce changes in consciousness had occurred before, mostly whenever there was a trade, like the record business, behind a cultural format. The textbook moment I always use to demonstrate this phenomenon is when Elvis Presley borrowed the blues from black musicians, put a hillbilly rock accent on it, and went on *Ed Sullivan,* swung his hips, and wreaked havoc with the rules against overt sexiness on the public airwaves. After all, in those days, TV married couples were still sleeping in separate single beds. But the more popular Elvis became, the more the makers of commercial brands that had been under lock and key—makers of condoms, birth control, sanitary napkins, and other products that hinted at human sexuality—could come out into the open and appear on drugstore shelves or up near the register. Suddenly, America changed its mind about what was risqué and what wasn't. And the next thing you knew, you had other cultural groups connected to new music bringing along the free-love movement of the 1960s, which had its own commercial beneficiaries that dovetailed right into the women's movement and radical changes in thought about reproductive and political rights.

Hip-hop, therefore, was following in the footsteps of others when the music's cultural reach began to ripple into commerce. Certainly, the practice of putting products and brands into the lyrical content of songs didn't start with rappers. The classic example goes back to 1908's "Take Me Out to the Ball Game," which went on to last over a century as an ad campaign for Cracker Jacks. I think for any imaginative lyricist, it's hard to pass up proper nouns and names, like Sister Sledge's 1979 disco hit "He's the Greatest Dancer," which went on a brand craze with "Halston, Gucci, Fiorucci," all in a row. The list does go on and on. Rap just did the brand-name-checking more often and more unapologetically.

It seems that the most frequently mentioned products in pre-hip-hop songs were car makes and models. In 1951, Ike Turner had a hit with what's been called the first ever rock 'n' roll song—"Rocket 88"—which songwriter Jackie Brenston penned about his love for the new luxury Oldsmobile 88. The Beach Boys sang about their girlfriend's daddy taking the T-bird away and their fondness for a little deuce coupe. Prince rocked a party with his red Corvette and the Pointer Sisters harmonized about their pink Cadillac.

And let's not forget that Motown, the most successful independent record company in history, was built from Berry Gordy's vision of having a hit factory that would churn out records and stars—just like brand-new shiny cars rolling off Detroit's busier-than-ever automotive assembly lines. With marketing and musical genius, Motown really wrote the preamble to tanning, creating the historic crossover from R&B to pop with the marketing slogan the company adopted, calling themselves, "the Sound of Young America." As I was reminded by John Demsey, president of Estée Lauder, who ran the MAC makeup division for years and who understands the power of culture in the marketplace as well as anyone, Motown taught middle America how to get their mojo on while driving their cars. The hit factory in turn transformed black teenagers from Detroit and beyond, like Diana Ross, Smokey Robinson, Marvin Gaye, and Stevie Wonder, into global superstars—musical icons and brands unto themselves.

So by the early 1990s it wasn't unthinkable that hip-hop artists would want to seize opportunities in product endorsement that those who had come before them had made possible. Yes, it's true that in the past the idea of pushing brands would have been seen as inauthentic, or something you did after your career peaked, or as some kind of selling out. But no longer. Why not? Why wasn't it selling out for rappers to embrace and promote Versace when it would have been seen that way for rock 'n' roll and R&B icons or pop superstars? Well, one reason, as we saw with "My Adidas," was that it's not a sellout when it's authentic to your taste and style anyway and you're already doing product placement for free. It was part of the art and far from selling out; Andy Warhol proved that when he painted iconic pop art portraits of products like Campbell's soup cans, paying homage to one of the most classic, enduring American brands ever.

When I asked Jay-Z for his insights, he pointed out that many of the rock musicians had come from sustainable backgrounds, seeking acclaim for their talent and a level of cool that playing music gave them. For rappers coming out of the projects, getting paid and bettering yourself is part of gaining credibility. Jay reminded me also that it's not selling out when a kid in the projects sees a guy rapping about Sprite or the Gap because they know he'll be getting the money and that feeds his or her own aspiration. It's not that being acknowledged for talent and great work isn't desirable, but getting paid trumps those goals.

I agree. I don't think many hip-hop fans ever subscribed to the concept of selling out, not when you come from nothing and a deal can become part of your rags-to-riches success story. Besides, if you were helping a company prosper by giving it a street pass and not getting paid, by the laws of the street that was *your* bad. After putting Kangol on the map, for instance,

LL Cool J expected the company would want to work a deal with him. They made overtures, but when Kangol didn't follow through on them and ultimately didn't bite, he quietly changed hat brands.

The other reason that endorsement opportunities made sense to hip-hop artists was because sports superstars had been aligning their winning images with top brands for years, scoring deals valued in the multiple millions without anyone batting an eye. Together, Michael Jordan and Nike began writing the rules of sports marketing starting in the mid-1980s, when Phil Knight signed the young Chicago Bulls phenom. What Jordan did for Nike and vice versa became the gold standard that reached its apex in the late 1990s, benefiting and employing the force of hip-hop in the process. To this day, I give infinite credit to Nike and their innovative advertising team, Wieden and Kennedy, for opening my eyes to the only-in-America story of how a celebrity athlete, Michael Jordan, turned a sneaker company into a global power.

It was all about the synergy. Oh yeah, by the 1990s, Jordan was the quintessential celebrity athlete endorser of any product, although the Nike swoosh went along for the ride, no matter what the brand. The mythology was indestructible. His ability on the court to defy gravity effortlessly was so extraordinary that once it was combined with the unique and well-designed Air Jordans, his signature line, the combination was unstoppable. With acrobatic dunks, championship buzzer-beating shots, prolific scoring, and an uncanny ability to win, all day, any day, Jordan seemed superhuman, mystical even. Sports anchors, fellow athletes, and fans alike were constantly dumbfounded. How did he do it? In one of the ad campaigns, Nike ventured to answer the question with the slogan, "It must be the shoes."

The moral of the story wasn't that Air Jordans would endow anyone with his ability to play or with his fairy-tale lifestyle. What people would get for over a hundred bucks a pair was another kind of uplift, a way to convey status, to touch Jordan's greatness via brand alignment. Or, as Phil Knight would say, he wasn't selling sneakers at all; rather, he was selling dreams.

The narrative of dream-seeking was so incredibly successful

that every brand associated in any way with sports—and even those that weren't—wanted in on the magic formula. And so the stage was set for athletes of all stripes to ride Michael Jordan's coattails and nab their own endorsement opportunities.

Because of the literal proximity in inner-city neighborhoods between ballers and rappers, it was automatic for there to be a kinship and an overlap of language, values, and style. When hip-hop stars began showing up in the most coveted and expensive courtside seats at NBA games around the country, the public accepted the symbiotic relationship as a given. The fact that most rappers might have fantasized about being on the court dunking the ball was matched by evidence that more than a few NBA players dreamed of rapping. Some actually did, like Shaquille O'Neal, who made two successful albums.

With most basketball players influenced by hip-hop culture, all to varying degrees, as the nineties wore on you could usually look at the court and see the latest reflection of fashion trends happening on the street—from piercings and tattoos to the ever-changing rules for male hair grooming and the dramatically expanding cut and size of uniforms. However the players were translating hip-hop's new rules for their look, fans in turn would reinterpret the style for street wear; then sports apparel manufacturers would pay unprecedented amounts to license team logos and colors and then go on to have a sales bonanza by mass-marketing apparel to consumers anywhere and everywhere. Besides the apparel companies that would come to life as the result of hip-hop's huge embrace of professional and college team attire, sportswear by existing companies such as Champion and Starter would become wardrobe staples. If you didn't have a Starter jacket, there was practically something wrong with you!

Like everything else about hip-hop, the potential for an economic impact as the result of the proximity between rap and sports wasn't taken seriously at first. Because it was not premeditated or mercenary to start, the intertwining of the two cultures really wasn't so earth shattering—until it was. Such was the case when NWA in South Central L.A. decided to adopt the warrior mentality, colors, and style of its favorite local team, the Raiders. NWA—which stood unapologetically for "Niggaz with Attitude" and included at various stages Ice Cube, Dr. Dre, Eazy-E, DJ Yella, and MC Ren—came onto the scene in the late eighties when hip-hop fashion was starting to explore the bright color palette. But wanting to avoid colors altogether, as L.A.'s most lethal gangs had commandeered them (especially red and blue, which belonged to the Bloods and the Crips, respectively), NWA opted to stick with all black. Actually, they opted to don the black and silver, with the logo of the pirate with a patch over one eye backed by a shield—the uniform elements that reflected their devotion to the L.A. Raiders.

It wasn't just the fact that the guys from Compton were loyal to their hometown Raiders; there was also the opportunity to identify with an unapologetic team that had a storied past. The team, in its own way, was from a hard-knock life, as a whole coming from nothing and then becoming crazy, badass champions. That was even before leaving Oakland in 1982, when they brought their black and silver to L.A. and won the Super Bowl the very next year. As Ice Cube would later say in *Straight Outta L.A.,* his documentary about the Raiders' twelve-year stay in Los Angeles before they picked up and went back to Oakland, his first impression of the team was that "they were violent and a little rough around the edges . . . and I think that's what I liked about them."

The Lakers, he would explain, were too glitzy and the Dodgers "out of reach," but the Raiders felt like family. As Ice Cube recalled, "It seemed like my uncles played for L.A."

Once NWA started wearing Raiders jerseys and other team-associated gear on their album covers and in publicity shots, the local boom for football-related apparel and merchandise was a done deal. The gear wasn't just for showing up at the L.A. Coliseum to cheer for the Raiders. For youth in Los Angeles, black, Latino, Asian, and white, it was like putting on clothing that gave you superpowers of attitude and protection—both the hard-edged, outlaw mentality of the rappers and the brash "Just Win, Baby" mind-set of the Raiders. The assumption at the sports organization's front office and in the press was that gang members had co-opted the Raiders attire—even though it was so much more beyond that. And not only in L.A. All of a sudden, there was a new entry point for consumers across many demographics and across the United States to identify with the take-no-prisoners playing style of both the football team and the rappers. Before the Raiders decided to pull up stakes and return to Oakland in 1994, the NFL's annual licensing and merchandise revenues went from $300 million to $3 billion—thanks mainly to what NWA had unwittingly caused!

All of that was accomplished without endorsement fees or any marketing deals ever being struck. Unbelievable! No matter how you personally felt about the bad-boy groove and the more violent lyrical content that was ushering in the era of gangsta rap, you had to admit that it reflected something completely authentic that was tied to real experience in consumers' lives. And somehow, when combined with the culture of football, the commercial translation became larger than the sum of the parts.

Ice Cube talked about his understanding of how this happened: "Sports without music is just a game. The music adds the same thing it does for a movie soundtrack. It tells your emotions where to be." And as for what the image and persona of the Raiders did for the music, he also asserted, "It changed the trajectory of hip-hop."

Because of the association firmly emblazoned in the mind of the public, across the demographics, all of a sudden if you liked football, really the quintessential American sport, it was okay to like rap music. Poetry. The tanning effect was swift and forceful, causing a quantum shift in how language from "the street" made its way to main street.

As early as 1991, executives from media to Madison Avenue to the music industry were starting to try to figure out how to handle the baby Godzilla of rap that was rattling its cage, trying to set itself free. The bad news was that nobody really had any clue just how powerful the market force was going to be. The good news was that the opportunities were plentiful for people who could serve as translators—people like me.

CHAPTER 3

FOR US BY US

On a Southern California morning at some point in early to mid-1992, or thereabouts, a future mentor of mine, Jimmy Iovine, held a history-making meeting in his offices at Interscope Records. A rock producer who had come up through the ranks of the music industry starting in the early 1970s, working closely with superstars like John Lennon, Stevie Nicks, Bruce Springsteen, and Tom Petty, and shepherding the fortunes of entities that ranged from U2 to Nine Inch Nails, Jimmy famously kept a pair of beloved old speakers hooked up to his office sound system that he believed were the only trusted means for listening to new artists. That day, those speakers would come in handy as he met with fellow Interscope executive John McLain and two guys named Marion and Andre—otherwise known as Suge Knight and Dr. Dre—who were then looking for distribution for their label, Death Row Records. The album they hoped Jimmy would decide to hear on his speakers was called *The Chronic,* featuring Dre with a new rapper by the name of Cordozar Calvin Broadus—better known as Snoop Doggy Dogg.

On that same morning, or in this general time period, across the country in the offices of RCA's record division, where I was then employed, a few back-to-back meetings were wrapping up that were definitely historical for me. Even though my path and the paths of everyone meeting on the West Coast would eventually intersect, the only common bond we had at the time was the confusing state of affairs in which the music business found itself.

By now, at last, in my early twenties, I'd finally given in to the pull that hip-hop had been exerting over me for years. After I let go of the idea that the mortgage business (or any of the other professions I tried) was going to be my calling, it seemed as if doors into the music industry kept opening and I kept getting the go-ahead. Well, at least initially. My entry point had been at the lowest rung of the ladder, not long after I'd befriended DJ Wiz, who DJ'd for the young, versatile rap duo Kid 'n Play. Besides their ability to rock a party, they were fresh, with killer comedic banter and funky dance moves—and, in the case of Kid, a distinctive hi-top fade—that made them instantly memorable.

What Wiz saw in me, I'm not sure, but he probably appreciated that I was an energetic fan who loved hip-hop and who maybe was curious to learn more about its inner workings. At any rate, he began inviting me to hang out backstage at performances and in the studio. Before much time transpired, I started pitching in and helping move equipment and run errands, and next thing I knew, they offered me an official spot as a roadie. A short while later, Wiz (a.k.a. Mark Eastmond from Queens), Kid (Chris Reid, from the Bronx), and Play (Chris Martin, from Queens too) decided to make me their road manager. In that capacity, they began turning to me for advice on all aspects of their broadening portfolio of work. However it happened, my insights and instincts were valued enough that I eventually stepped in as Kid 'n Play's manager. Wow. While being excited by the opportunity, I clearly had lots to learn. First came the crash course I was given in the intricacies of the record business. Next, because of Kid 'n Play's film franchise with *House Party* and its sequels, plus their various TV projects, I was fortunate to learn the behind-the-scenes basics of film and TV production.

With the entrepreneurial atmosphere that surrounded hip-hop, everything about it seemed to move at meteoric speed.

And as I learned from watching the mainstream success of Kid 'n Play, it became apparent that as quickly as you can gain a foothold in commercial popularity, you can veer just as fast into the territory of being considered soft art. Big alert. The experience would provide a cautionary tale for me down the road— both in entertainment and in advertising—that fortunes in the mainstream can turn on a dime and the change can come on as swiftly as a shift in the weather. Credibility in the pop culture marketplace is everything. It's a lesson worth underlining— <u>credibility is everything</u>.

And also, whether in niche markets or on a mass level, you can go from flowing as credible to ebbing into not being credible so fast you don't know what hit you. Once you've lost your credibility, it's really tough to get it back. Catching that first wave onto the public stage can be relatively easy. Not the second one. I would see this time and again with artists and with brands.

Before my stint managing Kid 'n Play was over, our production company endeavors expanded my network. So, in a case of good timing, I was able to segue out of management and into an executive position in the A & R department of the black music division at RCA. With the mandate to bring in new talent to their urban music lineup and also to oversee production, I could barely believe my good luck. Looking back, I realize that it was not just the nature of the music business that had allowed me to move up so quickly; it also had something to do with what I brought to the table.

For starters, I was and am enthralled with the creative process and have enormous respect for artists. That allowed me to advocate, first and foremost, for the creative forces and to be inspired by their daring to be different. At the same time, I understand how business works and have a "doer" mentality. Daring, dreaming, and doing became my threefold mantra early on, and it would serve me well at every stage of my career. The ace up my sleeve, however, was a knack for translation between the creative and business teams. With that, whenever there were murmurings that hip-hop couldn't survive much longer, I reminded myself that I would have job security nonetheless.

In some ways, I was very naïve. In the early nineties, major labels like Capitol Records and others were dropping or paring back their urban music divisions. The main issue was that along with the R&B sound changing there was a lack of understanding of the audience and how to develop and promote hip-hop artists. Another concern was corporate consolidation. During the eighties, most of the great indie rock and R&B labels became a dying breed. Recording outposts in Philadelphia and Memphis were on the way out. Smaller maverick operations like Sugar Hill Records were no more. In 1988 Motown Records was sold to MCA, and a short time after that, Geffen Records was also sold to MCA (later to be taken over by Universal and merged with Interscope). A&M had been bought by Polygram—which would later be part of Universal and also absorbed by Interscope-Geffen.

Independents could no longer compete with the bigger coffers of the five or six remaining major record corporations, especially when it came to signing top artists. Not only that, but with the corporatization/consolidation of media, the marketing divisions at the bigger labels had more leverage and much tighter control of what got played on the radio; corporations were also more tied in to advertisers and more beholden to their media buys. Of course, a huge stumbling block for the smaller, independent companies was the rising cost of music videos. Mini-movies that jumped off the TV and made you run, not walk, to your nearest record store, music videos were marketing necessities. And finally there was the issue that blinded the industry with its fool's-gold properties: the transfer from vinyl and cassette tape technology—analog—into the digital age. Compact discs. By 2001, cassettes would account for only 4 percent of music product sold across the board. CDs became the cash cow. The major labels that had spent their millions buying record catalogs reissued CDs in every genre and had a marketing field day. That is, at first. In the meantime, certainty and passion in developing and marketing new product for all audiences, especially for younger generations, suffered.

The result was what I would call the cynical pop imitation of rap that made household names out of MC Hammer ("Can't Touch This") and Vanilla Ice ("Ice, Ice Baby"). Nothing wrong, by the way, with being commercial and fulfilling the turn-of-the-decade market's need for dance music. But the tanning effect was nil. Musically at that time, pop rap was more of a regression in my view because a) in trying to appeal to everybody the sound was formulaic and homogenized, and b) it was bubble gum without the authenticity of culture and code that reflected honesty in people's lives.

In stark contrast, the hip-hop artistry that was evolving in more underground, countercultural ways in self-started, home-grown urban studios—with a range of credible alternatives to pop rap, including hardcore or reality rap—was anything but bubble gum. Most of the powers running the music industry had no clue how to market any of these latest evolutions of an art form they never expected to last as long as it had. Even with MTV's series *Yo! MTV Raps*—instituted in the late 1980s with none other than Fab Five Freddy as one of the hosts—most everyone assumed the drug-, sex-, and violence-laden lyrics and images of reality rap would never make it onto the airwaves. Why would it? Some of it really was too violent, obscene, jarring, insulting, shocking, and disturbing. True, but a lot of it was also incredible, original, brilliant, hilarious, prophetic, and musically and rhythmically addictive, and if you were culturally attuned, it was absolutely important.

At a time when I had an opportunity to sign voices of importance to the RCA roster, I was also eager to bring in up-and-coming production talent that included the likes of the Trackmasters, also known as Tone and Poke—Samuel Barnes and Jean Claude Olivier—and had set up a meeting with them at RCA to discuss the possibilities.

Tone—later to become one of my best friends—arrived first, even though he was running late for our nine thirty meeting. As he was coming in, I asked him to wait in my office as I'd been called into another meeting with my immediate boss, the late Skip Miller (blessings to his family), head of the black music division, and a group of guys from among the top brass. By the time I returned to my office, Tone could obviously tell by the horror-stricken look on my face that there was bad news. First, I had to tell him that, unfortunately, I didn't have a job anymore. Second, I couldn't steer him to anyone else because RCA was shutting

down its urban music sector completely. As a first step to getting out of the record business altogether, they were cleaning
house—quitting on the artists. Why? "They do not see the sus-
tainability," I told Tone, repeating what had been said to me.

Now I had to make a list of everyone to contact whose destiny and dreams had just been shattered. As for what I was going
to do next, I had no idea. For a few minutes Tone and I both sort
of shook our heads in disbelief that all of our rides to fame and
fortune could be coming to such an abrupt halt. Then a crazy
idea dawned on me and I turned to him and said, "Tone, let me
manage you."

Not missing a beat, he nodded and agreed to talk to Poke,
even though we both knew it was already a done deal. Out of the
frying pan and into the fire! As a manager and producer, as well
as basically becoming the third Trackmaster, I was also able to
seek out emerging artists and undiscovered talent for management. This was during the period when I first met a young artist
by the name of Nas who rapped about real experience with a can-
dor that was emotionally devastating. We moved forward with
his second album, *It Was Written*, which also yielded the big international hit "Rule the World."

Even though being independent was nerve-wracking, what
was liberating was that instead of having to temper my tastes to
those of higher-ups or conform to the standards of music that
was selling already, working with the Trackmasters meant we
could make the music we loved—and then dare to bring consumers in on the party. Why work so hard at having to cross
over when we could invite buyers to cross over in reverse? We
could also be subcontractors and shop our services to major
record companies with distribution capabilities. While we were
prepared for our approach to take a while to catch on and even
for a bumpy ride in the beginning, much to our amazement, we
flew out of the gate without a hitch and were soon unstoppable.
We landed on the charts hard and fast, following one breakout
hit record after the other at a rate of about every two weeks. The
work was incredibly satisfying and rewarding.

The kind of music I was signing as a manager and producer
represented a spectrum that ran from hip-hop with R&B roots

to old-school, from pop to novelty to hardcore rap, from world-music-infused hip-hop to plain spoken-word poetry and even some rock/electronic-funk-laced rap. The list of artists whose work came out of the Trackmasters years included Nas, Mary J. Blige, Big Daddy Kane, Heavy D, LL Cool J, Faith Evans, the Notorious B.I.G., Foxy Brown, Will Smith, Mariah Carey, and Jay-Z, to name a few.

RCA's decision to drop its urban divison was one of the best things that happened to my career. Now, as for the meeting in the West Coast offices of Interscope with Jimmy Iovine, that also turned out to be a great thing for a lot of careers. By his own account, Jimmy had no context for what he was hearing on his prized speakers when Dre and Suge played the first cut of *The Chronic*—"Nuthin' but a 'G' Thang."

As he would tell me in later years, up until that moment Jimmy had heard hip-hop at various stages and just felt he didn't understand it. The sound, to him, had always been interesting and well produced but he hadn't felt the magic of follow-through that would give individual artists or the genre its punch. However, because Iovine paid attention to consumers, he had made sure Interscope's early offerings benefited from hip-hop's more danceable grooves by releasing records from Latin rapper Gerardo ("Rico Suave") and Marky Mark and the Funky Bunch ("Good Vibrations"). The sales success of those releases from commercial artists, one Hispanic and the other a white group, boded well for the multicultural mixing that was happening at retail. But the truth was that those groups didn't represent Interscope's focus on leading-edge music, nor had they improved Jimmy Iovine's appreciation for rap.

Now he was listening to Snoop and Dre through his speakers and everything changed for him. All of sudden Jimmy f**king got it. As soon as "Nuthin' but a 'G' Thang" finished, he blurted out, "Holy s**t!" He admitted that he had heard Snoop before but now he was coming at the sound with a clean slate, with Dr. Dre's production, and after listening to the whole album it all came together so powerfully that he immediately said, "Let's do this!"

In his own personal tanning turning point, Jimmy finally had a cultural construct for what he was hearing. Describing the feeling to me, he later said, "It hit me then that I knew what it was." He felt that it was what the Rolling Stones had been when they arrived on the scene, what Guns N' Roses had been, what *The Godfather* and *Goodfellas* as movies had been when they hit a nerve with the public—"plus a little *Shaft* thrown in," he said. From then on, he compared Snoop and Dre to Keith and Mick as well as to Axl and Slash. To Jimmy Iovine, who knew nothing about the history of hip-hop or the culture it had bred or even the Main Street economy it was already beginning to support, this was no different from the most raucous, rabble-rousing rock 'n' roll from past eras—guys (or gals) telling gangster stories.

Everyone warned him against making a deal with Death Row Records. Besides the baggage from previous deals that would make it costly, besides the difficulty in getting *The Chronic* played on radio and MTV and favorably reviewed in spite of obscenity issues, besides the fact that Time Warner (then the parent company of Interscope) would withhold support, and besides everyone's certainty that there was a ceiling on rap's core (black) audience, they went ahead with the deal.

All the predictions about the challenges that *The Chronic* would face did come true, and then some. That is, except for one thing. There was no ceiling. Or, if there had been one before, thanks to economic forces, that lid was about to be blown off for good. The core audience, as only time would tell, wasn't black. It was tan.

Got Cool?

During the same time period when decisive meetings were happening at Interscope and at Trackmasters, it seemed that Madison Avenue, along with the rest of the advertising world and their counterparts in corporate boardrooms, finally got the memo that it was no longer the 1950s or '60s—back in the day when modern mass marketing began. Many of the up-and-coming baby boomer executives being handed keys to power at those companies had grown up in the shifting era that would be explored in the cable TV series *Mad Men,* which debuted in 2007. As a time in which the monologue in commercials and print ads portrayed a lifestyle that was idealized, airbrushed normalcy— a picture that rarely matched up with anyone's reality—in the fifties and much of the sixties you were led to conclude that your life would only live up to those ideals once you'd bought into the brands being marketed.

One of the few commercials that commented on race relations and attempted to reflect the real social and political concerns of the day was a Wisk detergent spot in 1963 that, shockingly ahead of its time, had two kids, one black and the other white, playing baseball together. For the most part, however, the color barrier would remain as firmly in place in advertising as it had been in the days of Jim Crow. Since the 1940s, socially conscious brands, like Pepsi, had developed loyalty in the African-American community with the inception of niche marketing—ads directed at black or other minority consumers—to great success. Sometimes there was backlash, as, for example, in the sixties when some of Pepsi's distributors complained the brand was too closely aligned to the consumer of color.

By the early 1970s, efforts to integrate marketing messages that would appeal to a general consumer reflected the widespread, potent influence of pop culture—music, film, TV, and other media that had an increasingly diverse audience. So at most of the top ad agencies, where women account managers were sprinkled among the men, you might have one or two African-American executives or maybe another nonwhite manager working with accounts to reach Hispanic or Asian-American or other ethnic demographics. Ironically, even as women and minorities were slowly gaining a presence in the boardrooms, instead of the corporate thinking and direction becoming more inclusive, lines drawn between consumer types were more color-based than ever. That said, the exciting news was the extent to which the advertising field did embrace a much more creative mode of communication, with a keener eye to smart storytelling— through music, jingles, slogans, animation, and especially the artful use of code.

In the 1970s, you also saw more enlightened attempts to

speak to consumers in less patronizing ways. Possible causes for the change in approach were a reaction to the past and a need for analysis—literally—about the stark contrast between the way life was portrayed in happy TV world and the way it was actually turning out. With therapy becoming more commonplace and a boom in pop psychology bestsellers on the bookstands, self-help was a watchword. For advertisers that meant courting consumers in a way that respected them as the best authorities on their own needs and wants, as well as a more thoughtful portrayal of reality. Fittingly, "The Real Thing" (coined on the cusp of the 1970s) gave Coca-Cola a slogan and brand identity that would have lasting resonance.

The 1980s made the term "branding" a marketplace verb. In an era of big and brash, the decade began with a famous brand battle in the form of the taste challenge Pepsi launched against Coke. After winning a series of highly publicized "blind" taste tests, Pepsi declared itself the victor. Consumers were given credit and embraced as part of the "Pepsi generation," alongside pop culture icons used in their advertising, like Michael Jackson and Don Johnson of *Miami Vice*. All in all, Pepsi's strategies were so successful that when everything was said and done, significant market share had been peeled away from Coke. Ironically, some of this had to do with the success of Coca-Cola's own brand divisions, Diet Coke, Fanta, and Sprite. Nonetheless, the hammering from Pepsi hit home in 1983 when numbers came in showing that Coke, still number one, had fallen to a dismal low—*below* 24 percent of the market. But instead of embracing its greatest weapon and essence as the Real Thing and pushing back, Coca-Cola responded with what became one of the greatest, costliest marketing blunders ever: *New* Coke. The campaign yielded a case study for everything any marketer needs to know about what not to do to reinvigorate a brand.

Let me start just with what I'll call the A's of marketing: *authenticity* and *aspiration*. After an alleged two years of top-secret research to improve the taste profile, Coca-Cola broke the cardinal rule of authenticity by changing the product so intrinsically— trying to be something they weren't, in this case a rival to Pepsi in sweetness—that instead of welcoming it as new, the public received it as *fake* Coke. As for aspiration, Coca-Cola's COO, Donald R. Keough, later admitted, "We didn't understand the deep emotions of so many of our customers for Coca-Cola." In trying to win back consumers who'd left them, no one thought about putting the most important question to existing and still loyal consumers—did they even *want* their product improved?

Touching on what I value as the B's and C's of marketing, the campaign strategy added insult to injury by nearly killing *belief* in the lasting power of the brand, which in turn meant losing all *credibility* that any claims of newness or nowness were valid. It's worth remembering that in feeling threatened by Pepsi's clear edge on the taste factor, Coca-Cola didn't just offer a new brand of Coke that was sweeter or that tested as tastier. What they did was announce and hype a totally new-tasting, partially new-looking product that was designed to *replace* the original. In terms of making the argument for their reinvention credible, the biggest blunder of all was the decision to first have a public introduction of *New* Coke and a few days later officially halt all production of *Original* Coke. The message? Something had to be wrong with old Coke if it needed reinvention. Or, not so dramatically, the message turned out to be a desperate, tone-deaf marketing pitch that consumers didn't believe. Worse, brand loyalists felt betrayed. Most of the public felt betrayed.

Coca-Cola was more or less dumping one hundred years of its own history as one of the first flavored carbonated beverages ever introduced in these United States of America or anywhere else in the world. (Of the early soft drink brands still on the market today, only Dr Pepper, branded in 1885, had preceded Coke's entrance in the marketplace by one year.) With New Coke, therefore, they were repudiating the heritage of authenticity and aspiration that millions had grown up enjoying and associating with their own individual and national identity. Indeed, Coca-Cola and its bottling plants and other subsidiaries often reminded employees that their product was more than a soft drink. Rather, it was as described in 1938 by Pulitzer Prize–winning journalist William Allen White as the "sublimated essence of all America stands for—a decent thing, honestly made, universally distributed, conscientiously improved with the years."

It took less than three months for the fiasco to be acknowledged as such. There were stories of frantic customers buying up truckloads of Original Coke and building basement warehouses to keep themselves stocked well into the future, and others hitting the streets to sell cases of the old brew for astronomical amounts. As Donald Keough later observed, they had been caught unawares by the passion for the original. "And that is the word for it," he emphasized, "*passion*. It is a lovely American enigma, and you cannot measure it any more than you can measure love, pride or patriotism."

Obviously, it would have been suicide for almost any brand to have appeared to be dismissive of customer passion and to have failed miserably to live up to the drumroll of expectations raised by its own advance marketing and the media's huge play of the remastered Coke. But with the resources to scrap everything, the company did just that, calling it Coke II, and keeping it around as a novelty for the few who preferred the sweeter taste. Then they regrouped and rebounded and went all in with a *Classic* Coke revival campaign, returning to their original taste, bringing back older-style labels, and ultimately restoring the brand to its former dominance. And then some. In fact, as time went on there were conspiracy theories suggesting that the company had intentionally developed *New* Coke to fail as a way of priming the market to rejoice at the return of *Classic* Coke. Such theories would be rejected by Coca-Cola executives. They would insist they weren't that smart—*or* stupid!

The big challenge for all marketers in the 1980s was how to interpret numerous old and new crosscurrents without misreading the cues—whether it was preppy Polo versus punk Madonna or women putting on their power suits, padded shoulders, and big hair versus the romantic understated elegance of Princess Di. In many ways, Madison Avenue in the Reagan years went back to old habits from the fifties and sixties of dictating brand worthiness to consumers and then portraying those values in over-the-top fantasy settings. With credit flowing like wine, as cheap and addictive as crack, the eighties' most powerful consumer group—baby boomers, whom Tom Wolfe called the "splurge generation" and portrayed as such in *The Bonfire of the Vanities*—had no reason to go against the marketing grain.

Fortunately, the advertising world's regression back to earlier days did not include the racial attitudes of those eras. Marketers at certain brands now understood that at least some of their bread was being buttered in communities of color. Minority representation in ads rose as a result, as did the number of smaller agencies that had particular niche markets as their focus—mainly African-American- and Hispanic-owned and -run firms with counterparts in media outlets in those demographics.

Coming into the 1990s, with new technologies and metrics for supposedly measuring who was buying what, the buzz was all about target marketing—with the dueling messages of the old-school experts on how to reach the masses versus the ideas from the younger players about how to use guerilla and precision methods for reaching targeted consumers. Neither had the secret. That is, until Sprite helped to identify it by hoisting the flag of cool.

By the way, there was nothing new about the need for brands to up their stock in cool. After all, as we know, cool is timeless and evergreen. However, in the late 1980s and early '90s, as the hangover from overamped consumption began to wear off, consumers wanted to come back to purposeful, conscious spending. So cool had to encompass being smart, stylish, and distinctive. Sprite was on that page early. What's more, Sprite perceived the potential marketability of the cool emanating from hip-hop culture around the same time that Adidas made a deal with Run-DMC. In the late eighties, not long after parent company Coca-Cola had gone so wrong with New Coke, Sprite went so right by creating the "I Love the Sprite in You" campaign. They designed directly for the urban youth market, making sure the sweetness in their taste profile was part of the design, and tapped everyone from Kurtis Blow to LL Cool J to Kid 'n Play. In this connection, as an artist's manager I had my first glimpse behind the scenes of the marketing world from the celebrity's perspective.

Smart, stylish, and distinctive, the campaign targeting the young urban consumer did incredibly well. So much so that in 1994, when the Cadbury Schweppes–owned brand competitor to Sprite, 7-Up, began to up its market share, instead of reinventing the wheel, the decision makers at Sprite stayed in the cool, hip-hop groove. At the same time, they added new faces to the marketing lineup, including less commercial, more serious rappers—A Tribe Called Quest, KRS-One and MC Shan, Nas and AZ, Pete Rock and CL Smooth, among others—together with rising star athletes like Kobe Bryant and Grant Hill. Where before the focus had been an invitation to party, the new campaign adopted some of the unapologetic tone of hip-hop, along with a dose of playful sarcasm that made fun of traditional marketing. The commercials were anticommercial, shot with handheld video cameras and made with the look and feel of freestyling rap, soon becoming the most distinctive advertising on the air.

Everything about the evolution of the campaign was visionary—with most of the credit for that going to Darryl Cobbin, whom I greatly admire for his marketing pedigree. Of course, Sprite knew what it was doing by having Cobbin, an African-American, as brand manager and backing his always innovative moves. Darryl Cobbin understood the core hip-hop consumer and why Grand Puba—not a mainstream artist—would be so much more meaningful than any of the better known hip-hop poets at the time. Grand Puba wasn't out on the *Billboard* charts, hadn't become MTV friendly, and never broke into the mainstream. But as a beloved figure in the underground of the culture, he was infinitely authentic and made you aspire to the cool Sprite lifestyle that his freestyling poetry embodied. In a spot Grand Puba did with his counterpart, Large Professor, all you saw was the green and yellow Sprite logo as the two rhymed back and forth while you heard the popping of the flip-top can and the sound of cold, refreshing carbonation being poured.

Having fun with it, Grand Puba talked about how he was grabbing his Sprite in his left hand and giving "a pound to my man" (code for a fist-bump) with his right hand, and then tagged it with "First things first: Obey your thirst." The tagline that Grand Puba may have well invented in the rehearsal for the commercial was so perfect, it carried Sprite for the rest of the decade and well into the next one. The point, made succinctly in the "Grant Hill Drinks Sprite" commercial that featured a kid trying to emulate a basketball hero spotted drinking Sprite, was that, no, drinking the brand wouldn't improve your game. The advice given to become a great player was to practice. "But," on the other hand, "if you want a refreshing drink, obey your thirst."

With all aspects of the "Obey Your Thirst" campaign a success that led to consistent improved market share year after year, Sprite and Darryl Cobbin had thrown down the gauntlet for other brands to get their cool on too. By designing into the market, speaking to loyal consumers in honest, humorous, imaginative ways—not just with commercials but also by later sponsoring hip-hop festivals and even creating a commemorative logo out of street graffiti—Sprite grew its consumer base within the target group, yet also outside of it. It was the fastest-growing brand in the soft drink industry for multiple years. This had been achieved by virtue of the core of the Sprite business being African-American and Latino youth dwelling in major U.S. cities. The reinvigorated domestic Sprite marketing strategy was then exported with similar success the world over. What? No one really saw that coming. It was tanning, once again, slyly at work.

Not surprisingly in a field where imitation is the highest form of flattery, the nontraditional thrust of "Obey Your Thirst" set off a spree of campaigns modeled on its elements. The "Got Milk?" ad campaign, commissioned by the California Milk Processor Board and created by the San Francisco advertising agency Goodby, Silverstein & Partners was a prime example. Meanwhile, Sprite had gained the attention of a handful of savvy brand managers who were beginning to track the power of cool. Among them were executives at the Gap. They apparently understood very well that in marketing to the young urban consumer, their coolness would be authenticated, and then, thus supercharged, would draw in every possible demographic of the 1990s before going global. And that's just what happened—but with a few twists along the way.

The Street *Is* Main Street

Tommy Hilfiger opened up his first business when he was eighteen years old while still in high school in Elmira, New York.

A white teenager rebelling against his parents' generation and their *Little House on the Prairie* values, as he would tell me, Tommy grew his hair long and wore bell-bottoms in defiance of the straitlaced, conservative styles and attitudes he saw around himself as a kid. With a dream to one day design clothes "for the people," he decided to name his first business, a retail clothing store, the People's Place. What began basically as a head shop that sold blue jeans, rolling papers, and rock records gained so much popularity that Tommy and his partners went on to open eight stores.

When Tommy later sat down with me to talk about hip-hop's influence on the design elements of the apparel, fragrance, accessory, and home furnishing lines that he ended up creating—and on his journey from rags to riches (pun intended)—he began his account in the mid-eighties. At that point in time, his jeans stores had closed down, following bankruptcy, and he had gone off to New York City. Armed with lessons learned at retail, after a brief apprenticeship designing at Jordache, Tommy found a backer, Mohan Murjani, then wanting to launch a male equivalent to Gloria Vanderbilt jeans. Going for it, before he had even made a name for himself in the design world, Tommy decided to build a clothing line—from the ground up.

"What I did when I started my company," he explained, "was based upon what I wanted to wear for myself." He wanted "very hip clothes that were not stuffy like Ralph Lauren but were still American classics." Taking cues from what he saw urban youth wearing on the street, Tommy Hilfiger began with more traditional designer looks and then revised and changed the apparel to make it hipper. How? "I redesigned the classics to make them oversized, wide, and colorful," he answered. "And they *were* hip." Not only that, but the business elements and style of marketing, with the red, white, and navy blue logo suggestive of a flag or a sideways H, had the same feel of a classic American company that was also fresh, colorful, and culturally inclusive. In almost no time, Tommy recalled, "people just embraced me."

So what was it that allowed the people to get to know him in the first place? Well, one of the most crazy, completely bold and daring instances of guerilla marketing strategies used by Murjani was to erect a big stark white billboard with crisp navy blue lettering in none other than Times Square. In keeping with the brash marketing approach of the 1980s, it was a classic positioning move but with an updated twist that was over-the-top even for those years. Putting him in the company of Ralph Lauren, Perry Ellis, and Calvin Klein, the billboard used code—initials only—for introducing somebody that nobody had ever heard of, stating simply: "The Four Great American Designers. R.L., P.E., C.K., T.H."

Everyone was quick to recognize who the first three names were. But the question running around sophisticated Manhattan circles was *Who exactly is this "T.H."?* Oh yeah, and when they found out, the answer came from the least likely of sources—kids from the streets. Those were "the people" that Tommy had begun to recognize as resources nobody else seemed to be observing. He started to pay serious attention to young urban consumers who were being inspired by hip-hop artists. After all, this was the same group that was also borrowing classic fashion statements and repurposing or reinventing them. Whenever he wanted inspiration, Tommy didn't have to look any farther for his research than the inner-city streets of the boroughs surrounding Manhattan.

As the company began to take off, whenever it was time to leave his office in the city and make the long drive home to Connecticut, he would often weave through the streets of Harlem to see how the kids were dressed. In addition to the profusion of hats, including baseball hats worn backward or sideways, one of the more obvious fashion statements coming out of the culture, especially for males, was wearing jeans that were lower than the underwear waistband.

Two thoughts occurred. First, he was reminded of his own fashion rebellion; so instead of seeing the style as ridiculous, he embraced it as fantastic. Second, he saw a design and logo opportunity. If kids were wearing their jeans low, he decided, why not design underwear with a super-wide waistband that prominently featured an oversized, bold Tommy Hilfiger insignia? How did he know that it would resonate with urban consumers? Because he understood the hip-hop impoverished mind-set and realized that wearing your pants low was a style that made you cool and in with the culture, especially if you could show the waistband of your underwear with a designer logo. It was a way of saying to the world, *See this glimpse of who I am? I'm badge-worthy.* By respecting that mentality and designing into it, making the logos big and bright, Tommy Hilfiger was translating from the streets and speaking back to the consumers, with nuance and all. That awareness infused the whole line, whether it was underwear, accessories, shirts, jeans, whatever item of clothing that a proud person would wear and show to the world as a statement and testament of who he was—*I ain't got sh*t, but look at my shirt.* It was code, as poetic as hip-hop lyrics, that was saying, *Look at my style! I may come from nothing but I'm not this held-back human being who merits being disparaged. I got something; I am somebody. Look at what I'm wearing, check me out, yo!*

Tommy Hilfiger was able to translate all of that into a clothing line that took off running, thanks to the urban market that responded with love and loyalty from the get-go. By the early 1990s, after seeing Tommy Jeans go from zero to $500 million in revenues over a matter of five years, and with every other denim designer soon getting in on the act, it became clear that the urban youth stamp of approval was echoing out across cultural and generational lines. Even as you started to see baggy pants and ball caps turned backward in white, suburban neighborhoods, Hilfiger marketing consistently honored the market that had inspired and supported the brand early on. There was, for instance, the 1992 cross-promotion with Estée Lauder for the Tommy men's fragrance that employed a print ad campaign, not with a celebrity or typical male model, but a handsome, strapping kid from Jamaica who wore big, funky dreads. Not your everyday mainstream image. But this hazy, crazy new idea—that images from the street were starting to become Main Street—was now coming into focus. Incredibly, the appeal of the ad earned so much attention for the fragrance that stores around the country couldn't keep it in stock. Tommy told me that for ten years in a row his line of men's fragrances held the number one, two, and three sales positions. "We won all the awards," he said. "It was unheard of."

In keeping with the cross-pollination of hip-hop and sports, the mainstream arrival moment for the brand was probably with the Tommy jersey. There was a bold proud jersey for every passion, as he recalled: "football jerseys, basketball jerseys, baseball jerseys." Hockey jerseys had never been part of street wear collections, mainly because of the high V-neck and oversized arms that were cut to go over the hefty padding worn by hockey players. Tommy saw an opening. "I did an authentic hockey jersey," he remembered, "and put them in Bloomingdale's for one hundred fifty a pop. Big numbers, embroideries, big logos, and labels. That was expensive twenty years ago for a shirt, but they blew up." From there Hilfiger started sponsoring hockey teams. Next thing everyone knew, brand sponsorships led to teams that were playing under the banner of Hilfiger basketball and football.

Although the streets were now converging and all leading to Fifth Avenue—or wherever its hip, high-style counterparts were in other places—whenever it was time to innovate, the brand always turned to the generation that first inspired it. For example, with these hockey shirts that came almost to the knees, Tommy and his design team saw that a lot of the kids would pull the crotch of their pants even lower. This presented something of a design challenge in terms of sizing. How could you put traditional sizes, say for a thirty-two-inch waist, on jeans when they weren't being worn at the waist? The solution, Tommy said, was to go get consumer feedback, in return for free clothing. Sometimes they'd literally go out into the streets and talk to teenagers and have them try on the clothes, and other times they'd invite groups of young urban guys and gals up to the offices to interview them about fit and style preferences. Everyone benefited. In return for their expertise, the kids were given clothes that they would wear into the clubs at night, promoting product at the same time.

Once it was rolling, the look became iconic—rugby silhouettes and unapologetic, oversized logos. Or then there was the stunning fold-out ad with the late Aaliyah. At the time, Tommy was starting to see a lot of urban girls in boys' clothes but with their own feminine touches. Photographed in big baggy jeans, hanging low with high underwear, Aaliyah's glamour was there, of course, with hair and makeup—and with her fingernails, which had been painted to spell out Tommy's name. So hot! Another important influence and celebrity authenticator for Tommy Hilfiger, as it so happened, was Grand Puba, along with other hip-hop artists tapped for marketing. There was Usher early in his career, the Fugees, Q-Tip from A Tribe Called Quest, and even edgy rappers like Method Man, who famously appeared in haute couture showings as a runway model for the brand.

Between this kind of hip-hop lineup—which would eventually include Notorious B.I.G. and, most notably, as we shall see, Snoop Dogg—and all the movement Tommy Hilfiger was getting from being name-checked in lyrics, he was golden. However, aside from the star power and really cool marketing and customer-friendly product innovations, there was a built-in ongoing campaign being run by young urban consumers. Tommy put it this way, telling me, "The street kids were my billboards. They were on every street corner and in every city in America wearing my name. You saw as many logos of mine on the street in the nineties as you did street signs or stop signs."

Actually, the only thing you might have seen on the street in the 1990s more readily than Tommy's logo or street and stop signs was Gap stores. With the exception of Starbucks, probably no other megabrand was as synonymous with the decade as the Gap was—with its khakis, denims, cool colored T-shirts, and other moderately priced, quality-made casual wear that wasn't too hip for the more brand averse but was still stylish enough for those who didn't want to be seen as completely out of it. With its various divisions that included the high-end Banana Republic and the lower-cost Old Navy, as well as Gap Kids and Baby Gap, the company was said to have grown 26,000 percent in profits between 1984 and 1999—26,000 percent!

Much of what it did to achieve such phenomenal growth was accomplished by paying attention to market and fashion trends, and then distilling the finer points and translating them into Gap's own special language. As a result they were able to draft off of everything that the top designers were doing. What they seemed to miss, however, was the creativity of the smaller street-run companies that were also flourishing with hip-hop's cultural expansion. And there was one such company, in particular, that the Gap hadn't noticed—although they really should have.

Known as FUBU, the company was founded in 1992 by Daymond John, from Hollis, Queens, along with a few friends, after they began buying T-shirts and hats in bulk and then selling them at local hip-hop concerts. While still working as a waiter at a Red Lobster restaurant, Daymond had picked up an interesting tie-top-style hat one day and then sat down at his mom's sewing machine to try to knock it off. The next thing he knew, he had come up with a product that everybody wanted to buy from him. Before long, he was making the hats in quantities, while also designing his own clothing and accessory line. When it dawned on him one day that he needed a company name and a logo, he thought first about the fact that he and his friends were making clothes for themselves and their peers, and as part of hip-hop culture they were in business to elevate through style. The name "For Us By Us" sprang to life—FUBU for short.

From there, as the story goes, he opened up a factory in his living room, still working his gig at the Red Lobster, and basically sold his wares out of the back of a van. That was until the FUBU executives managed to pool their resources and make it to their first trade show in Las Vegas—returning a few days later with orders for $400,000 worth of merchandise. And that was the beginning. Within a few years, FUBU had been embraced by urban consumers enough so that the company could afford to move up in the world—to an office in the Empire State Building. Much of the steady growth had happened by word of mouth alone.

Since there had been no budget for mass or local advertising, the key to exposure was in a kind of product placement effort that was fairly common in rap circles. If you knew someone who knew LL Cool J, for instance, as was the case with Daymond John, whose wife went to high school with him, you would show up wherever he was, remind him how he knew you, and then ask if he wouldn't mind putting on a shirt or a ball cap with a FUBU logo or a hanging tag and then snap a picture for a publicity one-sheet. That could get a clothing company huge mileage—just to have a logo spotted on a poet as prominent as LL Cool J, even in street flyers. Of course, the big get—whether you were Tommy Hilfiger or FUBU—was to achieve product placement in publicity or on television, that is, in a music video.

When Daymond started coming around so often, trying to get his latest designs to LL, the rapper was initially resistant. But being the early adopter that he is, and because he really liked the FUBU designs and colors, and especially because of the economically empowering concept of For Us By Us, he went along. Then one day, as LL recalled to me, Daymond brought him a shirt and asked him to wear it in a photograph. He was planning on getting it covered by *The Source.*

It was the 1990s and there was now a bible for anyone seriously interested in the doings of hip-hop, musically and culturally. *The Source,* founded by two white Harvard guys, was no mere gossip rag. Authoritative and opinionated, it was the only magazine devoted to rap.

LL felt that he'd given lots of free publicity to help out FUBU. So instead of asking for a fee to do the photo, he proposed that they give him a share of the company. With that LL Cool J earned equity and became an owner, just in time to help spur FUBU's healthy spike in sales. In addition to wearing the latest FUBU pieces in concert, in other publicity settings, and even on the NBC sitcom he did, LL also provided creative and design input.

Maybe because LL Cool J had been part of hip-hop's ride from the start, he may have had a deeper sense earlier on than most of us about what was happening in the minds of young Americans who were white and suburban yet being drawn to all aspects of the culture. He might not have had the language to speak about it yet in 1997 but my hunch is that the opportunity to help promote an African-American-owned and -run start-up like FUBU and help bring awareness to it from outsiders was an appealing way of being a cultural ambassador. Which is, by the way, what hip-hop was doing naturally, not by having to stage a self-conscious Benetton ad full of different colors of people, but by sketching an arc to take in all backgrounds.

Such a collective in which people of diverse ethnic heritage live can best be described with an anthropological term that we at Translation have updated and rebranded for its potent marketing applications. The word is "polyethnic."

> **pol•y•eth•nic (pol-ē-eth-nik): In twenty-first-century terms, this adjective refers to the individuals that form the new diverse culture in which we live. Because of America's ever-increasing numbers of interracial marriages and an unprecedented leap in ostensibly polyethnic births, we are giving rise to children whose ethnicity is often vastly different from who they are culturally.**

When understood in this context, it makes sense that the reason why the standard silos for African-American, Hispanic, General Market, and so on, began to no longer apply over a decade ago. Marketers who recognized the challenge realized that they needed new tools for cultural diplomacy, even if they didn't know how to use them. This was how the opportunity to be just such an ambassador arose for LL when he was hired by the Gap in 1997 to help them reclaim some of the luster of coolness that they were beginning to lose. And what LL Cool J did to seize the moment remains, to this day, one of the most unapologetic, bold, and daring things I've ever seen anyone do in my life.

Upon arriving at the set to shoot his commercial, LL happened to be wearing a FUBU hat, and as he came out of the dressing room in his Gap outfit, he decided not to take it off. A wardrobe coordinator might have told him to remove it, but when he didn't, nobody persisted. After all, the Gap executives were looking to him as a rap artist, a musician, not as a cultural force. Not having paid enough attention to the street, they had no idea what FUBU was anyway. Apparently no one looked at his lyrics before they shot the commercial. Did anyone check any kind of script he might have brought? Most likely, they didn't. So then, when cameras rolled and he did his bit, nobody knew what he meant when he threw in a rhyming lyric that went, "For Us, By Us, on the low."

What? When I saw it on TV, as best as I can remember, it was like being hit by lightning. Nobody did that! My conclusion was that none of the executives had a clue about code or that hip-hop could have its own language or that he had just piggy-backed FUBU onto the Gap's megabrand global mass-marketing ad campaign. This was the Gap, and there wasn't even a cul-turally connected person in the room or someone who knew a culturally connected person? That's how novice most corpora-tions were in their understanding of the force that hip-hop had become. The Gap executives in that case had no way to calculate that what LL Cool J had just done by shouting out another brand and telling listeners in code to buy "on the low"—via word of mouth, like a street drug—was about to unleash contagious con-sumer behavior at a mass level. The Gap must have wanted so badly to be part of the new tan culture that they were willing not to know or care what LL had said. As he would later report, they did eventually figure it out but weren't too upset. Why should they be? They were now cool by association. And FUBU went galactic.

There is only one other time when, I think, a strategy was pulled that was even more bold and more daring that caused a tanning shift that was truly seismic. The economic reverbera-tions of it can still be felt to this day. It also helped create a new tier of powerful hip-hop moguls who really did have a say on behalf of their generation, who lived up to the promise of "for us by us." That was back in 1992 when Jimmy Iovine master-minded a way to get Snoop Dogg and Dr. Dre what is known as day-parted on MTV. With a little help from his friends.

CHAPTER 4

ALL BUSINESS IS SHOW BUSINESS

When I first moved into the offices that my company, Translation, now occupies, I remember wondering what to do about a two-story white blank wall. Instead of hanging up a piece of art or having kids come in and do street graffiti on it, I decided to use the wall as a reminder of the power that culture can have in transforming hearts and minds and chose to have it inscribed with the words of Sidney Poitier. From a speech he delivered upon receiving an honorary Academy Award in 2002 for lifetime acheivement, the words are especially meaningful to me not only because of the seismic tanning shift Poitier created but also because of the towering barriers he overcame in his personal journey.

I never forgot the story of how, in 1943, at age fifteen, Sidney Poitier had come alone to the United States from the Bahamas, three dollars to his name, to find work in Miami. Unprepared for the indignities of racism, he was given a crash course over a short period of time. It culminated one evening when a job interview the following day meant he had to go pick up his clothes from a dry cleaner in a white part of town about ten miles from where he was staying. The bus got him there but by the time he paid for the dry cleaning, there were no more buses for the night. Not knowing any better, he tried to hitchhike back to the black neighborhood. The next thing he knew, Poitier had mistakenly flagged down an unmarked police car with five white officers inside. They took him into an alley, put a gun to his forehead, and told him that instead of killing him then, they would follow him all the way to where he was staying and if he turned back to look at them they were then going to shoot him dead. I can only imagine what must have gone on in his mind as he looked for their reflections following him in shop windows the whole way home.

Even though Poitier didn't speak about that experience in accepting his honorary Oscar or the fact that he was the first African-American to receive a Best Actor Academy Award (for *Lilies of the Field* in 1964), that story was undoubtedly part of the subtext when he spoke of the distance he had traveled:

I arrived in Hollywood at the age of twenty-two, in a time different than today's. A time in which odds against my standing here tonight, fifty-three years later, would not have fallen in my favor. Back then, no route had been established for where I was hoping to go. No pathway left in evidence for me to trace. No custom for me to follow. Yet, here I am this evening at the end of a journey that, in 1949 would have been considered almost impossible, and, in fact might have never been set in motion were there not an untold number of courageous, unselfish choices made by a handful of visionary American filmmakers, directors, writers and producers, each with a strong sense of citizen responsibility to the times in which they lived. Each unafraid to permit their art to reflect their views and values—ethical and moral—and moreover, acknowledge them as their own. They knew the odds that stood against them and their efforts were overwhelming and likely could have proven too high to overcome. Still those filmmakers persevered, speaking through their art to the best in all of us. And I benefited from their efforts, the industry benefited from their efforts. America benefited from their efforts, and in ways large and small the world has benefited from their efforts.

Therefore, with respect, I share this great honor, with the late Joe Mankiewicz, the late Richard Brooks, the late Ralph Nelson, the late Darryl Zanuck, the late Stanley Kramer, the Mirsch Brothers, especially Walter whose friendship lies at the very heart of this moment. Guy Green, Norman Jewison and all others who had a hand in altering the odds, for me and for others. Without them, this most memorable moment would not have come to pass. And the many excellent young actors who have followed in admirable fashion might not have come, as they have, to enrich the tradition of American filmmaking as they have. I accept this award in memory of all African-American actors and actresses who went before me in the difficult years. On whose shoulders I was privileged to stand to see where I might go. My love and my thanks to my wonderful, wonderful wife, my children, my grandchildren, my agent and friend Martin Baum. And finally, to those audience members around the world who have placed their trust in my judgment as an actor and filmmaker, I thank each of you for your support through the years. Thank you.

I wanted the speech to be on the wall as a reminder that the best storytellers—whatever their medium—are those who have that sense of citizen responsibility to the times in which they live. And I also wanted to be reminded every day of one of my heroes who embodies the transcendent power of popular culture.

For the world audience, seeing a person of color through the motion picture lens provided that transcendence. But it was a much different force that enabled hip-hop to finally overcome external and internal challenges to find its transcendent power. What was it? The answer is short and sweet: music television.

MTV

In 1987, when Van Toffler arrived at MTV and started moving through the ranks to eventually become president of MTV Networks—which today includes MTV and MTV2, VH1, among other cable channels plus departments for feature films, TV series, and video games—he had a vision that both appealed to advertisers and also scared them. Van was on a quest to make MTV the number one entertainment destination for the most sought-after yet elusive consumer demographic: youth comprised of 12-to-29-year-old viewers. What advertiser wouldn't love that goal? But the part that scared them was *how* MTV intended to attract and keep their audience. Unapologetically, Toffler and the team at MTV believed they could cultivate a discerning, loyal, constant viewership by offering culturally relevant music.

No, that didn't sound scary when you were talking about videos from mainstream rock stars. But issues came up immediately once rock started veering into grunge and heavy metal, or when pop artists like Madonna started pushing the envelope with sexually explicit content and images. Anything new, as usual, took advertisers out of their comfort zones and made them worry whether it was worth it to associate their brand with certain artists in order to win favor with the younger demographic but then run the risk of turning off other core consumers in older demographics.

From the start, Van Toffler was used to helping advertisers get past their issues. "For us," he explained to me, "it was always trying to reflect what the artists were seeing in the lives they were leading and the cultures they were reflecting. That's what we ultimately stood behind when talking to advertisers—that this is going on in the world. And musicians always set the cultural barometer for everyone else."

The strength of that argument had prevailed until edgier rap came along. Though the lines had long been blurring in the marketplace, the old divisions segregating black and white music that had confused the record industry were still impacting the thinking of music television programmers. As a result, videos by hip-hop artists tended to make it onto MTV by a kind of hit-or-miss process. That would change as the genre gained popularity and programmers and advertisers started to relax—at least with anything in the spectrum of the more rock-infused and pop-laced hip-hop. In fact, thanks to market testing, by the late eighties everybody arrived at the happy conclusion that white kids in suburbia who watched rock videos also liked rap. But then, right at the turn of the decade, red flags went up. Artists were being prosecuted on obscenity charges, some were fighting allegations of misuse of copyrighted materials, and all of a sudden hip-hop was back in the not-ready-for-prime-time category.

For a minute, as all of this was coming to a head in the late eighties, it looked as if the inroads that rap music videos had made toward legitimacy had come to dead ends. Not willing to give up, as Van Toffler recalled, the creative voices and programmers at MTV came together and made a strong case not to abandon the genre. Leading the way in the discussion was the late Ted Demme, then a recent college graduate who had begun his career in media as the host of a radio show on WSUC-FM. When Ted left the freedom of college radio—where he could mix music, talk, and comedy—he brought his underground, countercultural sensibilities with him to MTV.

Van noted that in 1988 he started hearing more and more from Ted and fellow up-and-coming MTV executive Pete Dougherty about how both the music and culture of hip-hop were percolating in urban streets across the country. In D.C., there was almost a dance subculture within the culture, known as go-go, and then there were the local underground economies on certain streets there and in Brooklyn where you could only find particular mix tapes in particular locations, just as in neighborhoods of Queens and the Bronx, all of them part of a phenomenon spreading similarly into different regions of the country. At a moment when the art form was about to be sequestered to the past, mix tapes were turning into the underground railroad for cultural expression. Ted and Pete argued that this new street music and culture, rich with language and customs of its own—something that was, as Van described, "really real with not that many filters"—ought to at least have its own regular MTV segment.

Toffler and the rest of the decision makers agreed. "Ultimately," he told me, "we felt that though we weren't going to be
the first ones to feature hip-hop and rap, we were going to be the
first big media company to shine a light on it and talk about it." In
those days, the network was developing weekly shows devoted to
certain "alternative" segments of their audience. The segmented
shows that were developed over the years included *120 Minutes,
Alternative Nation,* and later, *Subterranean.* Usually they would
air once weekly, later at night, not during peak viewing hours or
in regular day-parted programming. Basically, broadcast hours
are broken into daily blocks of time and programmers select content that is seen as most appropriate for that part of the viewing day. Getting day-parted at MTV meant reaching the general,
wider audience, the same times when advertisers saw the biggest
bang for their buck in reaching the best target audience for their
product. So the weekly nighttime shows were intended to build
an audience among a specific segment of viewers and also boost
popularity for each show's genre. Made sense. Rather than putting hip-hop music videos into general rotation, Ted Demme and
Pete Dougherty were given the green light to add a new series, *Yo!
MTV Raps,* to the lineup of segmented programming. While this
had to be a feel-good decision for the culturally curious, I don't
believe anyone had a clue as to how much the segment would
blow up. To mainstream eyes, the couple of other music video
outlets that were including hip-hop in their programming in this
period had seemingly not amassed much more than a fringe or
niche following. Over at BET—Black Entertainment Television—
in the late eighties and early nineties, after facing resistance even
from within the African-American community, rap videos were
now infiltrating the mix. But as a cable channel still in its infancy
BET didn't yet have the household count, exposure, or audience
reach to be a market force.

However, there was one other TV entity that predated all the
rest in its airing of rap videos and is too often overlooked in the
history books for everything that it and its creator, host Ralph
McDaniels, did to give hip-hop a footing—not just in music television but for its ultimate survival and growth.

Originally from Brooklyn before he moved to Queens—where

he cut his teeth in the early days of hip-hop as a DJ for local MCs—Ralph went on to pursue a formal education in communications and broadcasting. After earning a college degree from the New York Institute of Technology, he came up with a radical concept he called "edutainment" that would allow him to combine his passion for hip-hop with his communications acumen. His idea for creating a hybrid of education and entertainment was to layer rap music on top of news-style camera footage of the city's diverse street scene, complete with local interviews of artists and fans alike. Ralph is African-American, but his pitch wasn't about color, minority status, or the need to feature black music. What he was seeing, rather, was an emerging, important kind of American folk music. It was complete with a culture and an attitude that happened to be bubbling up ahead of the curve right there in the New York area.

Part of what really motivated him, Ralph explained to me, was the culture of B-boys, which was all about code: "The way you wore your sneakers, your hat, or cap to the side, and the colors. B-boys led the way. But they were outcasts. They were trendsetters, but club owners wouldn't let them in the club. And I saw this look nowhere on television." There were also videos being produced by the music companies for artists like the Fat Boys, Grandmaster Flash, and Whodini, as well as for Run-DMC, Rick James, and Michael Jackson. But as then twenty-two-year-old Ralph McDaniels realized, "There were no real outlets for them. They weren't on *Soul Train* or on *The Dick Clark Show*."

To do a local TV show on something that was beginning, something as transformational as ragtime was in its day—as one example—ought to have rung all sorts of bells with network affiliates in and around Manhattan. Nope. Not in the for-profit media apparatus. Fortunately, however, Ralph's energy and conviction were so appealing that the public station WNYC-TV, Channel 31, brought him on as an engineering intern. Ralph's fortunes changed one day when a promotional reel arrived from SOLAR Records, owned by Dick Griffey, with footage of the roster's mostly West Coast R&B artists. Ralph said, "The reel wasn't a video, just footage shot in the studio, not live performances at a venue." The label had simply sent out the reels to radio and

TV stations. Ralph proposed to his bosses that they use it during the annual station fund-raiser. "I rounded up more videos," he recalled, "and what we found was that when the music videos were played, we got more fund-raiser calls."

When he proposed to turn that into his big idea for a music video show, the station still balked. They did, however, opt to hire him as a host of a show that played an eclectic mix of danceable music called *Studio 31 Dance Party*. That went so well, by the end of 1983 when he pitched a public interest angle for his edutainment idea, it held sway with the station heads. Thus, *Video Music Box* was born.

Because there were so few hip-hop artists at the time with videos broadcast-ready, Ralph McDaniels often developed his own visual component to the music as part and parcel of his storytelling. Pioneer of music videos that he was, Ralph realized that the best place to do that was in the clubs. He remembered, "I'd go into the clubs and tape the acts." There was a rich diversity in the different outposts for cultural sharing—the hip-hop and punk clubs downtown at the Roxy, the uptown clubs where you had to have money to get in, and all the different neighborhoods where fashion was being created. His next brainstorm was to host the first ever concert lineup of rappers—with the likes of Run-DMC, Kurtis Blow, and a very young LL Cool J—and then to shoot video of that. From the very first performance, Ralph noted somewhat to his surprise that the crowd was composed of both inner-city kids of color and suburban white kids. Something very real and relevant was clearly happening.

Video Music Box soon became as much a part of the upbringing of area teens like me as *Sesame Street* had become for preschoolers. For one hour in the afternoon, six days a week, urban teens would rush home from school (or wherever we happened to be) and watch stories set to music that actually resembled and reflected our lives in ways nobody else was offering on mainstream TV. Out in the suburbs, as Ralph McDaniels realized, kids who weren't growing up in the culture also rushed home from school (or wherever they happened to be) to watch stories set to music that spoke to them too. Why?

And it wasn't just attracting kids in New York City and

environs. *Video Music Box* was so popular it gained national attention. When I asked Ralph how a local public access show did that, he explained that there was a signal from the station that was picked up in the D.C./Virginia area, as well as in North Carolina and in Detroit. Then, those viewers started recording the show onto VHS tapes and selling them around the rest of the country. That was how, he said, early hip-hop videos became a national phenomenon. Another part of the drawing power was that cable was in its infancy, and not everyone had access to MTV. And because public television was free—accessible to anyone with a television set—curiosity alone must have been enough to motivate teens of all backgrounds to check out a format completely different from anything on the other channels. For many, *Video Music Box* was where they could hear rap for the first time, with the added bonus of having visuals to go with the audio experience. Besides the appeal of poetry set to beats, Ralph's video footage provided a minidocumentary—a real, honest portrait of another world that existed not so many subway stops away. And the reason that it resonated both with those who were living it and those who were outside of it was not a fluke or happenstance. It had everything to do with Ralph McDaniels's prescience that there might be a tan mind-set waiting to be tapped by the possibilities of the new cable medium.

In time, the creator of *Video Music Box* would be affectionately known as Uncle Ralph for everything that he had done to provide a platform to up-and-coming artists, fledgling crews, and even nominal figures in hip-hop culture. With Uncle Ralph's man-on-the-street interviews, where he would stop passersby to say a few words for the camera, legend has it that Ralph McDaniels coined the phrase and practice of giving "a shout-out." Some of the shout-outs became local headline news—like who did somebody wrong, or the name of somebody's good-for-nothing ex about to be pursued with a paternity suit! Of course the language was part "localese" and part generational slang, both old- and new-school ghetto vernacular. All that code was now getting passed by *Video Music Box* to other neighboring locales, even to communities where the culture was very different.

Not every parent out in the sleepy safe suburbs was a fan

of their kids watching the gritty, urban, irreverent, and unpredictable show six days a week. Even if it was public television. From what those teenage viewers would later tell me, their parents weren't any happier when they started tuning into the more mainstream black music videos that BET was starting to air in the late 1980s. But then, interestingly enough, as soon as *Yo! MTV Raps* debuted in August 1988, first as a music special starring Run-DMC along with Jazzy Jeff and the Fresh Prince (a.k.a. Will Smith), then as an hour-long show shown once a week, hosted by Fab Five Freddy, suddenly, somehow, some way, parents didn't seem to mind as much. Even when the show expanded a short time later to include a daily installment hosted by Ed Lover and Dr. Dre, the general consensus by those who didn't love hip-hop was *Well, let the kids watch it, seems like they're just having fun.* Again, why?

Part of it was timing, and the fact that the MTV brand and banner gave the genre a legitimacy. Plus, my guess is that the segmented programming made it safe for visiting—just as advertisers were beginning to see it as safe for visiting.

As envisioned, the show didn't reinvent the wheel. It built on everything that *Video Music Box* and BET had started doing—but, like a petri dish, helped grow the culture by pointing out that what was happening in the Northeast was in full swing down in Atlanta, over in Houston, and out in California. Now the images and words were more regionally and culturally diverse—palm trees and skateboarders, graffiti that mixed Spanish and English, dance grooves locally branded, language with Caribbean, Asian, Middle Eastern, or other accents, or vocalized with a southern lilt or a western twang. The global exposure was a two-way street—with *Yo!* broadcasting from places, like Jamaica, where it wouldn't be lost on the hosts that the poverty of the 'hood there was so extreme, as they would say, that it was definitely the "'hoo-ooo-ood." One of the more memorable specials for me was shot in Japan. Here were 1990s Japanese kids in baggy pants with baseball caps on backward, listening to rap, break-dancing, popping and locking like they invented it. Proof positive of the global power of hip-hop and music television.

When I asked Van Toffler at what point he and the other MTV

execs started to recognize that the audience was much bigger than the segmenting would have suggested—and when they knew that white suburban kids were starting to emulate the language and the dress of the hosts and guests and the stars of the genre—he answered, "It was probably ten minutes after *Yo! MTV Raps* aired." The reaction from one and all, Van remembered, was literally, "This is the coolest thing I've ever seen."

With MTV's overall mission to tell real stories and provide the authentic narrative of life from the streets, *Yo!* acted as a cultural ambassador, as hip-hop had been known to do, for the entire network. Van's comment was, "Nothing connects more to the audience, whether it's told through rock music or folk or hip-hop, than real stories."

That popularity impacted a lot of careers, as I experienced firsthand. In the early years of the 1990s when I was going from artist management to working as an executive at RCA and then becoming a producer/manager—in tow with the Trackmasters— our success depended on whether or not we got played on radio and music television. Plus, *Yo!* gave exposure to artists as much as it did to their music.

Since most of the show was taped in-studio and there was lots of time to fill that wasn't about the music videos, the hosts were constantly coming up with entertaining bits, often inviting guests to freestyle right along with them or to engage in an unscripted megalogue with cameras rolling. The atmosphere was anything goes, wild and unhinged.

"Thank God it was taped," Van Toffler said about that. "It was uncontrolled chaos." One of the most famous instances of things getting truly out of control was Tupac Shakur's unsolicited rant about kicking the asses of the Hughes brothers—allegedly because of how they fired him from the movie *Menace II Society*. The hosts were practically tackling Tupac to get him to calm down. But to no avail. The Hughes brothers ended up showing that clip when they took Pac to court.

As boisterous as the shows got, Van Toffler knew that *Yo!* and MTV were benefiting from the excitement that those kinds of spontaneous outbursts aroused. Yeah, it was rough around the edges, but it was full of surprises, never the same, and a proving ground for emerging hip-hop artists like no other. Or, I should say, that was mostly the case except for the period of backlash against hardcore rap, right around the time in mid-1992 when Jimmy Iovine and Interscope were coming up with a bold, new strategy for how they were going to promote *The Chronic.*

The irony was that for all the liftoff that *Yo!* could offer, it was still segmented programming that wouldn't guarantee getting a music video day-parted and put into heavy rotation. The way for most rap or metal videos to keep from being limited to late-night airings was to first have a radio story—heavy growing rotation (a.k.a. "spins") and an expanding audience. And getting that to happen for hip-hop in those days—to climb to the top of the mostly still segregated R&B and pop charts—was next to impossible.

Just what was happening and why was revealed in the early nineties when new technology in bar coding for retail cash register sales showed what was actually selling in the record stores—as opposed to what stores had been reporting to *Billboard* and other trade publications. When the weekly syndicated radio show *American Top 40* (hosted by Casey Kasem and then by Shadoe Stevens) started basing the Top 40 list on a formula that included airplay but was weighted by these actual sales figures, it turned out—much to the shock of white-owned stations—that hits by black artists (rap, R&B, and pop) were dominating like nobody's business. The bar code scans also showed that besides black music, hard-core metal rock was booming. The other revelation in the scan reports was that there was completely unprecedented sales momentum for country music. Who knew? The data was contradictory to everything that programmers had been trained to understand about their advertisers and listeners. Country and metal were problematic but programmers could adjust. All that black music was another story. And so, when a significant number of stations threatened to drop *American Top 40,* a new formula for creating the list was established—weighted not by sales figures but by airplay as recorded among Top 40 stations. They jerry-rigged the formula.

Metal had a home on rock stations anyway and country music took lessons from R&B, first adding more mainstream pop music elements and then finding stations for brand-building for the genre on the AM dial. But what this did to hip-hop was throw it right back out into the cold, radio-wise, once again, after gaining legitimacy, back to being an orphaned street music—not fully suitable for black R&B stations, not welcomed on white pop stations (now being rebranded as contemporary hit radio), and not ready to be given its own station platform. Then we all turned around and a portal, as if out of nowhere, suddenly opened. It was crossover urban, called "churban" or rhythmic radio.

At Interscope, Steve Berman had just arrived at the company when the game plan for promoting "Nuthin' but a 'G' Thang" was coming together. Steve later explained to me how churban was invented by saying that even though hip-hop wasn't fitting any of the traditional radio models, "it was so powerful in terms of how it was moving, people and units and money, that they had to grow these other formats." Hip-hop had become such a powerful force for pop culture and for selling music that some of the radio stations that were paying attention to consumers and record stores in their own communities had no problem taking the leap.

A leading example in New York was Hot 97, an early adopter of churban programming. Not ready to be labeled rap or hip-hop, these types of stations welcomed a diverse audience of black, white, and Hispanic listeners. But even with this middle ground, there was trepidation that anything too cutting-edge would be off-putting to advertisers and some of the audience. When I recalled those days with Andre Harrell, the brilliant, pioneering entrepreneur who worked with artists at Rush Management before launching Uptown Records—where he would famously give one young hip-hop newcomer, Sean "Puffy" Combs, his first job in the industry—he could remember having to jump through those same hoops. Andre reminded me that a lot of the confusion in radio was a reflection of uncertainty on the part of the big record companies. They didn't know with clarity how to market the music.

So that was the tangled web of distribution obstacles in which Jimmy Iovine and his team at Interscope found themselves once the deal had been made to partner with Death Row Records. To complicate matters, as Jimmy recounted the story, everyone was telling him that the amount of money he would need to spend even to get the first single into serious rotation wasn't going to be worth it. In his words, "Everybody was telling me the sh*t is bigger than the cat." An expression that came from his father, its point was that if the cat is bigger than the problems, you keep the cat. But when the "sh*t is bigger than the cat, get rid of it." Well?

By his own admission, Jimmy was naïve. He had no resistance or baggage and was seeing only upsides. He was sitting in his office, continuing to listen through his prized speakers, and as he said, "I've never known from hip-hop before. I don't know anything about it. All I know is the Rolling Stones, Guns N' Roses, *Godfather, Goodfellas*."

And so Jimmy went all in. The first thing that he did was to treat the deal as if it was being made with superstar rock guys. The deal was unheard of at the time for several reasons but more than anything it allowed Death Row to own their masters— which was the right thing to do because they had walked in the door with finished product. What was so unusual was that Jimmy wasn't betting the odds. He was funding the fledgling record company, giving them their own identity and autonomy, with the cockeyed belief that this was the beginning of much more to come. Crazy? If history had turned out differently, yeah. But then again, this was Dr. Dre, one of the most prolific, authentic producing virtuosos ever to grace recorded music. And there was something about Snoop Dogg's voice on "'G' Thang," with its iconic tone and phrasing, and how it jumped off any sound system and into any listener's nervous system on the very first hearing, that could not be denied. Written by Snoop, the single reminded Jimmy Iovine of "(I Can't Get No) Satisfaction" by the Rolling Stones. Same structure, same vibe. It felt like a classic, he told me, even before it dropped.

In the meantime, Interscope had written another very large check for the music video that Dre directed for "'G' Thang." Jimmy confirmed the cost by saying that in those days it was "a lot of money." After appreciating early videos for being raw and real, viewers were getting choosier. But even the most aggressive hip-hop videos in the early nineties were in the range of

$50,000 to $70,000. For the first single video release from *The Chronic,* Dre had a budget on par with a Guns N' Roses video production.

Now it got really crazy. Given the era's landscape, as we've seen in the shifting sands of radio, guess what? No radio station, urban, churban, rhythmic, or otherwise, would even touch " 'G' Thang" with a ten-foot pole. Nobody wanted anything to do with "gangsta" rap. Despite Jimmy Iovine's comeback that it was art, fiction, a story about gangsters, just like rockers would tell badass stories about themselves, the truth was that in that market lull no really serious new hip-hop artist could get arrested. Not that Jimmy or any of his team at the time, like Steve Berman, had expected any differently. Actually that was the reason for spending so much on the video.

Time for something drastic, bold, and daring, as in gangsta. Jimmy went to MTV's head of programming, Rick Krim, and personally played him the video for " 'G' Thang." Raising all of the obvious objections, given the broadcast standards, Rick narrowed everything down to one issue: "Where am I going to play it?"

Jimmy then suggested that he put Dr. Dre and Snoop Dogg on in between Nirvana, Guns N' Roses, and Madonna. Translation? He wanted his video day-parted early. Rick Krim would have laughed him out of his office if Jimmy had not added, "I'll tell you what. Do it. And if it doesn't work, if I'm wrong about this, I'll never come in here asking you to play another Interscope record."

Without calling it as much, this was a go-for-broke strategy known in marketing campaign terms as total disruption. The approach breaks all the rules of branding, authenticity, and consumer preferences. When introducing a new or reinvented brand, it is the kind of tactic that will make you or break you. Kamikaze marketing!

Rick Krim and MTV, after editing some of the more risqué images and bleeping a word or two here and there, went for it and put the video into early day-parting, toe-to-toe with rock and pop's biggest marquee names. And it worked. By the end of 1993, "Nuthin' but a 'G' Thang" had become the third-most-requested video of the year.

But wait. There's more. Before that evidence came in, there were a few more moves in the total-disruption campaign that had to happen.

Although MTV immediately had success and increased rotation of Dre and Snoop's first video, reaping the rewards of an expanding audience and advertisers not about to miss the benefits of a phenomenon in the making, the next shocker was that radio still wouldn't play it. Oh yeah, as I remember all too well in my own promotional efforts, radio did not want MTV taking their hit-making power away from them. The unspoken agreement was that radio was supposed to lead, music television to follow. So what did Jimmy do?

What he did was, again, not what anyone in those days would have done in a million years. Jimmy went to his head of promotion and said, "Make me a radio spot that plays the hook for one minute." He didn't want any voice-over, any talking, just one minute of "'G' Thang." Then he gave the department a list of fifty radio stations, starting with the top tier in leading markets, like New York's dominant Z100 and L.A.'s KISS FM, and instructed his people to buy enough airtime to run the one-minute spot on each station ten times a day. For real.

Steve Berman, currently vice chairman at Interscope, remembers it well. None of the team questioned Jimmy Iovine's sanity. The logic was clear. He wanted people to hear the song. Sure enough, they heard it. In fact, audiences heard it at the same moment as program directors who wanted nothing to do with anything called Death Row Records (maybe understandably so)—as they were driving home and radio commercials came on the air, on their own stations, playing one minute of a song they wouldn't program. Next thing everyone knew, phones started ringing off the hook at radio stations across the country, with people requesting the song in multiple formats, including regular radio.

In March 1993, "Nuthin' but a 'G' Thang" peaked at number two on *Billboard*'s Hot 100, after topping the R&B chart at number one. By November 1993, *The Chronic* was certified triple platinum after hitting number three on *Billboard*'s list of the two hundred highest-selling albums. Artistically, most hip-hop aficionados consider the album to be one of the most influential of the genre.

But there was one other conversation Jimmy Iovine instigated that helped score the three loaded bases in the cultural paradigm shift of tanning that was afoot. Somewhere in the spring of 1993, with "'G' Thang" and follow-up single releases from *The Chronic* still riding high and Interscope gearing up for its Thanksgiving drop of *Doggystyle,* Snoop's debut album, which Dre was in the midst of producing, Jimmy called up Jann Wenner—the illustrious publisher and cofounder of *Rolling Stone* magazine.

With no preamble, Jimmy told Jann he had to put Dre and Snoop on the cover of the magazine. As the Iovine-reconstructed story goes, Jann Wenner's response was something along the lines of *Are you out of your f**kin' mind?* Then Jann, the rock 'n' roll journalism icon, explained more calmly, "We're not a hip-hop magazine."

Jimmy: "Hip-hop? This ain't hip-hop. This is *Exile on Main Street,* it's *The Godfather*! This is huge!"

Jann Wenner: "Whatever it is, this is not my customers." *Click.*

Actually, before Wenner got off the phone, he left the door open by suggesting that if Interscope and Snoop Dogg wanted to show him an idea for the cover, he'd be willing to look at it. So Jimmy went to Snoop and said, "Hey, we're going to get you on the cover of *Rolling Stone* and I want you to shoot it." Made sense. This way they would be more likely not just to get the cover but to have it shot with a feel and look that matched the genre.

Snoop: "Man, give me the cover of *The Source*. What the f**k is *Rolling Stone*?"

All Mr. Iovine could do was to assure Mr. Broadus: "Trust me on this."

In September 1993, Snoop and Dre appeared on the cover of *Rolling Stone* and, sure enough, it completed the grand slam that being day-parted early on MTV had begun. Even before the November release of *Doggystyle*—which would debut at number one on *Billboard*'s list of the two hundred top-selling albums—Snoop went to see Jimmy to tell him about the strangest thing that was happening. All of sudden, wherever he was, whenever he walked down the street, white kids were coming up to him, saying his name, "Snoop Dogg!" in greeting, as if they were connected, like they knew him. Snoop was like, *What the f**k is that?*

Obviously, having that kind of rapid, widespread fame is something that nobody can really prepare you to grasp until you've experienced it. But this was more than that. It was culture shock. As Jimmy pointed out, hip-hop up until that moment had already found an underground hip white audience. However, these weren't niche music consumers. They were white kids from regular, everyday, mainstream households. And the heads of those households, along with their counterparts in government and corporate America, were horrified.

The trouble began. Time Warner threw Interscope out and sent it, along with Death Row (until it shut down), into the arms of MCA, which was soon absorbed by Universal. Politicians, community leaders, and media figures representing the status quo went to war against what was seen as the dangerous Pied Piper of addictive beats and mind-altering poetry now leading their children astray.

As a disclaimer, I will say that during the years when the "gangsta" bravado was coming to a head—at the same time that I was becoming deeply ensconced in the record business—I didn't see how destructive it was. Only in hindsight can I attest that, yeah, it got ugly, particularly with the East Coast/West Coast nonsense that ultimately took lives. But I will also repeat that violence was not the true soul of the movement. A lot of the focus on beefs between leading hip-hop players was the result of propaganda—which artists would exaggerate to put themselves in the limelight because that was all that the media was covering. What was done for the entertainment value got carried away.

The best cultural parallel I can offer comes from what used to be called the WWF, World Wrestling Federation, which was later forced to change its name to World Wrestling Entertainment. World Wrestling Entertainment turned out to be more fitting since so much of it was staged to thrill and engage the masses. Cyndi Lauper told me a fascinating story about how she became part of that world. As a kid I used to watch the WWF and remembered seeing her on TV at the fights. When we met in recent times during a shoot for a commercial I was doing with Lady Gaga and MAC cosmetics, I asked Cyndi, "Why were you on those shows?"

"Oh," she answered, "that's how I broke my record." In the early eighties, Cyndi couldn't get any radio play for her song "Girls Just Want to Have Fun." Then one day she found herself on an airplane sitting next to wrestler and promoter Lou Albano. The two struck up a friendship. Although the fight world appealed to a mostly male audience, young males in particular, she got to thinking that the WWF might offer her an avenue to get some kind of TV exposure. As this was happening, Cyndi Lauper had raised all of $35,000 to make her "Girls Just Wanna" video and, being creative, was connecting with lots of people who were doing favors for her at no cost. Cyndi decided to have her new friend Lou Albano play the part of the dad in the video. The pop song had nothing to do with wrestling, but when it was shown on MTV and on other video music outlets, the kids watching who knew Lou got excited and before long Cyndi Lauper was one of the WWF's leading celebrities—and her song got tons of exposure with that audience. Doing that at just the moment when wrestling was getting onto cable was the knockout punch for the record to blow up beyond her wildest dreams—and from there she was golden. As she came into her own, WWF benefited from having a pop star of her stature in their midst, and she benefited from having access to a much larger audience than traditional channels might have allowed. Cyndi became such a part of wrestling culture that the template for what she had achieved was soon borrowed by record labels to break their hard-rock songs—with the hopes that wrestlers would use their music for making their big entrances or that producers would play their records for interstitial drama. It was just another way to get records spun without getting traditional airplay. This was especially true as time went on for breaking countercultural records by groups like Limp Bizkit—for whom the WWF was a launchpad.

Even though the majority of viewers of the WWE (as it's now known) and the growing millions of hip-hop fans know that the feigned violence isn't real—that it's being done for entertainment value—the possibility that it can spill over into the real excites human emotions. But that's why the ring is important and why an offbeat, super-talented girl singer like Cyndi Lauper could become beloved out of that mix.

Those comparisons aside, I agree some of the backlash against hip-hop was justified. There were, no question, offensive elements associated with the genre that unfortunately became hyped and underwritten by the corporate record industry, which figured out how to profit from those more controversial aspects. Those were the entities that in the mid-1990s had finally gotten the memo that hip-hop was about to be really big business. After shunning the genre as niche, they now wanted not only to get in on the game but to control it.

Too late. The uncontrollable genie was out of the bottle. How far and how wide it was going to go was in nobody's hands. Hip-hop, more than ever before, had taken on a life of its own—as witnessed by the world in March 1994 when Snoop was the featured musical guest on *Saturday Night Live.* Performing two of his latest singles from *Doggystyle,* he was attired in his Hilfiger best— with a long-sleeved, thigh-length collared jersey that had a bold brand ID across his chest that read TOMMY and a pattern of red, white, and blue stripes suggestive of the flag of the United States. Whatever you thought or had heard about the big, bad wolf of gangsta rap was not on your television screen being watched by millions around the globe with you. Cool as ever, with trademark humor, Snoop seized this seminal tanning moment for all it was worth and made history—as American and as lovable as mom and apple pie.

Tommy Hilfiger acknowledged to me that this was also the pivotal moment in the growth of his brand. And it was bigger than a brand. Hip-hop had arrived.

Much codification on multiple levels and playing fields had been responsible for setting the stage. It's hard to even quantify how important a role MTV had played in getting to this point. From the instant that "'G' Thang" was day-parted, there was no turning back. From a music distribution standpoint, it was an out-of-body experience for any of us in the business of promoting hip-hop artists and music—as if a switch had been flipped and all the doors you'd been banging on to no avail opened up and you were invited to come on in.

From a marketing standpoint, advertisers that might have been hesitant to spend money during *Yo! MTV Raps* all at once started jumping over each other to buy time connected to the airing of any hip-hop videos. Or, much better yet, to achieve some kind of product placement in them. At the offices of MTV, Van Toffler remembered, phone calls began pouring in from marketers asking how they could get in on any upcoming shoots. If videos could make a Cadillac cool, or whatever brand needed a pop culture boost, the right question to ask was, "How can I get in on that?" Some even made such pointed requests to Van as "Hey, I want Nelly to wear my sneaker, can you help me out?" Naturally, since they were the programmers, not the video producers, MTV couldn't do that. So the next step would be to pay to advertise in time slots when the top videos were airing and get some cool for their brand by proximity.

That's how powerful an art form music videos had become—especially with the influence of Hype Williams. The former graffiti writer who once dreamed of being the next Basquiat or Haring, Hype burst onto the directing scene in the early nineties, after having been mentored by none other than *Video Music Box* creator and hip-hop music video pioneer Ralph McDaniels. Hype was always a creative hero for me.

Iconic from early in his career, he quickly became the Martin Scorsese of music videos. There were two things you could be guaranteed if you had a Hype Williams video: a) It would be expensive, and b) MTV would put it immediately into rotation. In fact, the network started to look like Hype Williams television. That's how much content he delivered. Known for his wide-angle shots and the selective use of the fish-eye lens, along with outrageous color tints ranging from his own film noir black-and-white grainy look with a blue overcast, to jewel tones, metallic golds, coppers, and rich sepias, Hype could turn dark into light in ways filmmakers have yet to figure out all these years later. A small handful of the artists on his videography roster included Usher, Notorious B.I.G., Nas, Lauryn Hill, Jay-Z, Will Smith, Kanye West, Nelly Furtado, Mary J. Blige, and Coldplay.

Hype's breakout moment came in 1995 when Jimmy Iovine commissioned him for an unprecedented half million dollars to direct the video for Tupac's "California Love" (featuring and produced by Dr. Dre). Borrowing story and images from *Mad Max Beyond Thunderdome,* Hype took such a quantum leap with the visual poetry of the art form in that video, forget it—the seas parted. From then on, everyone who was anyone wanted that and had to have that. Not just hip-hop artists. When top rock 'n' roll bands started to see the impact, most of them started hiring Hype.

In terms of tanning, I see Hype Williams as the visual architect of its transformative power—just as Rick Rubin was its sound architect. Hype has been criticized for flash and overt commercialism, but I disagree. What he does is walk right up to the cutting edge, right into the gap—what we'll discuss more as the Thinnest Slice—into a space that changes the rules and thought itself, and where tanning happens. Moreover, by portraying his main subjects, the poets who had come up from nothing, from the streets, bathed in light, wrapped in luxury and all the trappings of seemingly limitless wealth, he only does for aspiration what hip-hop had done from the start. The new rules that arose dictated that as long as the artist and the video story had credibility, weren't a copy or the homogenized rendition of the real thing, they were still authentic and meaningful.

How did the executives at MTV react in those early days to the excess consumerism the videos couldn't help but celebrate? Van Toffler answered that question by saying that the innovations trumped the other aspects and "Hype's genius was to respect the culture of excess. He made brilliant videos and brought everything to a new level." Because of the honesty and respect for aspiration and the lack of artifice, the videos pulled everyone in, along with the culture, getting viewers together because, in Van's opinion, "everyone was speaking to each other in the same language of music."

In five years videos went from costing next to nothing to having price tags of fifty grand and then a few hundred thousand, until there was a true ticket-shock once the top-of-the-line music video could cost a couple million dollars. And like the old days of rap battles, the era of music videos each trying to outdo one another began.

At that point, by Van Toffler's assessment, the stars that shone the brightest in the galaxy ruled by MTV no longer came from rock 'n' roll. After the rock icons crested—everyone from Jimi Hendrix to Robert Plant to Bruce Springsteen to Axl Rose—there was a new polyethnic generation in charge and its stars were all from hip-hop. That was the power of video and the network that harnessed it.

And with this new medium of lush, visual storytelling, it was tanning on steroids, now drawing together the like-minded with a new set of values as to what really defined cool, glamorous, stylish, desirable, believable, and just plain old beautiful.

Ghetto Fabulous: Why It *Still* Takes a Woman

The sea change really happened in the mid-1990s. Underground music became mainstream, niche began edging into the general marketplace, and color and other traditional labels started to become unglued from the demographic boxes. For the next ten years, you would see the cultural youth movement—called urban but so much more—sweep the nation and merge with multiple aspects of the economy in a rising tide. Reminiscent of the Madison Square Garden moment with "My Adidas," the numbers had expanded beyond measure, with an endless array of brands being held up for celebration by an evolving slate of superstars, heroes, heroines, and antiheroes. Hip-hop was seeping under barriers, permeating all forms of art and entertainment—not just music, but comedy, movies, TV, theater, publishing, dance, sports, visual arts, fashion, beauty, and their related industries—slowly yet surely becoming nearly a synonym for show business itself. Not show business in terms of a false front or brute commerce, but the opposite—unapologetic, even over-the-top, in-your-face show business that still captured something real, credible, edgy, dangerous, or raw, yet also glamorous, seductive, and hopeful.

Somehow the storytelling in the best music videos managed to bridge those oppositions—and even offer some edutainment to boot. Andre Harrell saw this at his label, Uptown Records, in the 1990s during the start of these halcyon days, and gave me his take on how the videos became instructional. Because of the authenticity of the artists, and how and where they were pictured, the attitude projected in the videos was felt as real, and, Andre observed, it locked onto a similar attitude shared by the viewer. "Through the video image, they're taking in the whole life. Not just the dance," he commented. The viewer's next thought would then become, *I want to dress like that, be cool like that, to wear the earrings, do my hair like that, talk like that.*

Andre Harrell provided the larger context for the phenomenon, saying, "When you see urban culture become more than just a collection of pop records, it becomes a lifestyle drama—how to be in your life, how to solve your problems, how to go dressed up to an affair, how to talk to a woman—all defined by these young people in musical vignettes, which are how-to episodes." Better yet, America was being given a how-to manual for how to walk, how to talk, what to wear, and how to be cool.

The culture of hip-hop, through the videos, had decided without an invitation to be in all business. Because it could; because who was going to say no? Why not, Andre was arguing, have a say in what car to drive, what soap to buy, what cologne to wear? These how-tos were not just handing out advice about the latest brands or trends. On the contrary, the lifestyle dramas in hip-hop music videos had deeper themes, rooted in classic kinds of American entertainment—Westerns, romances, gangster and crime stories, horror, murder mysteries, gothic fairy tales, sci-fi, war sagas, legends from Greek and Roman mythology, Bible passages, family sitcoms, the nightly news, everything. With a few exceptions, the public had rarely seen the classic archetypes of heroes and heroines in those stories played by individuals of color.

Andre's insight about videos was that they were "four minutes of excellence in terms of how to be a country or how to be from Brooklyn or how to win a war or how to get a chick." Music video as an art form, in his view, also had a powerful message, delivered on the platform of what he identified as "network television for changing the attitudes of Americans in this continent."

The first visible measure of changing attitudes happened in communities of color, where, honestly, the videos did more for confidence building than any government affirmative action program could have. How? Well, as Andre explained, they "made us believe; we reached . . . and then we started moving around . . . we got to the places we'd never been, and we started emulating what we'd seen them doing in videos." Describing that as the "blueprint of the swagger," he compared the stars of the dramas, the rappers, to Cyrano de Bergerac, showing with the power of their words how to win in love—how to win, period. As Andre described it, "Words have power that manifested a new reality. Nuances count, and people listened—both black and white—the new American audience."

All of that said, I would argue—as would Andre—that the listening would never have happened on the scale that it did if it hadn't been for one artist in particular who closed the divide between R&B and hip-hop, for starters, and who struck an essential chord with the most powerful group of any market, any time, any place: women.

Mary Jane Blige began her Cinderella-story career as a teenager in the late 1980s and early 1990s at Uptown Records, where her then producer, Sean "Puffy" Combs, oversaw most of her debut album, *What's the 411?* Before he left Uptown to launch Bad Boy Records, Puffy had dubbed her the queen of hip-hop/soul— a distinction that goes to the heart of the discussion about how the genre would soon be coloring all of pop culture.

The blurring of the lines, in fact, had been happening at Uptown all along, thanks to Andre Harrell's direction and insights. Andre saw in the late eighties how the hard-edged drama of rap music, with the thumping drums and bass-heavy groove that were the signature of many Def Jam artists, was not incorporating all the rich cool smoothness and bright musicality that had built the house of R&B. The question he asked was, how can we make this less rough around the edges, give it more soul and R&B, put guys in suits and add glamour plus bring in the hip-hop element and beat but with a less dramatic emphasis? The answer turned out to be very basic: melody.

Andre Harrell, super-smart college graduate, who began as an artist in the rap duo Dr. Jeckyll and Mr. Hyde, had the insight to leave the rock elements in the mix but to find a way to turn up the heat on the R&B. Some of the efforts that arose from various camps didn't gel and lacked both the hip-hop authenticity and its commitment. Two artists who had the cultural understanding and the unapologetic aspect of it were R. Kelly and Mary J. Blige. They took that, kept in the beats, but also sang to it and brought the melody—putting the hip-hop spin on R&B and making it more palatable for radio. Eventually, you could look back and see how pivotal both were in bringing everyone under the hip-hop umbrella.

But in the beginning, at the point when churban wasn't ready to call itself hip-hop, radio stations initially still didn't know where to put cuts from Mary's *What's the 411?* What did you call it? Not pure R&B, not dance, not hard-edged hip-hop, and definitely not pop. But Andre Harrell finally had a marketing breakthrough to answer that question, as it so happened, when he was trying to secure one of Mary's new releases in the soundtrack for a film starring Halle Berry.

Andre was explaining to the movie people why Mary's hip-hop style of songwriting was more suited to their movie's storytelling. And then he began to put into words what she represented, "her attitude, her struggle, and then the fashion." Riffing away, he began to talk about her following, how Puffy had already dubbed her the queen of hip-hop/soul, because, Andre insisted, "she's singing about undying love, soulfully." Her image, he told these movie people, "hair done blond, jewelry dangling, Louis Vuitton this and that, big sunglasses, Billie Holiday blue," was, in short, "ghetto fabulous."

No sooner had he coined that very phrase for Mary J. Blige than almost overnight hip-hop music, culture, and marketing opened a new door that was as wide and as historic as the tanning transformation achieved by MTV's day-parting of Dr. Dre's

The Chronic. Andre Harrell asserted, "Ghetto fabulous allowed for women to get in it."

Mary Jane Blige, on all fronts, was for hip-hop what Diana Ross had been for Motown. Andre—who later went on to run Motown after leaving his own Uptown Records, around the time that I started working with Mary—framed the need for a queen of hip-hop/soul by saying that in the general marketplace, it's "women who are the first to take to minorities in a big way and let us in the house. Men ain't letting you in the house with a new thing. They want the old thing, the same styles. Women are in touch with their girl, and their girl wants to see every new shiny thing that sings beautifully or dances wonderfully or looks handsome."

In a marketing lesson not to be overlooked, the "ghetto fabulous" name gave Mary her own brand identity that sent her career skyrocketing, got women invested in hip-hop, and was infinitely merchandisable for all by all.

John Demsey, group president of the Estée Lauder Companies Inc., remembered how, when he was getting started as the head of MAC, ghetto fabulous fostered an aesthetic and values to urban culture that was the yin to the yang of what male rappers were doing. John told me, "All of a sudden hip-hop had a parallel track because the female side and the male side are very different." Talking about the macho aspect of rap as being more violent and gang oriented, he went on to note that the female side might have had the same swagger, but it cultivated the values of belief and respect and sisterhood. The women were in the minority because in the genre, men were having the big success, John observed, and the women needed to talk to each other about how the men didn't listen to them. The first time John went to a Mary J. Blige concert in her early years, he remembered it was about 90 percent women, mostly African-American, all of them pointing and screaming back when she was singing. "It was like a dialogue," he said, "basically like being in church, like a revival."

I had plenty of experience getting to watch the female bonding when I was working with Mary as a manager and executive producer of her *Share My World* album—by which point she had become the first woman I'd ever seen who could headline a show and have legions of men show up too. Hard-core hip-hop guys would come to see Mary J. Blige. Why? Well, it didn't hurt that they could say, *I'm going to bring my girlfriend out for this*. But the fact was that Mary J. was embodying the essence of hip-hop—the beats that brought the feeling, that let you dance and show your authenticity, and the subject matter that she was speaking about was generally not too far from a man's understanding. Mary was speaking about it with a hip-hop tone, giving voice to issues that were in the rap code, not to mention that she had songs with rappers. In that big tent brought to you by Mary J. Blige, it was all coming together. Guys were going, women were in the mix, and tanning was about inclusion however you wanted to look at it.

As would become abundantly clearer to me in the later years of the 1990s when I went on to head up a division of Columbia Records (part of Sony Music Entertainment) and then landed the presidency of urban music at Interscope, those boxes and tags for genres limit their relevance. What name an artist or a brand of music or a product has is important, and production values do count, but why tanning happens en masse has to do with the fundamental truth that you can feel in the voice and hear in the lyrics. Mary J. Blige had lived the ghetto life that gave her the undeniable truth, that made her a pain icon everyone loved, along with the gifts of her amazing vocals and powerful poetry.

The Thinnest Slice, a term I employ, is that fundamental truth; it's what doesn't need to cross over to the mainstream because the mainstream comes to it, like moths to the flame. You can't hit it all the time. Rare artists and certain influencers do. Sometimes all the coordinates come together and the flame happens and all are drawn to it.

Ghetto fabulous took in everyone—women, men, rappers, soul singers, athletes, comedians, movie stars, TV hosts, everybody. One of the most iconic images that later appeared to encapsulate this time (when the battle to out-ghetto and out-fabulous each other kicked into high gear) was by photographer

David LaChapelle. As the story goes, after LaChapelle took this caramel-tinted photograph of Lil' Kim wearing nothing but a Louis Vuitton hat over blond hair, and showing her completely bare body stamped all over by the same Louis Vuitton logos, it was included in a gallery exhibit and spotted by then editor-in-chief of *Interview* magazine, Ingrid Sischy. As she was being shown David LaChapelle's work, the moment Ingrid laid eyes on the Lil' Kim photograph, she immediately said, "Take it down." She wanted it for the cover of *Interview*. And when it appeared as a cover, as I can well attest, it stopped cultural time. This was blatant, unapologetic consumption mixed with fine art and the rare moment captured was a visual masterpiece.

And it galvanized attention in the midst of the heyday of party and champagne and bling culture. The power of Lil' Kim appearing with these logos on her body certainly did more for Louis Vuitton than anything inside or out of popular culture at the time. Those who were attuned read the image and thought that if she believed enough to have the logos on her in a way that said, *Look at me, this is how much I'm down for this brand, this is how much it means to me,* then it had to be important and worthy. It was certainly powerful whenever hip-hop artists vocalized their love for luxury brands and thus became walk-ing billboards for them. Again, the fact that they came from the ghetto and had fabulous taste plus money to make luxury choices made the brand powerful by association. So the fact that Lil' Kim was literally wearing the brand and nothing else was a watershed moment, catapulting Louis Vuitton and doing so much for Marc Jacobs in the process, but pushing luxury brands further into prominence. What's more, it pushed the psychology of needing luxury brands even further into the cul-tural mind-set that already embraced the idea of needing luxury brands to establish who and what you stood for. The statement was that important. Not an endorsement deal, not an ad, not a record promo. Just a statement about starting in one place and journeying to another on the cover of probably the most prestigious, elite, cultural magazine of the era, expressed in one image, in code.

Long before that cover appeared, MAC cosmetics—through

the reading of consumer cues by John Demsey—had understood where pop culture was headed and how the ghetto fabulous sensibility was the perfect match for the brand. Seizing the moment before anyone else, MAC leapt on the opportunity to use both Lil' Kim and Mary J. Blige in the first strongly supported ad campaign featuring female urban artists. From a marketing perspective, John remembered, "Up until then, no one had ever embraced hip-hop as being glamorous." But the MAC team recognized that "urban music had become the music for everyone and urban culture had become the culture for everyone."

Just as important—and what is too often ignored by Madison Avenue, corporate America, and the celebrity artists (brands unto themselves by this era)—is that MAC's company values were naturally akin to those of urban culture. Not only because of a shared consumer demographic mind-set but, more to the point, because of what John Demsey described as a shared consumer psychographic mind-set. Before Estée Lauder owned the Canadian-born company that became MAC, as it turns out, it was a business built by a professional hair care entrepreneur for the professional market that catered to the ethnic community— in partnership with Gladys Knight. John explained, "Their first product line was actually called Knight." After distributing mostly through hair shows, "the makeup came as a side development for professional makeup artists."

When Estée Lauder bought MAC in the early nineties, they kept a part of the professional line but made the consumer market their bigger thrust without losing their heritage of appealing to communities of color and to the makeup pros in the world of show business. With those professional roots, MAC was already known for having a huge array of pigments and shades. John went on, "That means whether you are porcelain white or darkest of dark, we can match skin tone, which most companies can't do."

When John Demsey was given the MAC brand, he was told by the Lauder family "to go figure out what made it successful." John understood that it embodied a beauty aesthetic that was in the company's original DNA from when it was born in Toronto, Canada. The ethnic community in Toronto—"the place where you go when you can't get into the United States as an immigrant"—was disproportionately large and included populations from the West Indies, India, Africa, different parts of Asia, and so on. In that multicultural mix, there wasn't the "notion of the traditional porcelain beauty." So Demsey understood that being in an alternative market was part of what made MAC successful. Second, he also knew that the line already shared a following with "black divas" from the entertainment world. Besides Gladys Knight, many women of color in the music and movie business had been introduced to MAC by their makeup artists. Plus, it was known that the top drag queens in the eighties, like RuPaul, frequented the hair shows and were well acquainted with the line. In fact, one of the first campaigns that the Estée Lauder–owned MAC brand did was with RuPaul, looking, as John said, like "a glammed-up Amazonian woman."

Without all that history, Demsey might have had trouble convincing the Lauders that for their big breakout campaign going to the hip-hop marketing well was certain to build on that success—as opposed to a more mainstream star, say, perhaps, Halle Berry. But the minute TLC name-checked the brand with a line in a song that said, "It doesn't matter how much MAC you wear," John Demsey made the connection that hip-hop was the way to go. The bold, fierce persona of Mary J. Blige was the psychographic match for MAC and, he added, "we accelerated with the statement that we were the brand of record for any woman of color no matter what her ethnicity." Mary J. and Lil' Kim bringing the ghetto-fabulous energy was not any old moment of tanning. In the words of John Demsey, "It was earth-shattering, earth-shattering."

The list of other brands that were brought along on the ghetto-fabulous ride, either free of charge or through endorsement deals, is epic. The money definitely got poured for all to partake—making for some very cautionary tales in the process.

Let the games begin.

PART TWO

THE POWER, PITFALLS, AND POTENTIAL OF TANNING

(act·i·vā·tion)
[*ak*-tuh-**vey**-shuhn]

(a) turning on, making active, setting into motion
(b) stimulation of activity (in organism or chemical)
(c) call or drive to action by an inner spirit or force or
principle (d) making a brand active through strategies
deeply rooted within the brand itself (in marketing)

CHAPTER 5

MARKETING CDS WITH SHOELACES

What made you decide to leave the record business?"

That was the question asked of me by a lot of different people—especially in the early days of my first testing the waters in the advertising world. Sometimes I would try to explain my interest in how all the tanning and code-shifting had taken place by answering, "Cultural curiosity!" Or other times I'd go into a longer explanation about how, after more than a decade in the music industry, I'd been lucky to make it to the top and it was important to go in search of new adventures and new challenges. But most of the time I would simply say, "Sunglasses"—which is a story coming right up but that first requires some background.

Getting the Drums Right

Not too many years ago when I was skiing in Aspen I had an interesting conversation with a group of kids. In their late teens and dressed in a combination of urban cool and the latest athletic ski-wear, this group of white kids was next to me in the parking lot while getting ready to head up to the slopes. Because I heard them playing Wu-Tang Clan in the car, I was curious and gravitated toward them. At first, I assumed that one of them had probably downloaded a Wu-Tang song or two and had been playing it for his friends as a hip-hop authority.

Downloading? Yes, that term wouldn't have had much relevance back in the mid-nineties, when record executives' bonuses were reflecting all those CD sales we've talked about. Technology had always been the friend of the music business, prompting innovation in the studio and new ways to market existing catalogs as well as new product. But when the technology came along that would make file sharing possible—and in fact digitized music to fit a compact digital file, so it was a natural target—nobody reacted with alarm or stopped to consider how this could be the demise of an industry. Executives who ought to have used their own resources and found ways to control the kinds of things that Napster and later iTunes were doing, unfortunately, were complacent. As a result, unbeknownst to much of the business, the timeline for music sold mainly in physical units was coming to a close.

Meanwhile, these kids in Aspen hadn't just downloaded a Wu-Tang single or two. Quite the opposite. One of the guys told me, "Other than Biggie, all we listen to is Wu-Tang . . . ," and then proceeded to detail the life and times of the late Notorious B.I.G. and how the best video ever was for "Hypnotize" (on his last, posthumously released album), which immortalized Biggie as a ghetto-born James Bond out on his yacht surrounded by players and hot women before speeding off in a motorboat over the high seas in a chase against villains in helicopters.

Clearly, these kids weren't casual or status culture consumers. And what was it they loved about Wu-Tang? They thought RZA's beats were "sick" (as in great) and Method Man was just "the sh*t." And one of them talked about how crazy but likeable the late Russell Tyrone Jones, a.k.a. Ol' Dirty Bastard, had been. He had recently dropped dead on the street of what was determined to be a lethal mix of drugs in his system.

Then another one of the kids pointed out that Wu-Tang never lost the whole countercultural feel, or the aspect of what used to be called "gangsta" (a term that in 2004 had fallen somewhat out of favor, and with certain acts was really just superfluous).

My friends heading up to the ski slope knew the chronology too, how the East Coast/West Coast feud came to a violent head in 1997, when Biggie was shot and killed, after Tupac's shooting death in '96. They even knew that things had settled down for the most part with everyone's realization that keeping the peace and empowering the community was not only more in line with the values of the movement but better business for one and all. Insiders were starting to accept the truism that with power comes responsibility, at least among some of the more socially conscious artists, producers, and prominent hip-hop voices. Many did feel it was time to do more to combat the violence.

As the decade wore on, that stance triumphed over hip-hop's more dangerous elements. Not that it stopped the media from promoting the feuds. Nor did it change the code about what made a rapper credible.

One of the artists that I signed during my tenure at Columbia/Sony was 50 Cent—who was dropped from their roster but was later brought on board at Interscope after being championed by Eminem and signed by Jimmy Iovine. During the interim, 50 had been shot nine times and lived to tell about it in his album *Get Rich or Die Tryin'*. There was nothing about him or his music that lacked credibility before he got shot. But the truth was that it wasn't that distinct. After almost dying, not only did he have something to talk about that authenticated who he was, but, bizarrely, as a result of how one of the bullets hit him in the jaw, his voice actually got better and became more unique. It helped him tell his story better and elevated the sound he was delivering. Dangerous? No doubt. But talented beyond question, 50 Cent could now use his fame and his voice like a megaphone for the multicultural rockin' party that America wanted to have "In Da Club."

The Sony executive, Don Ienner, with whom I battled over the signing and who unceremoniously dropped 50 Cent—as well as Alicia Keys—was indicative to me of Sony's general lack of cultural curiosity and, specifically, an apparent contempt for hip-hop culture. This was partly a reflection of the corporate atmosphere at Sony overall, which never seemed comfortable with hip-hop as a music genre either. While it's true that Def Jam had been at Sony, controversies connected to the group Public Enemy had led to that label being dropped from distribution. The upshot was that the corporation would dabble in hip-hop but didn't want to invest in it. So those were some of the land mines that I was trying to dodge and still advocate for artists and music.

You can imagine the uphill battle faced by Mariah Carey when hip-hop began to inform her artistry. At first it was just bringing in the rhythm, as Mariah did in "Dreamlover," which used beats from "Warm It Up," a Big Daddy Kane record. In the video, the choreography for the guys dancing to that hip-hop-infused rhythm was based on a Jamaican dance-hall style of dance called "the Bogel," then becoming popular with urban kids but not yet known to the general public. It showed how much Mariah was paying attention to where culture was. For hip-hop fans, this was very cool, but it went right over the heads of the executives. Nothing could have prepared them for what happened next when Mariah wanted to include a collaboration with Wu-Tang Clan's Ol' Dirty Bastard on her album *Daydream*. After all, she was the label's top-selling pop recording artist at the time—not to mention their superstar who would sell more records than any other American artist across the entire 1990s. For her to take her own music into the genre of hip-hop as far as what Ol' Dirty epitomized, in the company's eyes, was too far.

And truly, with as much as she had to lose, Mariah Carey was putting the most at risk by wanting to tap into the future of tanning that this fusion of different music styles and culture was creating. Mariah knew exactly where the mainstream tan mind-set had already arrived, and she knew in 1995 how important serious rap was to the evolution. If her instincts told her to ride hip-hop as far as she could while still bringing her R&B/pop fans along, why not? Well, a big reason why not was there was no promise that they would come along. That was a considerable risk that she believed was important to take. So when executives tried to dismiss her instincts it had to be offensive, both to Mariah and to her then husband, Tommy Mottola (who was a much valued friend and guide to me, especially in navigating the murky waters of the industry at the time). Refusing to be dissuaded, Mariah Carey and her "Fantasy (Bad Boy)" remix featuring Ol' Dirty Bastard gave us a tanning juxtaposition like nothing we'd ever heard. Besides its global sales success, critics recognized that it was the new paradigm for how R&B/pop and hip-hop could harmonize. Many believed it was the most important single of Mariah's songwriting career. As for Ol' Dirty Bastard, it gave him a mainstream outing that blasted off and went into permanent orbit.

Allow me to confess that for all I knew about how far and wide hip-hop sensibilities had spread, I still couldn't help but be delighted by the kids on the slopes that day. They were not passive consumers visiting culture; they had been fully activated by it. They were a big reason why I had ventured out of my comfort zone into the marketing world. True, the shorthand answer for why I got out of the music business was "Sunglasses" (as I'm setting the stage to elaborate upon soon). But another reason had been to solve the mystery of how kids and young adults like the ones I met in Aspen (who would not be considered hip-hop's core audience) had become so connected to urban culture that they co-opted it as meaningful to their lives.

The question wasn't academic. For years fellow record business insiders and I were mystified by skewed sales numbers that showed units moving in zip codes where those singles weren't on the radio—so it was odd how they were doing that without exposure. We also saw a tanning effect happening as rosters started to sign hip-hop artists who were also white, Latino, Asian, and from other ethnic backgrounds—selling in supposedly African-American-only zip codes.

When I asked Steve Berman at Interstate what clues he had been given earlier on that the music was attracting a much more diverse audience than anyone expected, he reminded me of how the various retail accounts around the country—in the good old days of record stores—reported those trends from the start.

"Remember the Box, in Florida?" he asked. Of course. The Box was really, truly video on demand—before its time. The Box was on cable networks in a lot of the major cities and consumers had a chance to call the 1-800 number and order any music video that was selected. Radio was being circumvented because kids were at home, paying the $1.99 (or whatever it was) to watch videos that they wanted to see—and that's how it was getting into the house. It was video on demand (what the Internet offers to us today for free). This was the way that music distribution and marketing would be going, only it was too premature to be commercially successful. But what it did do was explode record sales after kids had ordered the videos from the Box—wherever it was available. A retail eruption followed next, with big-name independents or regional chains that had as many as thirty to fifty stores all reporting sales of hip-hop in non-urban locations to non-urban kids.

Back to radio, I still wondered why was there such resistance to playing the music when retailers were tracking sales of that magnitude. Steve's feeling was, "Took time to get there."

Throughout my career in the wild, wild west of the changing music industry, one of the most important general marketing lessons I learned was the value of local advertisers. Why? Because those mom-and-pop businesses are on the front lines of cultural understanding and have their ears to the ground as to who their customers are and what their tastes are. Because of proximity, local advertisers—used-car dealerships, stationers, florists, whatever—tend to have a better gauge on whether the stations where they buy ads play the music their customers like; if not, they recognize that those listeners will move on.

In describing these patterns, Geoff Mayfield, a high-profile analyst now at Universal's music group, formerly *Billboard*'s director of charts, emphasized, "Radio is the first line of defense for advertising. If Z100 is not playing the songs that kids want to hear, the local auto dealer isn't getting the ROI that he wants." Since getting return on investment is the sword by which marketers live and die, that was logical. The example Geoff offered for the nineties was, "When radio starts playing Michael Bolton for too long, the advertiser goes elsewhere." Therefore, credit for helping rap break the glass ceiling in radio belongs to the power of smart businesses putting pressure on stations to update their programming. In turn, the local advertisers started seeing a direct translation to a more active, loyal consumer base. That was one of the first unexpected transmissions of cool I witnessed in action.

Not everyone was happy when advertising showed its power or, for that matter, when consumers leveraged their preferences and hip-hop began to dominate the radio dial. Scholars of pop culture and rap purists and hip-hop's old-school voices predicted that surely all the commercial success and mainstream explosion would be the death of the art form. There was an assumption that once hip-hop artists no longer had to battle for legitimacy—now that they were rolling like royalty, becoming unapologetic capitalists, and showing off their bling and their rides and their cribs—everything in their DNA that had come from poverty, hard times, pain, dysfunction, and the outcry against social injustice would be suppressed.

But that didn't happen to the art form, which was still evolving. For one thing, hip-hop always had to fight for legitimacy. For another, all this really meant was that record companies were finally putting money behind talent and newcomers were given real opportunities. So it was really a recruiting poster to continue building the army.

Not everyone could claim the stature of being a folk hero and folk artist. Those who did were the true storytellers. When Jay-Z, for instance, came out with his first album, *Reasonable Doubt,* it was literature written in code—a poet speaking three or four levels down into his Brooklyn past growing up in the Marcy Projects. The entire album was conceived as his effort to explain to a judge why he took the actions that he did, providing evidence of reasonable doubt, saying, *Look at where I live, put the light on that experience and tell me, what am I supposed to do, because all I want is to change my situation.* He's saying, *The prayers aren't working, the schools are failing, the parents are breaking, so we will raise ourselves up, live with the consequences, do x, y, and z, and we're getting the hell out of this.*

The storytelling was all the more riveting because of the originality of the language being used for it. Thunder did not crash and lightning didn't strike when a New Orleans rapper—Lil

Wayne at fourteen years old—created and first used the phrase "bling bling" in a Cash Money Records video and song, but it was still thunderous when it went on to be a description of jewelry and riches understood worldwide. The strength and the power of the colloquialism to spread that far that fast was proof once more that art transcends barriers and causes this tanning to forge on. As an artist, an older Lil Wayne could come back and speak to more serious concerns, as he did in a nine-minute piece of oratory in which he took older generations to task about the need to tackle racial differences differently—stating plainly, *"Humanity is helping one another, no matter your color or your race."* The record wasn't commercial but it was Lil Wayne using his popularity, his platform, to talk about diversity and helping every race, color, and creed to promote the value of people coming together.

This messaging revealed a marketing miscue on the part of record companies and marketers who didn't know colloquialisms or code. Everyone loves to talk about selling CDs, obviously. But marketers miss the point that content is a platform for artists to speak to their audiences, for connection—which is the art's reason for being. Artists like the validation of selling lots of records but that also means they're speaking to a lot of people.

And so, the message of tanning was starting to become a conscious one—a message of one mind-set, one mental complexion, one America.

When artists started saying that racial bias and stereotyping based on color were not acceptable, on both sides, they not only elevated the medium and gave it a social conscience but they were giving props to their audience—those consumers from all backgrounds who were showing them love and buying their albums, like the kids on the ski slope. Artists understood that their art was being valued by white fans who were not beholden to what their parents thought of African-Americans or other ethnicities, to the old ways of judging someone based on color and the old thinking of putting them in boxes and in branded compartments. The artists were activating a generation that didn't think in those terms.

Of course, the mainstream wanted to treat it as a trend, not as an evolving and ultimately enduring art form. This wasn't new. We saw it when Bob Dylan, as the poet of his time, would speak about details of life at a depth other songwriters couldn't reach—saying things that others might think but couldn't say, using vivid pictures and feelings that the words triggered. Certain hip-hop artists went there too and put their blood on the page and the stage to speak of what they had lived through, in similarly riveting images. But what changed with hip-hop was that there was no war between high art and what the mainstream liked, primarily because of the beats.

Kanye West once explained to me how one of his most provocative songs, "Jesus Walks," never had trouble getting spins. In the song he talked about religion being the only taboo subject and that otherwise you could rap about anything, "guns, sex, lies, videotapes." Basically, Kanye explained, he had learned that in hip-hop you could pretty much say anything, "as long as the drums are right." With that, the mainstream would move and dance to it anyway and bleep out anything overtly offensive. So when the drums are right, the lyrics either go over the head of listeners who aren't attuned or stream into the frontal emotional lobe of those who are. If you did know what the rapper was saying, however, it was pretty funny when you had Jay-Z on MTV using code like "It'll sell by night" and "It's eggshell white" to boast about the superior quality of a dealer's drugs; you wouldn't know that, unless you did.

Dr. Dre always understood the power of getting the drums right in a way that was multilingual and epic. His production of *The Slim Shady LP*, Eminem's debut, shows that. And as for Eminem, I contend that he is one of the best things that ever happened to hip-hop. Why? Because the level of scrutiny he received from within the field and outside of it forced the masses to pay attention to the lyrics for the first time. There were other reasons I believe he activated tanning and that make him important as an artist, as a proxy for white kids who grew up on Run-DMC and Ice Cube and who, in adopting the dress and the language, had been unfairly labeled "wiggers" (slur for "white nigg**s"). With Eminem, the response came—*No, that's how I dress and the way that I talk, and I'm no less credible because I'm white.* And as a storyteller,

Eminem epitomized a twist on what many of the rappers were talking about, because he had all the same issues, only set in a different world. Add to that the fact that he was trying to break into a flock of black and brown sheep as one of the few white ones.

When I was working with Eminem at Interscope, and ended up becoming an executive producer on *8 Mile,* I wanted to portray the challenge of his breaking into the club to be as difficult as it had been for John Travolta in *Saturday Night Fever.* Because if it wasn't, and if he didn't have to prove himself as an artist, it wouldn't ring true. Well, ultimately that's what happened in Eminem's career.

No, he didn't have to sneak in a side door or come through the back. He walked in through the front door with "Hi, my name is . . . ," with an album that had a mass pop appeal but also had some seriously dark sh*t underlying it. And his arrival on the scene made everyone stop to listen to his every word. Thank God for hip-hop's sake that he's talented! It would have been a bad day for the art if he wasn't gifted, with everyone suddenly paying attention. But from the start he was brilliant. His peers benefited from him too once lyrical content started to be judged differently, and they embraced him because he spoke to the common experience—about parents and authority figures being hypocrites, pretend do-gooders blaming kids for getting high while doing the same, asking, *So how come you point your finger at us? F you!*

Dr. Dre gave Eminem the beats, built the authenticity, and everybody ran to him, bought the CDs, and then listened to the words, including insiders, and, as I said, he rhymed his ass off. The verdict was *Wow, this kid is good.* Eminem went on to sell more records than any artist in the first decade of the 2000s. How? Tanning. Yet he was always respectful of the artists who got him where he was, and he gave to the black pioneers of his art form exactly what Elvis Presley didn't return to his—acknowledgment.

Once hip-hop proved that it could earn its keep, it wanted to grow, and through a handful of artists it found another level to make what they were doing as transformational as Basquiat. Not just painting. Not pop art for pop art's sake, but pop art with a vision and depth and texture that you can put up against anybody. I can take lyrics from Eminem and Jay-Z and put them up against Edgar Allan Poe and Shakespeare. I can put them up against Bob Dylan all day.

These observations having been made, I have to admit to being surprised by the numbers represented by tanning that were captured in an article that appeared in February 1999. It was a *Time* magazine cover feature titled "Hip-Hop Nation: After 20 Years—How It's Changed America." With a team of contributors from all over the country, *Time*'s music critic Christopher John Farley unapologetically broached the subject of urban culture's economic impact:

> Consider the numbers. In 1998, for the first time ever, rap outsold what previously had been America's top-selling format, country music. Rap sold more than 81 million CDs, tapes, and albums last year, compared with 72 million for country. Rap sales increased a stunning 31% from 1997 to 1998, in contrast to 2% gains for country, 6% for rock and 9% for the music industry overall.

But the real eyebrow-raising data came a few lines later:

> Hip-hop got its start in black America, but now more than 70% of hip-hop albums are purchased by whites. In fact, a whole generation of kids—black, white, Latino, Asian—has grown up immersed in hip-hop.

So if you are someone, like me, who has cultural curiosity and you read in 1999 about this incredible, relatively untapped, diverse, superpowered consumer group, in numbers you'd never expected to see before, the next question you'd wonder about is, *What else are they buying?*

Cool in Translation

Thanks to an earlier experience, I definitely knew one of the answers, and that, as previewed earlier, was sunglasses.

No, not just any sunglasses. I'm speaking, of course, about the iconic brand that had been developed by Bausch & Lomb back in 1937 after World War I and II pilots complained of damage to their eyes from the harmful rays of the sun. After a patent was developed for an antiglare lens that reduced the ill effects of infrared and ultraviolet rays, a prototype was produced. With a lightweight, durable metal frame and a style that was more function than fashion, the sunglasses were marketed as Ray-Ban Aviators. Embraced from the beginning by the U.S. Army Air Corps and the brass of other branches of the military, including none other than General Douglas MacArthur, Ray-Bans were soon synonymous with a proud, brave, and mighty nation that had returned triumphant from wars against evil. And in the decades that followed, that winning American brand identity stayed, even as Ray-Ban diversified and came out with a variety of looks and styles that allowed the company to appeal to a wider market without sacrificing quality or losing elite status.

Starting in the early 1960s, after the Ray-Ban Wayfarer II sunglasses were worn by President John F. Kennedy—probably our first president to benefit from very early tanning—Hollywood fell into lasting love with the brand. In that same era, we saw Audrey Hepburn in Ray-Bans in *Breakfast at Tiffany's* and then in '69 Peter Fonda wore Ray-Ban Olympian Deluxe sunglasses in *Easy Rider.* Clint Eastwood made the Ray-Ban Balorama part of his Dirty Harry uniform, while John Belushi and Dan Aykroyd wore Wayfarer IIs in *The Blues Brothers.* In the eighties, after NBC's head of programming, the late Brandon Tartikoff, launched *Miami Vice* from two words he scribbled on a napkin—"MTV cops"—Don Johnson wore Wayfarer II Ray-Bans in the early seasons. Tom Cruise then wore them in not one but two eighties blockbusters, *Risky Business* (Wayfarer IIs) and *Top Gun* (Aviators).

Clearly, the product placement agency that the company had retained at one point when Ray-Ban hit a revenue low had done a formidable job. By the mid-1990s, however, Bausch & Lomb started to worry that maybe their Ray-Ban division had gotten as far as it could go just by appearing as the ubiquitous cool sunglasses in movies and on television. Being a top eighties silhouette was also problematic. Not only that, but in these boom

years of bling with steep competition within the designer eyewear market, Ray-Ban's classic allure was verging on antique.

This was not a challenge that could be so easily remedied
by just having the sunglasses placed in yet another movie. That
is, unless the movie happened to be *Men in Black,* starring Will
Smith and Tommy Lee Jones, which Columbia Pictures, a division of Sony, was readying for release in 1997. As fate would have
it, a short while before the production deal for the movie came
together, I had gotten my start as an executive at Sony. Coincidentally, one of the areas in which I had done very well was overseeing the production and marketing of soundtracks, and CDs
with music tied to movies. And in that capacity, I would be able to
watch and learn from how the fortunes of a brand of sunglasses
were about to be changed in dramatic ways. Because of Will
Smith and where he was in his career, paired with Tommy Lee
Jones, at the right time, in the right way, with the right vehicle,
Ray-Bans weren't just getting to be seen and appreciated. They
were about to benefit from tanning by becoming part of the story.

In these years, by the way, Will Smith was not yet firmly
established as the world's number one box-office draw movie
star as he would be soon enough. But his success had already
given him the powers of a brand and a cultural force. Of course,
in my future career, I would gain a much greater understanding
of how celebrities become brands and to what extent that allows
them to be a beneficiary and/or an activator of tanning.

Having mass popularity and being iconic—to the point
that your name is known in short or your silhouette alone is
recognizable—are components of being a brand. But they do not
necessarily help bridge a cultural gap and create a like-minded
connection that is required for tanning activation. An artist's ability to be both a brand and a cultural driver comes down to belief.
The public has to believe in you and, because of a certain authentic voice that you have, believe that they can depend on what you
say and what you represent. Some of it is popularity, definitely,
but without authenticity, the offering falls flat. For you as a celebrity to, say, wear an outfit and have others try to duplicate what
you're wearing, people have to believe that it's intrinsically you;
they have to perceive that you wore it because you believe in

the look as cool for you and that it's part of your creed, your distinct interpretation. People don't want to believe that you wore it just to make a hit song or, by extension, to sell a product. Yes, if you wore it because of your belief, and if, along the way, your record is a smash and you ignite a trend, wow, that's dazzling and inspiring and cool. That's where you become a tastemaker, a thought leader, and even an agent of tanning. In twentieth-century pop culture, Madonna understood this proposition better than almost anyone and because of the integrity of her own brand, she changed how people saw differences in color, class, gender, and sexuality. Even though Madonna's music couldn't be categorized as hip-hop, her influences come straight from Motown and R&B, giving her linkage and impact in urban culture.

The artists who became brands in the cycle marked by the growth of hip-hop were the individuals who moved the ball forward because their contribution represented something culturally meaningful so that others could collectively nod and say, *Yeah, this is cool, this is significant.* Originators like Run-DMC or Dr. Dre who are legendary figures today didn't know they were becoming brands at the start. That was never the intent. Making good music was the intent, along with the hope that people would buy it. But when you make good music that touches people's souls and beings over a period of time, when there's a look and a feel that's consistent with that sound, then you became a brand.

Artists as brands bring expectations and assumptions. LL Cool J's brand early on included his confidence, which brought expectations about him as a masculine figure who could speak to women with a certain cool and swagger. And over time, whether you saw him in a Kangol or FUBU hat or drinking Sprite, there was an expectation and an assumption that he would do that only because he believed in it. The expectation is that whether it's music or a product or a cause, it is sincerely felt. And if you are believed too as a brand artist, you are trusted and given a level of respect reserved for those who have earned it over time. Those artists as brands were very important on this cultural journey of tanning. If it weren't for those brands, the hip-hop genre would have been about only the popularity of the drums and would have become just dance music.

Will Smith, without question, is one of the most crucial players in tanning, but not so much because of his early days as a rapper coming out of Philly—although that did give him his authentic hip-hop, urban roots. At the same time that DJ Jazzy Jeff & the Fresh Prince were coming into their own, the edgier trends in the genre made him have to fight hard for legitimacy as an MC. And Will did. He talked about growing up middle-class and the authentic struggle caused by the generation gap. But he did face backlash when the first ever Grammy Award for rap went to him and Jazzy Jeff in 1989 for their single "Parents Just Don't Understand." The other nominees that year were LL Cool J for "Going Back to Cali," Salt-n-Pepa for "Push It," Kool Moe Dee's "Wild Wild West," and JJ Fad's "Supersonic." There was a feeling, right or wrong, that though fun and entertaining, "Parents Just Don't Understand" didn't best capture the essence of rap at that time.

But on the other hand, the whole vibe of "Parents Just Don't Understand" helped Will Smith reveal a persona that pushed tanning to a completely new level with his TV show, *The Fresh Prince of Bel-Air.* Just like *The Cosby Show,* what it did was show an African-American family on the mainstream stage—which by itself was significant. The family was affluent but Will's character, a fish out of water, wasn't; and, in fact, he had the hip-hop point of view of someone who came from nothing, from the impoverished inner-city experience. And so, by some kind of alchemy, Will took the slice of hip-hop credibility he had earned and put it on this gigantic mother ship called NBC with his show and blew the doors off. Besides what it did for him as a brand, when the next wave of rappers-turned-actors started hitting TV shows and movies, they benefited as well. From there, Will has only gotten better at the tanning process with what he's done on film in a range of characters completely different from each other, all of whom he makes authentic and believable over and over and over again.

Just how powerful a global tanning effect Will Smith was providing—as far back as the late 1980s—was really brought home to me recently when I had a chance to talk to him about those early years with his longtime manager, James Lassiter.

When James first started working with Jazzy Jeff and the

Fresh Prince back in Philly, he had actually begun his management role after growing up as Jeff's best friend—although it was a vision of seeing the world as bigger than Philadelphia that he and Will truly shared. James recalled, "We wanted to see it *all*." They never limited themselves, nor did they see rap as a short-lived niche phenomenon, as did most of the music industry. James explained that he and Will believed everyone would buy their records for the simple reason that Run-DMC had proven it was possible. They made up their minds that "we're not just selling records to people here, we're selling records everywhere."

So was making records as popular as Run-DMC their goal? No, James said, "We were trying to make records that were as popular as Michael Jackson, asking how can we reach the same audience he reached." That idea, he went on to say, was probably encouraged by Jive Records founder Clive Calder who kept telling them, "Don't make records only for America. Hip-hop is gonna break around the world." Clive would edit their records, cutting them down to two minutes by taking out verses so that they could get radio play overseas. Will and James didn't know that until the first time they traveled internationally and heard the records on the air. But they were hitting the charts and beginning to build a mainstream international following, even before Jazzy Jeff and the Fresh Prince had become top hitmakers in the United States.

The extent of their recording success and Will's worldwide appeal, however, didn't register until *The Fresh Prince of Bel-Air* began airing in places like Spain and it turned out to have a 50 percent market share there. Crazy! The Super Bowl here in America doesn't even have a domestic 50 percent market share. Even crazier was the experience that James and Will both described when they traveled to Spain in this era. As the story goes, when their plane landed, there was a huge crowd of excited fans holding up signs and lots of paparazzi waiting at the airport. Will and James assumed it had to be for some big star on the plane. "Wow," one of them asked the other, "did you see anybody famous on the flight?" No, neither had seen anyone. Well, lo and behold, as they got closer to the signs that the fans were holding up, one word jumped out, *¡PRINCIPE!* That is "Prince!" in Spanish.

And that was a pivotal moment that made Will understand he had become a global star. It didn't stop there. That night fans stayed outside the hotel calling for him to come down and sign autographs. All of a sudden, they needed a police escort to get around because sightings of Will Smith were stopping traffic.

In spite of the worldwide recording success that Will had achieved with Top Ten hits and Grammy awards, even with the international stardom he had attained as a television star, when it was time to go and promote the movie *Bad Boys* overseas, the studio didn't want to spend the money to have Will go on a major international tour. Why? Because, the marketing experts hired by the studio insisted, African-American stars could only garner five million dollars in overseas box office receipts. No matter what James Lassiter did to try to convince the studio they were missing a great opportunity, they wouldn't move. That is until Will was invited to appear at an MTV event at Cannes and did so well in his interviews with the foreign press—these were then picked up all around the world—that the studio agreed to give him the chance to go promote the movie. The end result was that *Bad Boys* did 138 million dollars in worldwide box office receipts. So much for those experts who predicted a fraction of that.

Part of the cultural misread had to do with the generation gap. Those experts, after all, based their predictions on the track record of international stars like Sylvester Stallone and Arnold Schwarzenegger. They were out of touch, no doubt, with their own kids, who were now seeing Will Smith as the earlier generation saw Sly Stallone. The experts were so disconnected from culture that they avoided not just traditional assumptions but hard-core statistics like Will's TV show share in Spain and the global fan base established from his recording career.

But once the entertainment industry caught on to the trajectory of Will Smith's journey and observed the worldwide tanning effect he had caused—because he reflected the hip-hop attitude—it altered the playing field for everyone else who followed. Again, this is why, when you look at key factors of tanning, you can't discount how far ahead of the game Will was and you can't underestimate everything he had done to drive global culture.

One other thing that I personally feel is significant about Will Smith is that the longer he holds a seat at the table at the highest levels of the entertainment industry and the more mainstream he has become, the more clear it is that always and forever he will never lose his blackness. Because of Will making it part of the conversation, unapologetically, the understanding that African-American culture is popular culture has become accepted. And because he understands his own proximity to culture, Will Smith has never tried to change himself because of trends—to put on the "gangsta" leather jacket to fit in.

Will fortunately saw very early how tanning was activating the public because he genuinely had the mental complexion of someone who was both urban and suburban in his sensibilities. He naturally appealed to those populations, who were being drawn together. He didn't try to appeal to them; that's who he is and what he is. If he had tried to become more thuggish, that would have been false and the trust in him and his brand would have been diminished. Instead he stayed in his own lane musically, and when things lightened up in hip-hop, in 1997, his time came again.

During his waiting-out period, Will's original label, Jive Records, offered him the option to get out of his contract, and I thought that was a mistake. But as the saying goes, Jive's loss was my gain. Not only did I know Will personally from my days working with Kid 'n Play but from the moment I arrived at Sony, I was hot to do more to build their soundtrack business. Besides the fact that you can sell them to multiple markets, soundtracks come with a ready-made marketing campaign, not to mention that the film company provides your budget. Plus, when I signed Will to the record label, he was in the successful throes of the soundtrack for *Bad Boys* and there was a sequel in the works.

I will say, however, that it was crazy when we finished recording with the song for *Men in Black,* and because of the gangsta mentality's dominance, many of the female hip-hop artists we tried to hire for the background voices on the song felt it would hurt their credibility. SWV got the gig and their lead artist, CoKo, didn't even want to be in the video—so as not to be seen with the clean-cut Will Smith. Hard to even believe in hindsight. But that was how hard-core the mentality was at that moment in music.

Frankly, I wasn't banking on Will selling a certain number of records with any given movie, but, staying positive, my instincts told me we could definitely build momentum with those soundtracks. None of this prepared me for how many CDs we would sell with *Men in Black*. Cresting at number one on the *Billboard* Top 200 chart and staying there for two weeks, it was quickly certified triple platinum for sales over three million copies and would go on to far surpass that in the years to follow. A soundtrack!

There was only one thing that happened throughout this fairy-tale story that made me stop and question possibilities for myself. How much better could it have been than to have an array of gifted artists on an album that was attached to a major Hollywood blockbuster spawn four single hits, win Grammys, and sell that many copies? Well, the one issue that caught my attention was how Ray-Bans and the program conceived by Alyse Kobin of Kobin Enterprises—where the idea for partnering the sunglasses with *Men in Black* was hatched—had made out from their product placement opportunity. Given the challenge of fading cool that the brand had been facing, instead of going with any of their more classic silhouettes, the Ray-Bans they chose to use to revive their image in the movie were the insanely cool, superpowered, streamlined wrap-style Predator II sunglasses. When Will Smith and Tommy Lee Jones put them on after telling us that they were "the first and only line of defense" in ridding the planet of alien scum, and after repeating, 1) "We work in secret," and 2) "We dress in black," and Will adding the big one, pointing to his sunglasses and saying, "And I make these look good," the Ray-Bans instantly took on the attributes of the movie heroes. In no time, the Predator IIs went on to become the top-selling Ray-Bans ever. And though the soundtrack sales represented close to a 100 percent improvement over the last big Columbia movie release, the movie's promotional program ultimately increased Ray-Ban sales 500 percent!

Retailers like Sunglass Hut, which had moved 13 percent of

the Ray-Bans and saw a 19 percent jump in their stock price, had their economies instantly benefit from the movie. For Columbia Pictures, Ray-Ban's in-store advertising support was estimated to have been worth $20 million. In a win-win-win, Ray-Ban expanded its popularity with 25-to-39-year-olds into the previously untapped teen market.

This wasn't one of those moments when lightning struck and I decided to give up my day job and go in search of the Holy Grail for marketing. In all honesty, my thinking was still driven by CD sales and I made a mistake, a blunder that taught me a great lesson. If rap was that popular, I figured, and all it took was someone famous behind it, that was enough for me to go off and sign a superpowered icon—Kobe Bryant—and produce him rapping in a remix with Brian McKnight. What a rude awakening when we finished a couple songs on him and then made the first video, at which point the project stalled.

Though I had to learn that lesson, there was another insight from *Men in Black* that opened my eyes to opportunity like nothing else. When all was said and done, I couldn't help noticing that all the folks from Bausch & Lomb/Ray-Ban and their advertising and product placement people were having a private celebration. And they were having it at enough of an arm's length from show business that they didn't have to be immersed in it all the time. From my vantage point, it suddenly seemed very appealing not to have to deal with egos, coordinating logistics for all the heavyweights in the music business with their entourages and private planes and assistants and agents and managers and lawyers. It was just selling sunglasses. Hmmmm.

In the past, I had always seen a main-tent event in pop culture as the equivalent of a concert, where you're just selling tickets and posters directly related to the event. But now I saw that the main-tent event with something like a blockbuster film and a megastar could put the Midas touch on whatever else came into contact with it. Like sunglasses, for example.

How exactly it could do that, I wasn't so sure yet. But two years later when Bausch & Lomb sold their Ray-Ban division to an Italian company for $1.2 billion dollars, I was determined to find out.

Proximity to Culture

One of the first things that I noticed in surveying the landscape where advertisers were looking to use the hip-hop Midas touch for their clients was how little most of them really understood about the consumer they were trying to reach.

From my take on it, consumers wanted to be able to invest the same trust and belief in their brands as they did in their heroes and favored celebrities. Where advertisers seemed to be missing the mark was with the formulaic approach that assumed if you put Hip-hop Star X together with Corporate Brand Y you were going to yield Power Z that would conquer the marketplace. In reality, there is no formula. What's essential is that there are shared values between that star and the product the star is being asked to put him- or herself on the line for.

The subsequent case of Dooney & Bourke provides one of those cautionary tales of a company that tried to chase after cool credentials without having any shared values between their brand and the celebrity they engaged. The maker of a beautiful, classic line of handbags, accessories, and apparel items, Dooney & Bourke had been launched in the mid-seventies and had done well for years in boutiques and fine department stores. Wanting to expand their customer base and online business, while engaging the forces of pop culture to attract the youth psychographic, they selected actress Lindsay Lohan as their standard-bearer. They trashed their brand in the process. Maybe with another, perhaps funkier or more unpredictable brand a Lindsay Lohan marketing strategy could have worked. But Dooney & Bourke, trying to be something that they weren't, confused and ran off their former customers, putting their brand at utter risk.

Another instance that would come up down the road was the clear mismatch between Angelina Jolie and St. John's, the elegant, professional women's clothing line. What went wrong? Nothing and everything. It must have seemed smart in theory to have one of the most gorgeous women in the world—known in her film roles as bold, dramatic, sensual, and exotic—draped intimately on the page in the understated elegance of St. John's.

But it wasn't believable for her or them. In my opinion, the campaign was a debacle, much like the tree that fell in the forest that no one was there to witness.

When there are shared values between companies and celebrities, as so many of the hip-hop artists who were name-checking brands in their lyrics were discovering, the exchange is almost always fruitful and robust. That's the Midas touch, when there is proximity to culture and it sets off a chain reaction of consumption. Sean "Puffy" Combs, as we'll see shortly, manages to do this almost in his sleep. An impresario who produces, directs, writes, MCs, acts, and builds cottage industries one after the other, he has cultural instincts that rival those of P. T. Barnum (the godfather of all show business). The prime example is when Puffy was featured with Busta Rhymes on the memorable "Pass the Courvoisier," which name-checked almost every luxury libation on the market—Hennessy, Rémy, Cristal, Moët & Chandon, you name it—with the idea that they'd take any of those too but still preferred that you pass them the Courvoisier.

Within a year after the record and the video dominated the airwaves, Courvoisier sales increased 30 percent, the largest jump in the history of the three-hundred-year-old brand. Meanwhile, overall annual cognac sales in the U.S. had topped a billion dollars. Seventy-five percent of that had come from hip-hop-generation consumers (legal drinking age up to thirty-four). That is proximity to culture.

Not every brand wished to be included in the party. Later on, in 2006, the chief executive of Louis Roederer, the maker of Cristal champagne, told an interviewer, in effect, that he viewed hip-hop culture's embrace of the brand as unwelcomed attention. "But what can we do?" he asked the interviewer. "We can't forbid people from buying it. I'm sure Dom Perignon or Krug would be delighted to have their business."

Jay-Z promptly released a statement with a response, saying, "I view his comments as racist and will no longer support any of his products through any of my various brands including the 40/40 club nor in my personal life." In addition to boycotting Cristal in his clubs, replacing the bottles with Dom and Krug, Jay-Z then invested in his own line, Ace of Spades, made by Champagne Cattier, which three years later would be rated the best-tasting champagne in the world. The hand of the consumer that Cristal had bitten followed Jay-Z's lead and changed brands too. Not surprisingly, Cristal's market share plummeted and has not returned to its former glory since. Ace is now the champagne of choice in clubs and has replaced Cristal as the champagne of fine taste and status.

There were some brands that, though not averse to the business and the benefits, still never made the attempt to acknowledge and gain proximity to their customer. Timberland fell into that category. As part of the fashion and the culture, artists and consumers alike would wear Timberland boots like sneakers, driving sales around the world, making outdoor rugged footwear into a type of fashion, and yet the brand never showed their appreciation. Timberland didn't acknowledge that they had a loyal, activated consumer group that was supporting their brand. Executives just sat there and reaped the benefits of their spiking revenues and yet had no investment in managing or promoting the culture that made them rich. When the trend began to wane, at the last minute the brand tried to design into the community without any input from the consumers and the result was a goof, but still insulting. This was the same error committed by Adidas when they failed to give Run-DMC design input and blew the ongoing benefits of their endorsement deal.

Gaining proximity to culture, by the way, is not some one-shot deal that allows you to have insights and then conclude you've done all your homework in order to keep your relationship vibrant. Retailers, often the intermediary between brands and consumers, see this all the time. A very interesting account of how this urban/suburban like-minded consumer group evolved into the powerhouse it is today came to me from Mitch Modell, the CEO of Modell's Sporting Goods Inc.

Founded in 1889 when the first store was opened in lower Manhattan by entrepreneur Morris Modell, a Jewish Hungarian immigrant, Modell's is the oldest family-owned chain of its kind. Run by four generations over its history, Modell's boasts a massive online business and over 140 brick-and-mortar stores scattered across the Northeast and mid-Atlantic states, all stocking different inventories that reflect the neighborhoods where they're located, urban and suburban, ethnic, mixed, and not.

From the start, the company prided itself on providing excellence in terms of products and customer service, at a reasonable price. By selling a varying combination of outdoor and athletic gear, with army-navy supplies as well as casual apparel, the different stores over the decades had avoided becoming seen as an impersonal chain and were able to retain a connection to their distinct communities. But in the mid-1980s, with changing demographics due to reverse gentrification in their urban settings, in particular, Modell's suddenly found themselves without an active consumer base and with sinking sales figures.

Bewildered, the Modell family members and executives couldn't understand how a template that had worked for almost a century was now failing. Doing what most businesses did in the 1980s, they hired different consultants to give them answers, most of which indicated the need for an image overhaul but didn't explain how such changes would reflect the wants and needs of consumers. So it was at that point, Mitch reported, that they commissioned a huge $50,000 study to look at different locations, do customer surveys, and come up with a blueprint for whatever overhaul was needed.

Funny thing was, right when the study was commissioned, Mitch heard that one of their employees, a seventeen-year-old, African-American stock clerk by the name of James who worked at the Modell's on Jamaica Avenue in Queens, had volunteered helpful information to the store managers that would explain why their business was in serious trouble. Excited for answers, Mitch heard everything that James had to say and was stunned. But he heeded every word.

And the gist of it was: "Mr. Modell, I would never shop here." Whenever he had purchased items in the store, James admitted, he was embarrassed. He said that he would use a bag from another, more cool store in order to walk home without being ridiculed. James explained why he would never shop there for anything other than a few sundry items, saying, "Look at the way you merchandise your product, you don't make it look fresh, you don't make it look right." And then there was the issue that the brands being offered had no connection to cool.

Stunned though he was, Mitch Modell knew James was right

and went to work, acting on the insights of a kid who knew more than all the experts—especially with regard to what brands they needed to start selling. While in the middle of doing that, the customer surveys that had been commissioned started coming back. Mitch recalled, "Everything that James told us, our customers told us. Either people had never shopped us and told us why they wouldn't go to us, or people who used to shop us told us why they wouldn't shop us anymore." Mitch Modell knew they had to change within the year or they were sunk.

Among the brands that customers were going elsewhere to purchase were such names as Cotler, Starter, Bugle Boy, Champion, A.J.'s Jeanswear, Russell, New Balance, and Avia. These were the lines that early hip-hop culture had been adopting and giving the equivalent of the FDA inspection stamp of approval. Modell's needed to be authentic in the way that these brands were seen. And the most important brand of all that they hadn't been offering was Reebok—the early-eighties king of all cool footwear.

Ironically, the very brands that Modell's most needed to get into their stores would absolutely not sell to them. Why not? Their image. Reebok was the lynchpin. As long as Reebok wouldn't sell to them, none of the other brands would. The fact that some of Modell's stores sold army-navy supplies and others had discount inventories, the brand wholesalers believed, would disrupt the perception of their distribution powers. They were right.

Mitch said to them, "If we change our image, will you sell to us?" Everyone said back to him, "You'll never change." Well, eventually that was disproved and the media covered it with headlines proclaiming how they managed to not only change their whole image but also create great excitement in the marketplace. And the rest, as they say, is history. But what never became history was the crazy, bold, and daring—as in gangsta—machinations that were required by Mitch Modell to get Reebok to sell to him.

This points out yet another cultural rule that commerce always has to manage, especially in a shifting economy—the fact that the flames of aspiration are fanned by scarcity. How does the brand control that? Very carefully!

No matter how much leverage Mitch used with the sales rep, no matter how much begging he did for just a dozen pairs of Reeboks to put in one store, he was told, over and over, "No" and "Never." At a trade show, he even went directly to the CEO of Reebok, Paul Fireman, the gregarious visionary who had taken the British shoe company to the pinnacle of the footwear world, and Modell pleaded with Fireman to grant them a personal favor and let them put Reebok in their stores. Unfortunately, word was out that some of the Modell's stores were still very much army-navy and selling batteries and had inventories with irregulars or discounted merchandise. Paul Fireman couldn't interfere with his rep's decision.

Mitch Modell then came up with a kamikaze strategy to scare the rep into changing his mind—which meant almost going broke to get sneakers shipped from Germany and making it look like Modell's was going to discount Reeboks and hurt the sales of the big-name department stores like Macy's and Bamberger's. In the end, after sitting there with a fortune in sneaker inventory, the bluff worked and he didn't have to do that. Between the sales rep and Paul Fireman, Modell's was okayed as an account and within seventy-two hours all the other brands opened up accounts for them. Mitch said, "If it wasn't for Paul, I wouldn't be in business today. I'll never forget it."

Within six months the new and improved Modell's was booming like never before and growing like wildfire with stores opening up left and right. Reebok was that powerful, that magical, that cool. Not just in the urban locations where James had helped Modell's become responsive to their local consumers but, as time went on, in their other stores everywhere. After almost biting the dust, they became key movers of the athletic and other apparel that by the late eighties and early nineties was part of the hip-hop look.

I could well remember my teenage years when their store on Jamaica Avenue was suddenly the coolest place to shop. Run-DMC got their sneakers there! Forget about it. All the eighties rappers from the Bronx, old-school before there was such a term, shopped at Modell's. Jamaica Avenue back then was a destination of glamour and excitement—where you'd go to get gold teeth and big flashy jewelry and also pick up the coolest brands, like A.J.'s, Pony, and KangaROOS, at Modell's.

When I asked Mitch Modell what evidence he saw that the urban customer was driving mainstream consumption—at what point the kid in Greenwich, Connecticut, was buying the same shirt that the teenagers in the boroughs were wearing—he answered, "We were always an urban retailer that transitioned into suburban." Initially, just as with the early days of only finding the music on certain ends of the dial, that meant some of the nonurban, nonethnic consumers who crossed from the mainstream before everyone else were actually making the trek to Jamaica Avenue and other urban Modell's.

At first, there had been Modell's Sporting Goods in the city and boroughs while the Modell's Shopping World stores, the discount operations, were out in New Jersey and Long Island. Then in the early nineties, with the rise of massive discount superstores, instead of battling for survival, they turned all their suburban stores into Modell's Sporting Goods at just the right moment. Mitch Modell described their unique, fortified place in the marketplace by saying, "And so we became an urban/ suburban brand."

Because they had been authenticated by the cool of their urban influences, with urban culture driving sales in suburban doors, Modell's was at the perfect intersection to witness how trends moved. Starter was a brand that Mitch said began with athletes spotted by fans in the stands, followed by rappers anointing the look, and then it kept building like a wave in a stadium. As we saw with NWA's adoption of the Raiders' uniform and colors, the blurring of the lines between hip-hop and sports had been there from the start. As time went on, team affiliation was important, but as the trend widened, the mass appeal of sports-influenced fashion had much more to do with colors borrowed from teams. Color was king. Kids would sometimes buy as many as five of the same item in different colors. This was true whether it was Starter jackets or New Era hats or pro-league licensed jerseys or Reebok sneakers.

Coincidentally, when I finally made the decision to begin to transition out of the music business and into advertising, one of

my first major accounts that was facing a grave challenge and
was in need of the Midas touch was Reebok. After a decade and
a half, they had lost proximity to culture. It was to the everlast-
ing credit of Paul Fireman that he was willing to give me a shot
to try to pull off what needed to be a total disruption strategy.
And then some. There was only one solution that I knew could
work. Hip-hop culture was going to be the magic bullet I could
use to help Reebok with the reinvention and activation required
for relevancy.

How could I be so sure?

Well, right before I officially left Interscope, where I was
still overseeing projects that had been in the works for a while
under my auspices, I had done a favor for a friend at Motorola
by asking Jay-Z if he wouldn't mind giving them a shout-out. Lo
and behold, on *Dynasty,* his very next album release, on the single "I Wanna Love U (Give It 2 Me)," there was the line *"I'm too
cold, Motorola, two-way page me."* When the video was aired,
the magic from that one name-check happened instantly. The
shared values of the brand—what was one of the coolest phone
texting/e-mail and paging devices technology had as yet delivered—and a poet/entrepreneur/icon who stood for all that was
real and possible, the coolest and most hopeful path of all, registered overnight with consumers. Sales went through the roof.

With that, I finally decided to go into the advertising world
full-time. My mentor at Interscope/Geffen/A&M, Jimmy Iovine,
gave me his blessing to go forward with my new endeavors. My
attitude was that it would hopefully all work out as long as I
could take all the lessons taught to me by the music business and
put them to use. For starters, I was going to think of this first big
mountain to climb simply as marketing CDs with shoelaces.

CHAPTER 6

MIRRORS AND THE VELVET ROPE

From the moment that I sat down to meet with Reebok CEO Paul Fireman in late 2000 and presented him with a fairly blunt assessment of the main challenges facing his brand and what my team and I would propose we do about it, I had a strong hunch that we were going to make marketing history together. Why? Because when I told him my ideas and admitted, "Nobody's ever done this before," he was sold. That's all Paul wanted to hear.

Clearly, Paul Fireman hadn't built his brand by betting the odds. He not only seemed able to find comfort in the discomfort of doing things differently from the rest of his industry but from the start of doing business with him I learned a lot from how he kept instincts and intellect in balance. Paul also commands a most admirable characteristic of leadership that I have identified as the ability to know what you don't know. Too many seasoned entrepreneurs and executives are more interested in self-validation of what they know than in paying attention to what they don't. Reebok was never run that way. As a result, cultural curiosity and a mission to be relevant—"to make a difference" as the brand puts it—had been part of the company's values from early on. In addition, Paul Fireman's belief in research and his willingness to invest time and money in product development meant that, historically, one of the company's core competencies was superior design.

Our first strategy meeting was at the offices of Reebok, which were eerily quiet at four P.M. as most of the once bustling building had emptied for the day. Not a good sign. Paul and I went over Reebok's history and how it figured in a storied past as epic as the brand battles of Coke versus Pepsi and McDonald's versus Burger King, otherwise known as the Sneaker Wars.

No Business Like Shoe Business

A native of Brockton, Massachusetts, where Reebok's offices were, Paul Fireman had more or less grown up in the sneaker business while working in his family's sporting goods store. After attending Boston University, Paul dropped out in 1975 to take over the store. Then, in 1979, during an overseas business trip to a London trade show, he spotted some interesting European makes of athletic shoes that didn't yet have American distribution. One of them, made by a tiny, three-generation-old British company named J.W. Foster & Sons, was the Reebok line of custom-designed running shoes. Paul and his wife decided to seize the opportunity and borrowed $35,000—putting up their house as collateral—to invest in the company, and, as part of the deal, to become the exclusive North American distributor of Reebok.

Globally, the two most dominant sneakers in those days, Adidas and Puma, were not just brand competitors. The two companies had originally been one and the same, having been founded in the 1920s by the German Dassler family, which had come to a fork in the road when brothers Adolph (Adi) and Rudolph had a falling-out. Parting ways after that, Adi's Adidas and Rudolph's Puma were subsequently run on two sides of a river with their companies locked into a family feud. One brother allegedly accused the other of arranging for Hitler to send him to the front lines during World War II, while the other was said to have retaliated by informing Allied forces that his brother was supporting the Nazis. After the war, their brands survived, and both companies grew rapidly. At the same time there were bizarre accounts of how the Dassler brothers remained with their families in one villa for many years and how villagers were divided by whose company employed them—and were identified by which of the two brands of sneakers they wore! However, by the time Adidas and Puma reached the shores of the United States, both sneaker brands were quickly embraced for their fine design and for their reputed enhancement of sports performance—which both companies marketed by endorsements obtained from a variety of celebrity sports heroes. Although the feud eventually caused most of the next generation of Dasslers to lose ownership in the companies, not much of the infighting was ever known to the American public.

In fact, until Nike started to come on strong in the midseventies, Adidas and Puma together accounted for 60 percent of the U.S. sneaker market share—with Adidas controlling most of that. But by the early nineties, Adidas had fallen to less than 3 percent of the American sneaker business, in spite of the nice but brief spike they were given from the Run-DMC relationship. Puma managed to stay alive on the global scene but dwindled almost to nonexistence in the U.S., although it maintained its elite status as the maker of a superior soccer shoe; ultimately, Puma's survival was only possible when it was taken over later by a French company that had also bought Gucci.

This is all to say that in 1980 when Paul Fireman was just getting started, Reebok ought to have been the longest of long shots for even getting on the map. Nike already ruled the roost. When outdoor jogging had suddenly become an American pastime and Adidas didn't see it as something that could last, Nike had ridden that wave almost solo from the midseventies, when they were doing $14 million a year, to the start of the eighties, when the company went public and was taking in a reported $270 million a year as the top-selling sneaker in the U.S.

Then a funny thing happened. Just when Adidas was figuring out how to climb back to the top from second place and compete with Nike's ever-increasing market share, jogging got cold for a minute as skating started to heat up, and, in 1982, as if out of nowhere, an indoor aerobics craze seized the nation. Nike, then immersed in the development and marketing of a sneaker called the Air Force 1—a piece of artwork if you ask any serious footwear scholar—opted not to concern itself with aerobics. Adidas also made no move to take advantage of the aerobics boom and thus missed their chance to capture a rich, emerging group of newly activated sneaker consumers: women. Well, guess what? As Reebok's luck would have it, they had a woman's shoe—white leather oxford style, low-tops, with the brand name in baby-blue lettering and a regal stamp on the side of the shoe showing Britain's Union Jack. Introduced in 1982 as an aerobics sneaker, it was fashionably dubbed the Freestyle.

At almost sixty dollars a pair the price would have seemed excessive even by most of its high-end competitors' standards. Yes, that was a lot for a sneaker—at least from the point of view of those companies mainly targeting male consumers. But for women ready to get their groove on at the gym, in a social and experiential context, the cost only elevated aspiration and status. Very smart. And before long the Sneaker Wars became a battle of innovations and higher costs.

Recently, while catching up with Paul Fireman, I recalled the Freestyle moment in footwear history and asked him to give me a sense of the economic impact. During his first few years with Reebok, he had actually gone into more debt and had initially lost money. "What people today don't realize about the footwear business," Paul explained, "and what they don't realize about what Nike did, what Reebok did, and originally what Adidas did, is how much was spent on design, development, and research. We spent a ton." Losing money in the short run, however, gave them an incubation period that would pay the greatest dividends. Paul described the early years as a time when coming up with new product required working three years out. "And what you're looking to create, you don't know. You just needed to get people stimulated to look for new possibilities, create new possibilities, to have conversations for new possibilities."

Such was the thinking that put Reebok on a path to becoming

the number-one-selling sneaker brand of the 1980s. Sure enough, by 1983, women and aerobics catapulted the company into annual sales of $13 million, and by the following year, Paul Fireman and his partners, Pentland Industries, bought Reebok from J. W. Foster & Sons for $2 million. In 1985 that investment was richly rewarded with the $64 million he collected when the company went public. Two years later Reebok was reporting annual revenues of $1.4 billion—beating Nike out on almost every measure.

Many factors were important in that success story. Certainly one of them had to do with a vital aspect of hip-hop culture's love for discovery—for being the first on the block to show up in new kicks that nobody's seen yet and that come with a luxury price tag. To keep the power of that coolness going, as we saw when Reebok wouldn't sell to Modell's until they upgraded their image, takes an incredible level of discipline. Paul Fireman put it this way: "What happens with urban kids in the world is that they are fundamentally creating fashion. They start the trends or they enforce the trends." Either way, he pointed out, "They're more provocative, more daring, more willing to stand for something. And I think that's an important factor in how fashion goes. Now the problem in urban trends is that if you're not careful, you can allow the urban trend to eat you up alive, because they want to move on quickly."

My question to Paul, relevant no matter what the decade or the brand battle, was, "How do you stay new? Because if you're not new, you're dead."

What Reebok learned, not only from watching its competitors but by observing the early battles between clothing designers like Hilfiger and Polo, was, as Paul put it, that you have to avoid going through the system too fast and burning out. When Tommy Hilfiger was the contender going up against the über-brand Polo, "all of a sudden Hilfiger got adopted and pulled by urban culture. If they are pulling you, you're in great shape. But you must resist that pull. The current wants to pull you, but you are fighting the other way."

Translated into the cautionary tale drawn from the grand love affair between hip-hop and Tommy Hilfiger, that suggests that when you go so far, so fast, so big without pulling it the other way, you're always in danger of killing the golden goose: aspiration. But in Tommy's case the complication in this mix was the baseless rumor that started in 1996 and that had gone viral overnight suggesting he had gone on *The Oprah Winfrey Show* and had said, in effect, that he wished people of color wouldn't wear his clothing line. Beyond a shadow of a doubt it was not true—as Oprah would emphatically insist a decade later, it was "a big fat lie that never happened." Though Tommy had denied it—and in spite of the fact that he had never gone on the show and that there was no evidence, ever, that he had made the offending statement, and in spite of an extensive PR effort to combat the rumor—it lingered. Why? Partly because his response wasn't big enough, fast enough, or far-reaching enough. But I think it was mostly because of the closeness of the relationship between the Hilfiger brand and the culture that was there from the start, such that even a baseless rumor felt like marital infidelity. Even when you've been told it didn't happen, you can't get the offending image out of your head. Interestingly enough, it wasn't only people of color who backed off the brand. When urban kids pulled back, their white suburban peers followed. The company then lost more generations of mainstream consumers whose mindset was sophisticated, politically correct, and usually brand-savvy. The street, more and more, was Main Street.

Knowing Tommy as a person and an entrepreneur, I can attest that he would never say or even think anything along those lines. What's more, I watched him rise above the fray with a lot of grace. Things didn't turn out too badly either when he sold his company in 2006 for $1.6 billion or when it was sold again in 2010 for about twice that much. The purchase by Phillips–Van Heusen put Tommy Hilfiger under the same roof as one of the brand's former rivals, Calvin Klein. Strange bedfellows? No longer. The power and pitfalls of the tanning effect could be seen at many of those turns.

What Paul Fireman was learning with Reebok in the mid-eighties was how to stay engaged with urban consumers—showing the love but without being too available. He commented to me, "Nobody wants it when they can have everything. When it goes too far, people want to get rid of it. Now, it may sell a lot of volume but it's no longer driving the show and that's what you don't want to be in. You don't want to be common." Whether the consumer is urban or suburban, he went on to say, "the fear is that you let the early adopters become multiplied too fast and they take over. You lose your whole purpose for being." In Paul's estimation, the brand that understood how to be in the current without letting it move them through the system too quickly was Nike.

In other words, other factors in Reebok's 1980s success were lessons learned from how competitors were managing to thrive. To stay on the side of newness, the brand then followed the demure, simple styling of their original aerobics Freestyle with a high-top version that included the signature two Velcro ankle straps and also came in hot, flashy colors like pink, orange, and cobalt blue. These sneakers weren't just must-haves for the gym but gave girls and young women their funky uniform for school, work, parties, hanging out, and completing fashion statements.

One of the many distinctions of the Reebok sneakers was that they were made with very expensive leather that was considered to be ladies' handbag leather or glove leather. As such it was thinner and softer than most athletic footwear and tended to wrinkle—like an elephant. Well, somebody in the company saw the wrinkling as a problem to solve and recommended the use of a thicker and smoother leather that cost less too. Made sense. But as soon as sneakers without the wrinkles started hitting the stores, sales began to slip. And Paul, being the smart entrepreneur that he is, insisted that he didn't care what it cost— they had to use handbag leather again. Companies miss these lessons all the time when they're so concerned about making money on the margins and trying to cut costs that they don't see the enchantment that consumers have with the product. In the case of Reebok, handbag leather, wrinkles and all, was a detail that authenticated the brand.

The affection that female consumers had for the Freestyle ran so deep that the shoe earned its own local colloquialism. In New York girls called them the "5411s." Wonder why? Nope, it wasn't the model number on the box. That was exactly what a pair of Freestyles cost when you added tax: $54.11. Reebok 5411s were code for being in the know in the best sense of the word. And meanwhile, as that phenomenon was building an army of female consumers, Reebok also made significant inroads into marketing to male consumers—thanks to new technologies.

Paul tells a great story about something that happened at Reebok headquarters in Brockton one day when he found a pair of boots in the wastebasket. This was a situation when after all the conversation that had been going on about looking for new possibilities, he realized that sometimes your company isn't going to invent it but that someone else will. And in those cases, Paul stressed, "you have to see the product, recognize it, and then transform it into something that can work."

The pair of boots had been jerry-rigged—as Paul Fireman put it—by an older gentleman, a World War II veteran turned inventor, so that the insoles provided added cushioning in the form of two "humps." Apparently someone in the office had opened the mail and had no idea what to do, so they had chosen to dump the prototype for the "Pump" technology into the dustbin of history. Instead, Paul rescued the boots and met with the man, who described his invention as "energy air" that was not so much for high-performance sports but for good old-fashioned walking. In another twist of good timing, during the late 1980s one of the fastest-growing footwear categories was walking shoes. So Paul made a deal with the man to take the technology into a product that promptly sold seven million pairs a year.

That was only a glimmer of things to come. Similar technology, as it was, further developed for high-performance athletic sneakers—allowed you to apply pressure to a basketball-shaped pump on the shoe and customize how much air cushioning you had. The Pump was spectacular, as was its sequel, the Double Pump, which offered one of Reebok's most memorable slogans: "Life is short. Play hard."

The Pump really was a phenomenon. Not only was the design hot and the concept fresh but it impacted the game of basketball—as witnessed during a famous televised dunk contest in 1991 when an unlikely contender, the Boston Celtics' Dee Brown, a kid from Jacksonville, Florida, wore his Reebok Pumps to the contest. When it came time for Dee's turn, he backed all the way up, and before he took off, he kneeled down and started pumping the shoes. And this blatant endorsement of Pump technology that was going to improve his dunking sent him flying into the air with a no-look dunk—that enabled him to come from nowhere and win the contest—and simultaneously put the shoe on absolute fire.

After that, Dee Brown used to joke that there were only two basketball players in the NBA with legendary sneakers—him and Michael Jordan.

True. During this period, Nike had definitely not been idle. And Reebok wasn't the only sneaker getting help from rarified air. One of the ironies in this whole saga is that in 1982 when the Freestyle was all anyone talked about, Nike's stunning original Air Force 1s had been overshadowed and overlooked by almost everyone—with the exception of a loyal urban following who felt personally dispirited when it was dropped and never stopped hoping for its return. The reason for dropping the Air Force 1 was to make way for bigger and better—the Air Jordan. The press suggested that not everyone at team Nike was sure that the sneaker would sell. When the five-year $2.5 million endorsement deal was made to bring in Michael Jordan—then a rookie first-round draft pick by the Chicago Bulls out of the University of North Carolina—there were out-clauses for the brand in the event that the Air Jordan failed to lift off. In the black and red team colors of the Bulls uniform, the sneaker sold an unbelievable $130 million in its second year on the market, transcending anything ever achieved by a mere athletic shoe before. The Air Jordan had magic in it. Perhaps it was a reflection of the brand that had been named for the Greek goddess of victory or that the sneaker embodied the energy of the Nike swoosh logo drawn to represent her wing. It also stood for the entrepreneurial genius of the brand's creator, Phil Knight, and the gravity-defying ability of an athlete destined to become one of basketball's greatest players of all time.

On top of that, Air Jordans were a cultural departure from the classic NBA uniform look, just as Michael himself was unlike the gold-standard heroes in the mold of Larry Bird and Magic Johnson. Jordan was frequently threatened with being fined for wearing his Nikes on the court because they weren't regulation. As Adam Silver, now the NBA's deputy commissioner, recently reminded me, the rule at the time was that sneakers had to be all one color. The fact that Jordan risked the fine and wore the sneakers anyway—bucking the system—made Air Jordans all the more desirable by mirroring the authentic, unapologetic attitude of the youth generation. This reveals an often overlooked yet pivotal role that Michael Jordan played in tanning. Not only did he have a great-looking sneaker—with a beautiful, new-to-market silhouette—but he embodied hip-hop culture's antiestablishment attitude at the same time that he was a baller who played out of the stratosphere.

Magic Johnson and Larry Bird were undoubtedly adored as athletes. But they didn't convey the same cultural codes as Jordan did, codes that were starting to resonate—the use of one-on-one moves, for example, or wearing a gold chain during dunk contests. Basketball fans who wished they could play like Magic or Bird but didn't have the height found aspiration through Jordan that came from sharing his against-the-grain attitude. With these attributes, he captured the values of the hip-hop cultural creed at a critical moment when a generation was redefining how it saw and experienced the world. If kids were wearing no shoelaces or fat laces, Jordan was in sync with them—by refusing to have his Air Jordans fit the definition of an acceptable NBA sneaker.

And so, by 1990, in spite of Reebok's sponsorship and licensing traction with the NFL and other major league men's sports teams, Nike was back in the lead as the top-selling brand across the boards. In some ways, the Sneaker Wars now resembled a battle of the sexes—with Reebok doing at least 50 percent of their business with women, while males overwhelmingly favored Nike in most categories, none more so than basketball.

Paul Fireman and Phil Knight had never made any pretense of being fond of each other. My impression was that Paul loved going up against the behemoth that was Nike, even if it meant not always winning. Paul's motto was "Nobody holds all the cards at any given time, and that's what makes the game so much fun." Phil Knight didn't appear to see anything fun about the competition or any reason to have to like his rival. Nike was out not just to win but to crush all contenders for the throne. Phil's guiding philosophies included the saying that it's important to "play by the rules but be ferocious," and "It's okay to be Goliath but always act like David."

From the underdog's standpoint, Reebok probably figured that the reverse was just as true. In the role of David in the brand matchup they managed to sign a literal Goliath by the name of Shaquille O'Neal to an endorsement deal that really heated up the Sneaker Wars. Shaq's newness in the NBA—and even the looming question of whether he was ready to go up against the big boys or not—was smartly woven into a "Don't Fake the Funk" commercial campaign. Besides being funny, irreverent, and always comfortable in his off-the-court persona, Shaq gave Reebok credibility in its bid to become more of a hard-core athletic sneaker and in connecting to a younger generation of males. With a language and attitude that was hip-hop-infused, he brought some added cool to the mix in 1993 when his first rap album, *Shaq Diesel*, went platinum, and a year later the follow-up album went gold. Despite Reebok's success with Shaquille, Nike still kept its top-dog status—but with only a little breathing room. A 1995 *Fortune* magazine feature about the Sneaker Wars reported, "The company regained the revenue lead from Reebok in 1990, $2.24 billion vs. $2.16 billion." In 1994 Nike's earnings were $299 million on $3.79 billion while Reebok's numbers were $254 million on $3.28 billion in revenues. *Fortune* noted, "Together the two companies sell more than half the athletic footwear in the U.S. and they control over 40% of the global market. Only Adidas, with about 10% of global sales, remains a significant competitor." Other indicators had suggested that Nike was overextended and that sales were actually slumping—enough so there was a significant restructuring warranted.

That was basically where things stood around '95 when Paul Fireman decided he needed to free himself up from the day-to-day activities of running the sneaker business to take over the direction of other companies that were in Reebok's expanding portfolio such as Rockport, Boston Whaler, Avia, and a line of footwear designed by Ralph Lauren. In addition to new opportunities in the booming global athletic footwear and apparel business (plus an interest in investing in health and fitness clubs), there was also philanthropy to run and, who knows, a memoir he was thinking about writing. No doubt, Paul had stepped aside with the assurance that younger ideas and hopefully the more culturally attuned leadership he left in place would keep Reebok right at the top.

Five years later, after watching the stock price plummet and the brand lose its former sparkle, Fireman couldn't take it anymore. While he had been on the sidelines, instead of sustaining and building momentum, Reebok had suffered a stunning and thorough reversal of fortunes. By 2000, not only had Nike conquered the global market as well as the U.S. sneaker business, but Adidas was back in action. After almost facing bankruptcy in 1993, they were now Adidas-Salomon (after being merged with a ski gear maker), ranked second globally, and in the U.S. controlled 17 percent of the sneaker business. In short, Adidas had outmaneuvered Reebok on two fronts—in high-performance sports shoes and in delivering style in terms of newness and cool to the young urban/suburban consumer.

In Paul's absence, Reebok's executives had not lived up to the brand's values. On the one hand they hadn't kept in tune with their base of women consumers who had made Reebok a phenomenon and helped it change the industry. On the other hand, like many corporations run by directors that rarely leave the boardroom, the brand had no connection to the one make-or-break consumer segment for marketing sneakers—young adult males and teens, this polyethnic group whose tastes, as we've seen, were now driving urban as well as mainstream culture. There was a paralysis, understandably so, from not wanting to do anything that might turn off the traditional Reebok consumer or hurt the legacy of a global corporation doing $4 billion a year in business with ten thousand employees worldwide. Another issue was that instead of investing in new ideas, research, and development, the company was being run by the numbers— with efforts to save money, for example, by ending deals with inventors and trying to copy designs or retrofit older technologies. No originality, no creativity. That assessment, along with the other concerns, had been enough for Paul to return to his post as CEO and take back the reins—and to come to us.

So the challenge was straightforward: to define a strategic position by which the brand would connect to the lives of young adult males and to increase Reebok's overall profile, product alignment, purchasing consideration, and urgency within the retail environment. Translation? The brand needed more than cosmetic surgery. It needed to be reborn, as Paul Fireman agreed, through a total disruption marketing strategy, different from anything tried before. Paul also agreed with my reasoning for why, as in this case, marketing is sometimes best done in product creation. And finally, because of the background that he had provided us, when I explained the importance of mirrors that we would be using to reflect real lives and consumer cues—along with the intention to employ the velvet rope to bring back aspiration—Paul Fireman was game.

The Sound and Rhythm of Sports

During my initiation into the field of marketing it had been my observation that a lot of the men and women working in creative positions in advertising were frustrated screenwriters. Their interest had nothing to do with solving companies' problems but more with crafting flashy commercials to put on their reels so they could break into the movie business or win awards. Yet I also knew there were younger and/or less conventional creative people who actually wanted to be in marketing and had proximity to pop culture but weren't being tapped. Since I had always seen my role at Translation as keeping us focused on being a solution agency in service of clients, regardless of whether we were doing product development, brand design, strategic insight, or traditional media, those were the creative people I wanted to bring on my team. Whatever the solutions, I was determined to find the way to fix my clients' business concerns. And doing that is the only way, in my view, to say you've been successful.

Again, the baby boomer era and the *Mad Men* advertising

attitudes still running the show didn't hold up the right mirror to the multicultural, multigenerational, polyethnic consumers that we can now call the millennials. By 2001 the millennials had become the most informed, most discerning consumers ever to appear on the planet. At this stage, factors going into purchasing consideration had also changed. No longer could a brand get away with doing the autocratic monologue to cram down their message. No longer could the language be verbalized as talking to the mass audience; the focus was now on individuals. No longer could slogans or jingles be force-fed because even though they might be catchy, they didn't necessarily entice you to buy the product.

We had arrived at that point in time when it was imperative for brands to issue an invitation. Consumers wanted to be allowed in, to have a point of view in the matter. Elements that needed to be emphasized were social, experiential, and then, finally, retail. In the old days, all advertising had to do was push retail. But now other considerations—the social-status entry point and the experiential/emotional entry point—had to be woven into the invitation. A very gentle relationship, I might add. What's more, with this choosier consumer, design aesthetics were influencing purchase consideration more than ever.

In a challenging retail environment, the payoff for a radical disruption strategy is never guaranteed. With a new product, brand, or organization being launched into a crowded marketplace, it may be easier to expect you'll attain the desired goal of gaining a certain amount of attention. But when it's a strategy for reviving a brand that has lost relevance and is on its last gasp, a radical disruption strategy is like applying the defibrillator paddles to a patient on life support. When your brand is not performing, risk and disruption are among your few assets. When you are performing, you are naturally risk-averse. Yeah, true disruption is a complete risk, loud, bold, multitiered, without guarantees, and extremely expensive. But for a dying brand, if you don't try it and you're dead, then it wasn't a risk, right?

We knew that Reebok lacked any credibility when it came to communicating with its target consumer. Whatever new, fresh values it was embracing wouldn't be perceived anyway and the chance to connect to passion points would be denied. We had to relieve the brand of the baggage it was shouldering and come correct, believable, with something new. The solution was to create what in some circles is called a brand extension but flies on its own as a new, alternative brand—not an offshoot or pretender to follow in Reebok's footsteps but a satellite brand that could chart its own course and direction.

Explaining this disruptive strategy to Paul Fireman, I had to remind him that anything we did couldn't overlap or in any way be seen as like Nike—which we all accepted had the monopoly on performance sneakers. "Paul," I remember telling him early in our planning, "we aren't going to do anything to make people believe our sneakers are going to make them jump higher or run faster than they will in a pair of Nikes, so let's not even go down that path." What kids did want were color options to match their apparel—brightly colored soles, for example, to coordinate other arhcles of clothing. That mattered more than performance.

He understood. Likewise when my team and I pointed out the futility of trying to remake Reebok without an alternative higher-end brand, he saw that made sense too. The model we used as an example for this new brand we wanted to create was what Toyota did when they wanted to veer into the luxury end of the auto market. Realizing that consumers couldn't wrap their heads around such a radical shift in how the Toyota brand represented itself, it created Lexus as a stand-alone brand to house their aspirational and luxury values. In no time, Lexus was a well-established top name brand in the higher-cost bracket. Most of the public didn't know the two were even related. But for auto experts, when Lexus was introduced it came ready with an outstanding automotive track record in its DNA. Later, when we saw the Toyota brand get killed almost overnight—once the raft of acceleration problems and recalls met their tipping point and hit the news—Lexus as a brand was pretty much spared. It didn't have to rebuild its good name the way that Toyota did.

Needless to say, getting the right name for a new satellite brand for Reebok wasn't going to be easy. We got lucky. As it turned out, the perfect name was on the tip of Paul Fireman's tongue. In 1985, when he took his company public, the stock symbol for traders had been denoted by the abbreviation RBK. Reebok without the vowels? It was current and sounded cool. I loved it.

We now had a brand name that embodied its roots in sports footwear and that reflected hip-hop culture's penchant for abbreviations. Taking it a step farther, the next goal was to link the athleticism of sports to a visual profile of hip-hop music and its icons. This presented a multitude of possibilities, as Paul Fireman had always sought, to develop the main theme. We dubbed the platform, "The Sound and Rhythm of Sports." The underlying story premise came from a fact of life that I'd observed since childhood—rappers want to be athletes and athletes want to be rappers.

Little had changed in the long-standing affinity between hip-hop and most forms of athletic competition. So much code-sharing and switching had been taking place across the eighties and nineties—with the language and customs of hip-hop permeating the field of sports and vice versa—that the mentality was filtered in a two-way process. Brands, of course, had accelerated the distribution of the style and cool that was being cross-bred. The urban look, from the cuts of clothing to the cornrows and tattoos, was being adopted by a diverse mix of players as readily as they were importing/exporting the language being adapted by athletes. This was a tanning effect on the global level, turning the code into a conversation to be used by black, white, brown, yellow, red, whomever; it was also being shared with the growing numbers of foreign-born athletes learning to talk hip before knowing literal translations of words. The use of playing-field colloquialisms rarely prevented players (with college degrees or not) from being able to speak into microphones to millions of fans while addressing the finer points of the game without being a) inappropriate, or b) inauthentic.

Kobe and Shaq weren't the only ballers who took their shots as rappers. *Basketball's Best Kept Secret*, released in 1994, boasted the rhyming of nine NBA stars—including Jason Kidd and Gary Payton. Deion Sanders, the Florida State phenom who went on to play pro baseball and pro football, had a mid-nineties rap album with a single that got some spins, "Must Be the Money."

The French-born Tony Parker of the San Antonio Spurs would do very well in the later '00s with a hip-hop album performed in French.

Meanwhile, attempts to cross over from music into sports were not as common as were the number of ballers trying to rap. But it happened. There was Master P, for instance, the New Orleans artist/producer/entrepreneur whose hip-hop entertainment empire built in the 1990s once included a sports agency, No Limits Sports Management. They represented several professional players (including the Heisman Trophy winner and star running back Ricky Williams—who was drafted fifth overall by the New Orleans Saints and later went to the Miami Dolphins). While Master P had enough skills to earn serious tryouts himself with the Fort Wayne Fury (Continental Basketball Association) and the NBA's Charlotte Hornets, he never made it to regular-season play.

These particulars would give us fuel for "The Sound and Rhythm of Sports." But the more we looked at the possibilities, the greater our consensus was that our most effective marketing was going to happen in product development. In other words, yeah, cool name, crazy ideas for *how* to sell, but first, *what* was RBK going to sell? We knew what we had set out as the brand's strategic intent and mandate: "to be relevant to global youth by creating innovative products and marketing that connects sports with the sharp edge of music, fashion and entertainment." What we didn't know was the details.

Once again, we were lucky. Reebok already had the shoe series and the basketball star that had been waiting in the wings for RBK. Perfect. The original shoe in the series was undeniably cool. It was simple, with a super-appealing toe shape; they had made a limited number of them with a color wave framing the front part of the sneaker and had distributed lots by specific color in only certain cities. That way, if you were in L.A. you could have only red, or in Boston only blue, and so on. Paying attention to consumer cues, the line reflected the awareness that kids didn't want the soles of their sneakers to get dirty, so they too were made in colors that hid the grime—and for owners of multiple pairs they could be traded out to go with other colors they were wearing as far as hats and jackets. The rest of the design elements weren't fussy; the line was edgy by going against many of the bells and whistles of some of the signature sneakers everyone else was promoting. How fitting for Allen Iverson of the Philadelphia 76ers, who was edge and rebellion personified.

Iverson was considered by some to be the anti-Jordan. If that was the case, it wasn't the worst thing to be when there was no way RBK would win in a contest against the wholesome, safe face of Nike. But I would also argue that Iverson was following in the footsteps of what Michael Jordan had begun earlier by defying the status quo. With his nickname, "the Answer," Iverson represented the underdog mentality of a guy who was barely six feet tall but who could still dunk and hit three-point buzzer beaters to win games while running circles around opponents. And he took the antiestablishment stance even further, not just with his cornrows and tats all over his body, but as the first NBA player to vocally refuse to wear short, fitted basketball shorts and get into trouble for going against the grain. At 180 pounds soaking wet, in his baggy shorts that looked two sizes too big, he could have been any kid from any urban neighborhood or someone you knew. And those kids who shared the same dream of making it to the NBA might not have made it but Iverson gave them hope that it was possible. After "the Answer" broke the ice, other players and fans alike began adopting cornrows, tattoos, and baggies, which were soon showing up on courts across America at every level. It was all part of hip-hop culture's embrace of individuality and the power of marching to your own beat.

For some brands, an unapologetic bad boy like Allen Iverson would not have been the right marketing fit. But for RBK, at that point in the brand history when it needed to come out into the market with a massive splash and have some rags-to-riches appeal, Allen Iverson was a way of putting a mirror up to a figure like Rocky Balboa. Whatever the obstacles, the message implied, they could be overcome—as long as you had some of that cool.

Plus, with Iverson and our mantra that all rappers want to be athletes and all athletes want to be rappers, we had another case in point. He, in fact, had recorded a single, "40 Bars," and was working on an album. Neither would be released, mainly due to NBA commissioner David Stern's concerns about offensive language. Still, that didn't take away from Allen Iverson's credibility as a basketball star who conveyed the look and attitude of hip-hop—as well as the rhythm of the sport.

Now Reebok could get ready for the launch of the first Iverson sneaker to go forth under the RBK banner. All we needed was the sound, as I had promised Paul, that would make our efforts different from what everyone else had tried before. The goal was to find an unlikely voice to pair with Iverson. Because the airwaves had been so saturated by iconic sports celebrities repping brand-name goods, anything reminiscent of a monologue was not going to work. With a pairing, the linkage between sports and music—emphasizing the aspiration of rappers to be ballers and vice versa—could be given a visual profile. It would also be a kind of dialogue that consumers were being invited to join. When I recommended Jadakiss, an up-and-coming rapper from the group the Lox, at first the honest answer was that most of the men and women in the room had never heard of him. The only ones who knew—and who nodded—were all under twenty-five. Right on the money. Since we wanted to lace elements of newness through the campaign, Jadakiss fit the bill. He wasn't mainstream. He was a rap superstar. He also had big talent, a husky voice, humor, and fun. Jadakiss was our guy.

For the commercial we didn't have to rely on luck because we brought in the reigning superstar of hip-hop video direction, Hype Williams, and then he worked his magic. When we designed the commercial, I wanted to make sure that it had the feeling of a soundtrack. We decided that the rhythm of sports would be based on the squeaks from the sneakers, the hot new A5, and that Allen Iverson could dribble to the beat—and that Jadakiss could rap to it. The commercial was shot in black-and-white with splashes of color. Even before the reaction from the launch, we knew we had a winner on our hands. From that day forward, Paul Fireman always referred to RBK as his "music shoes."

In keeping with radical disruption, we needed the RBK launch to be especially noisy to create a sense of urgency for purchase consideration. And loud it was. The spot officially debuted on Sunday, February 10, 2002, during the NBA All-Star Game, after a press release bombarded media outlets everywhere and anywhere promoting the commercial as a "cutting edge fusion between hoops and hip-hop." On BET, Reebok products and references were being celebrated through placement and programming integration, starting with "RBK Freestyle Fridays" on one of the most popular shows, *106 and Park,* a video countdown.

Like I said, we knew the commercial was hot. But we couldn't have imagined its sound and rhythm would be so addictive and authentic that radio stations in NYC and Philly started putting it on the air as if it was the latest hip-hop single—a commercial! Those DJs had no issue with giving free play to an ad because they got the boost for discovering it. Listeners even called in requesting it. Before long, the commercial track ended up on mix tapes. Unbelievable.

Even before any of this rolled out, I had thrown a private viewing of the RBK line for Foot Locker buyers and other retailers to place their orders. Instead of a hotel ballroom or retail setting, I used the conference room at Universal Music's New York City offices and set up displays of the shoes mounted on pedestals in between gold and platinum records. For these buyers who were used to the conventional trade show booths—seen one, seen 'em all—the cultural immersion in the music business was like nothing anyone had experienced before. It was flying to the moon. The conclusion wasn't just that RBK had resurrected Reebok but that by taking on elements of music marketing, it was elevating the whole sneaker business with it.

With all the advance work, when the new line landed in stores, it was like the arrival of a much anticipated blockbuster movie. Throughout urban America, on billboards near basketball courts and on buses and inside subways, RBK beckoned. Now that we had set the stage with mirrors connecting the real lives of consumers with authentic brand values, it was time to bring in the velvet rope—literally. For anyone who has ever lined up on the "by invitation only" side of a velvet rope, whether standing on the red carpet of a Broadway opening or a limited run of a special museum exhibit or waiting in line just hoping and praying the bouncer will let you into the nightclub, you know that the experience taps something primal in most of us. It is more than aspiration, I would say. The feeling of being special, a VIP, I believe, is a need that is universal.

With that in mind, we made a deal for the RBK campaign with a retail chain that wasn't in the footwear category at all. Instead of marketing in the obvious venues, we created this once-in-a-marketing-lifetime arrangement with FYE, a music retail chain, and other big box music retailers, to exhibit RBK sneakers in more than 1,500 stores across the United States. *Record* stores. The locations were selected for their proximity to footwear stores that were specifically "authorized RBK sneaker dealers"— where consumers could easily find them to go purchase shoes, or, because they were being issued in limited amounts, they could go order them in advance so as not to miss out. At each of the FYE and other authorized stores we placed a single, gleaming RBK sneaker in a protective Plexiglas box high atop a pedestal— with lights—as you would display priceless, untouchable gems. And then for the final detail, we cordoned off each display with a velvet rope.

The code could be read in any neighborhood. RBK, because it merged values of sports and music, found its way into distribution channels that had previously been unthinkable. The satellite brand was such a smash out of the box that when the dust finally settled, Reebok overall found itself not just off life support but on its way to regaining enough market share to take away gains from Adidas and to start to eat into Nike strongholds.

We had only just begun. For true radical disruption, there were still some really out-from-left-field strategies in the works for the campaign's phase II.

Sneakers as Cultural Ambassadors

There is an unwritten law in the hip-hop code of ethics, woven into the belief system—the urban/suburban religion being spread worldwide through tanning. And that is the rule that always and forever you gotta represent what you love. And the truth is that I, as a consumer, as grown-up urban kid Steve Stoute, and as a marketing expert, happen to really love Nike.

And the love of a brand, as often as not, can be tied to experiences that happen when we're young and the most impressionable. So whenever I think of Nike from those days of growing up—when your sneakers defined your cool or destroyed it—the image that comes to mind is that of the Air Force 1 that was on the market so briefly, back when I was twelve years old. Then, in the early '00s, a miracle occurred. Nike released the Air Force 1 in all-white. In the record business, where I was still working at the time, for artists and executives alike, the return of "the 1s" in all-white was like a religious revival. Clean, understated, with a thick sole and low cut, the sneaker was mandatory. And with a pair of jeans and a white T-shirt, the Air Force 1 was part of the ubiquitous uniform for cool.

More variations in colors and materials and updates would come each year but what made the white sneakers especially powerful was that they belonged to the hip-hop generation, to the architects of the culture who never forgot them. They were like collector's items. Definitely not common. All the care that we regularly took of our sneakers had to be intensified to make sure our 1s didn't incur even the hint of a wrinkle or the suggestion of a smudge. We would not only put tissue in the toes when we weren't wearing them but some of us actually left tissue in the sneakers when we wore them. Nope, it wasn't comfortable but it was what you did to care for sneakers that might be tough to replace. Because if there was a wrinkle or the shoes looked dingy in the least, you had to replace them. Well, the solution to that was to buy multiple pairs.

Here's where it got really crazy. With Nike's keen understanding of the marketplace, they intensified demand for the Air Force 1s by putting them out in a limited release. As the proverbial eight-hundred-pound gorilla of the sneaker business, Nike had the retail relationships at Foot Locker and elsewhere to institute "only one pair per customer" rules. The only recourse for those of us who needed to stock up was to become very good friends with our local Foot Locker sales staff—making sure that we had

tickets to concerts and sporting events to show our appreciation for being allowed to purchase twelve pairs at a time. That
was the culture.

All of that said, over its history, though Nike had paid attention to the influence of hip-hop music and culture, it had kept
almost at an arm's length from it marketing-wise. So it was not a
problem as time went on to love Reebok/RBK a little bit more for
a few reasons, especially for its willingness to go all the way in its
embrace of the consumers who were changing the brand's fortunes. How Nike was reacting to Reebok's resurgence was hard
to read at first. Eventually, however, a showdown was inevitable.

One of the issues Nike could not have been happy about was
the news in 2002 that Paul Fireman had ended up taking a page
out of his own playbook to score the seriously lucrative contract
to outfit all twenty-nine teams in the NFL with uniforms—and to
be lead licensee for selling official team apparel and merchandise to the public. Two years earlier, just back on the job after
watching the Reebok stock price plummet, Paul had gotten the
NFL contract in an unusual way. In those days, several brands
had NFL contracts. In some cases, teams like the New York
Giants might have deals with four different top brand apparel
companies—causing overlap, confusion, price gouging, and falling profits for everyone, including the football teams. If you went
to a sports apparel store for a Giants jersey, there might be four
different shades of blue for that same team, none more official
than the other. Nobody was winning that contest.

When Paul was informed that everyone's contract was up
for review and renewal and that a visit was going to be paid to
Reebok headquarters, he told them all he wasn't interested. The
only way he would throw his hat in the ring is if the commissioner, coaches, and owners would come see him last—after
they had met with the other manufacturers.

When the NFL brass arrived, Paul Fireman welcomed
them—as he reported the story to me—and then told them up
front, "Before I begin, I'm going to tell you something, and you
can leave, if you wish. You can leave any time you want. You
can get up and be outraged with me. But I have to tell you that
you've abused manufacturers for years." He went on to detail

how the NFL had taken advantage of brands and lost people their jobs and gotten away with it because—well, because they could. What's more, he believed that the product line was terrible and he asked for a show of hands to see who disagreed. Not one hand went up. Then Paul held up those four different colors of blue Giants jerseys to emphasize his point. He proceeded to tell them he could fix it and that if they wanted him to give them a proposal, he would.

Because he had gotten their attention in such a blunt fashion, Paul explained to me later, "they now knew they had to listen to the next chapter." In making the proposal, his ultimate recommendation was that for every football franchise, all the teams together, the business needed to be overseen by one licensee—one leadership, one set of business systems—which would mean consolidating everything into a relationship with one manufacturer. Otherwise, with brands working at cross-purposes, everyone was being dragged down in the process. Initially, owners and commissioners decided they would like to split the business, with Reebok overseeing the American Football Conference and Nike the National Football Conference. Or the other way around.

Fireman said, "Give it all to Nike. Let them run it." Even though they worried that might change the brand they wanted, he told them, "They'll still run it better." In a very short turnaround, they came back and asked Reebok to run it all. Amid much back and forth, a ten-year contract was scored.

Incredible. When I first got the account, I was rolling in football jerseys. The Philadelphia Eagles made a jersey for me that said "Stoute" on the back. How he could have told them to go with Nike was beyond me. It was just brilliant.

Paul Fireman said, "I knew that they'd resist if I said they should give it all to me." Suggesting they give all the business to a competitor was "very simple math," per Fireman. "It's called a gamble."

Before Reebok consolidated the business, the NFL's merchandise revenues had fallen from $700 million to $300 million annually. Paul's recollection was that after taking over he was able to drive revenues up to about $750 million per year. And unlike before, the revenues were split evenly between all participants.

Not surprisingly, when it came time for the NBA teams to review their contracts for uniforms and licensing, they sought out Reebok's core competencies and made a similar deal to begin as soon as the other brands' contracts expired.

With RBK's success on top of that growth, brand revenues had been raised $100 million for 2002. The Sneakers Wars had heated up again, especially when RBK put out a limited edition of an all-white shoe we called the I3 Pressure, as part of the Iverson lineage. Though the toe was different, it was a similar price and looked so much like the all-white Air Force 1 that sparks really began to fly.

The commercial we did with Fabolous and DJ Clue had a guy eating a jelly doughnut and watching the dripping jelly fall slowly in an overdramatic way to accentuate the message: Don't get any mess on your white shoe! Not the smartest spot ever but it appealed to the mass of kids who wanted the look of the all-white sneaker but could never get their hands on the Air Force 1s. Now they could without a barrier—and with Allen Iverson's stamp of approval promoting an all-white shoe that was clean and fit the cool uniform. Was this stealing Nike's thunder? Absolutely. And because of the command and control that Nike had been exerting over Foot Locker and other retail stores with their limited editions and their only-one-pair-per-customer rule for the 1s, the opportunity for the I3 Pressure to gain momentum in its limited run was huge.

The launch was at Foot Locker. As Paul reminded me, they sold a million pairs immediately. Nike went ballistic, as he recalled. After all, he noted, RBK was "eating up the market, coming on like a freight train."

And what did the power player in this matchup do? They told Foot Locker that if the retail chain didn't stop selling the I3 Nike wouldn't sell them any more Jordans. Foot Locker, caught between a rock and a hard place, couldn't lose their Nike business. They proposed to Reebok that they would drop the I3 but put those dollars into another sneaker. Paul Fireman refused to budge at first but Foot Locker kept upping the ante, promising an additional $50 million and twice that if only they could get out of the Sneaker Wars diplomatically.

We even went through a period when Paul Fireman wanted to get into mobile retail, actually to rent RBK trucks and pull them into parks so we could sell the sneakers that had been banned by Nike and Foot Locker. After everything was said and done, as Paul would say, he blinked and agreed to pull his I3 business from Foot Locker. As he himself had said before in other ways, "You can't win them all."

Thankfully, given what I had in the works for phase II of "The Sound and Rhythm of Sports," the relationship between Reebok and Foot Locker was preserved. But there was another concern having to do with Nike that I had to approach very carefully.

My vision for consummating the marriage of RBK and hip-hop—and for the grand finale of the total disruption strategy— was, again, to do marketing in product development. But this time, I wanted to have the sneaker line be for a hip-hop artist. The story that had begun with the tanning moment back in 1986 at Madison Square Garden and Run-DMC being given an endorsement opportunity with Adidas had never truly realized its potential. It was time to follow through on the opportunity to impact culture even more powerfully—to explore the possibilities of having the first nonathlete receive an endorsement deal on par with superstar sports heroes, a signature line of sneakers, and the fervent marketing support that one of the top global brands could provide.

This was just the next logical step in the lineage that had begun with Michael Jordan and Allen Iverson pushing culture on the court, coming at the premise that all rappers want to be basketball players from that angle. The momentum of music, hip-hop culture, and a sport that was going global like never before was creating a harmonic convergence energy. To make an impact worldwide, of course the basketball players had to be great athletes and the rappers had to be great poets and musicians. Not everyone could be that. But the attitude of coming from nothing and turning it into something, as well as having an antiestablishment mentality, was accessible to all. The possibilities for me, when you could get all those elements working in tandem, were incredible. There were three artists I had in mind for fulfilling all the possibilities. But nobody could rise to the occasion to hit that first home run better than Jay-Z.

Paul Fireman needed little convincing. Between everything we'd already accomplished with his "music shoes" and in making RBK a reality, he saw only the upsides of an endorsement deal with Jay-Z. The decision wasn't brain surgery. Jay-Z, referred to by many as the CEO of hip-hop, had one of the longest careers as a rap artist of anyone in the record business. By 2010, he would have sold forty million albums worldwide and would hold the record of having the most number one albums on *Billboard*'s Top 200 of any recording artist in history. If that wasn't compelling enough, the point I made to Paul was that the sneakers we had the chance to develop for Jay-Z were about pure, unadulterated cool. Sticking with my mantra, I said, "We should make a sneaker for the kid who doesn't want to jump at all. He's just going to stand still and look good in his sneakers." Period. The end.

Except for one detail. Jay-Z loved Nike. He followed the code that you had to represent what you love. Those Air Force 1s were part of his look that he had written about in his lyrics and that had been seen on his platform blasted far and wide to every corner of the earth. How would it be believable that he was now going to wear Reeboks? Then again, as I thought about it, the truth was that Nike had never returned any favors to Jay. Maybe they had sent him free sneakers or added a logo of his choice to the shoes. That was the standard practice of giving swag to celebrities, including even hip-hop artists who religiously wore Nike and made the brand a fortune. But as for seeking him out to do an endorsement deal and invest their brand's core equities in his brand, Nike had not shown that cultural curiosity to date.

One thing that I didn't have to worry about was whether Jay-Z's role as part-owner of Rocawear, a hip-hop fashion brand, would prevent him from partnering with RBK. Since Rocawear didn't make shoes, that wasn't a problem. In fact, the parent company never conceived that an artist—versus an athlete—could sell footwear, so they had placed no restrictions in that area. Once that was cleared up for me, Jay and I sat down to talk about what I had in mind. Without having the language yet to describe tanning, I presented it as an opportunity for him to connect to his audience, the multicultural mix of consumers who were urban/suburban/global—to let sneakers be cultural ambassadors, bridging differences.

This raised another unwritten law in the code of ethics that hip-hop had given us—and that is about the power to change in order to grow. This was not the first or last time that the theme of change would come up for Jay-Z. But that rainy day toward the end of 2002 when he came to my office and we talked about the possibilities, it made all the sense in the world to him. He knew that I wasn't going to let Reebok do anything that wouldn't align with his values. And the deal was simple. A fifty-fifty joint venture, it stipulated that the ownership of the logo and trademark would revert back to him over a period of time after the deal ended.

As an opportunity to grow and change, Jay-Z loved the idea of calling the sneaker line the S. Carter Collection—in tribute to his given name, Shawn Carter. Unlike with the Iverson line, RBK didn't have a sneaker in the pipe ready to be launched. We went through a period when I drove everyone crazy at the company turning down their ideas. Jay-Z was very Zen about the process until one day he announced, "I have an idea for the design." It was inspired by a vintage Gucci sneaker. Even finding an original had not been easy. Sneaker aficionados hunt for them all over Europe and on eBay, and those who owned them back in the day, the illustrious and notorious ballers and dealers, usually had their Guccis stashed away, kept under lock and key. And when we all saw the prototype of the S. Carter, with just enough changed to make it new and authentic for RBK, it took our breath away.

We pulled out the stops, taking radical disruption marketing to places it had never been before. Nobody could even fathom that a sneaker could be marketed like a Hollywood blockbuster movie. On the global launch, we wrapped a private jet in S. Carter logos, took off from New York, and in the middle of the night landed at London's private airport near Heathrow, where hundreds of screaming fans and press stayed behind the velvet rope upon our arrival on the tarmac while throngs of reporters

Whenever I am asked about what brands now fighting for survival in tough economic times really need to do, I point them toward all the choices that Paul Fireman made in building a company from the ground up and then re-empowering it even in the face of slim odds. If there is one particular rule that made the difference, it is the reality that doing business by the numbers, with focus *only* on the bottom line, is an economic death trap. During our work together, I distinctly recall that Jay Margolis, then president of Reebok, who had come aboard for that position after successes elsewhere, was resistant to many of the strategies that connected the company's fortunes to culture. Paul chose not to bank on what others insisted the trends were going to be, but instead focused on making sure that the sneakers held up a mirror to the lives of the consumers who gave Reebok life from the start.

I loved every second of it. My favorite moment would have to be the night of April 18, 2003, when one thousand or more people lined up behind a velvet rope stretching down several blocks from the entrance of the Foot Locker shoe store on 125th Street in Harlem. Police guarded the main doors, which had not yet opened, and upon becoming concerned that the crowd was growing more and more worked up by the minute, they decided to shut down the busy street to keep it clear of traffic. Inside the Foot Locker store, I was watching all this unfold as a local radio station broadcast live and reporters from local and national media outlets buzzed around waiting for Jay-Z to appear and for the unveiling of the S. Carter by RBK.

For a minute, it all seemed surreal. Who would have ever thought that a sneaker could galvanize so much attention? Then out of the recesses of memory, I heard an echo of some lines of poetry from "My Adidas" by Run-DMC and all I could do was smile.

and photographers formed a press line to greet J
descended the steps of the plane, walked briskly to t
in his S. Carters, spoke into the mic to greet the fan:
questions from reporters about the new sneakers an
else was on his mind. Then he waved good-bye to
turned around, headed back up the steps and into t
jet, and we flew right on into the night to Italy—where e
crowds awaited.

As Paul Fireman later recalled, Jay-Z's instinct not
pose the line but to keep the quantity down and elevat
was so smart. The S. Carter thus became the fast
shoe in Reebok's history. When we shot the commer
appeared in it with 50 Cent, setting the stage for the
and teasing it with the G-Unit, 50's sneaker, which ha
been released. And when the G-Unit did hit, forget it
every sales record in the book. We were ready to f
again with rising star rapper/singer/producer/designer
Williams and his Ice Cream sneakers. Both the S. Carter
G-Units outsold any of Reebok's athlete-endorsed snea
of that period.

In August 2005 the announcement that Reebok h
acquired by Adidas-Salomon for over $3 billion was a st
ending for the brand revival we had undertaken not t
years earlier. When Paul Fireman had returned to picl
reins again at Reebok and we started working on it, stocl
had been trading at the sub-basement price of $6. At the
the sale they were paid $59 per share. From as low as 6
of market share, Reebok had rebounded during Paul's ov
to as high as 17 and even 18 percent. Most analysts pr
that the Reebok and Adidas merger would be mutually a
geous, pointing, in fact, to the opportunities opened up t
outreach to younger consumers through music. Intere
enough, Nike was following suit with their own embrace
sounds and rhythms of urban culture gone global. Wit
holding steady at about 36 percent of U.S. market share
combined Adidas-Reebok still around 20 percent, analysts
that the rising brand to watch was—guess who?—Puma, c
on strong. So much for the Sneaker Wars.

CHAPTER 7

FUTURE SHOCK REMIX

Pop culture, like nature, abhors a vacuum. This is to say that only by responding to the events and movements happening in the times that the culture serves can there be truth and relevance—which are necessary in order for the culture to go on. Hip-hop, as both the driver of tanning and the beneficiary of it, had proven early on that it could take advantage of opportunities and be resilient in the face of challenge. And that was long before it was recognized for its profitability. Now, in the 2000s, with dramatic change happening almost on every level, each of those capacities became more evident and more needed than ever.

Those had been my thoughts in the fall of 2001 when I still had a foot in the music business but the other already in marketing. One of the trends in the record industry that wasn't hard to notice in those days was the fervor for Latino artists who were dominating pop as well as the Latin music charts. In 1999, Puerto Rican–born Ricky Martin, already well established with record releases in Spanish, debuted his English-language album and broke it out of the box with the single "Livin' la Vida

Loca," which became a global number one, followed the next year with "She Bangs"—another international smash. Between Ricky Martin, Marc Anthony, Jennifer Lopez, and Enrique Iglesias, the influence of Hispanic artists was such a significant phenomenon that it drew attention to what was the actual changing complexion of America.

The 2000 census reported that in the largest one hundred cities in the United States, (non-Hispanic) whites—for the first time ever documented—had become the minority population. Within forty years, the Census Bureau went on to predict, more than half the population in the country would be comprised of the three most populous ethnic minority groups—Hispanics, African-Americans, and Asian-Americans. Between 1990 and 2000, the Hispanic population in the U.S. grew by 58 percent. That was thirty-five million Latinos in this country—what market research companies estimated to be over $45 billion in buying power growing at twice the rate of general consumer groups. In 2000, seven million Americans categorized themselves as "multiracial," a literal translation of tanning, and this was so notable that within two years, a few trade groups would begin to study the market forces in a polyethnic way. Multicultural buying power in 2002 would be estimated to be worth $580 billion. And one of the most telling statistics for future trends was the fact that the fasting-growing group, the Hispanic-American population, was younger—more than a third under the age of eighteen—as opposed to the majority of the U.S. population, which was aging.

This isn't to say that Latin music in the United Sates was news to the record business. In the 1970s, *Billboard* magazine started tracking sales of Spanish-language Latin artists domestically and abroad. In 1994, *Billboard* starting charting Latin pop to account for the growing potency of English-language music by Hispanic artists. By 2001, with "Livin' la Vida Loca" charting a full-blown crossover to mainstream pop, the hinges of the doors had been knocked off. None of it was a fluke or a passing fancy. The music was hot. Young people who loved hip-hop, pop, R&B, country, you name it, embraced Latin pop en masse. They loved what and who it represented and they loved the beat for the feeling, flavor, and fun of it.

As it so happened, Ricky Martin and Shakira were signed to Sony, my former employer, now my competitor. Then they signed Jennifer Lopez and Marc Anthony, after they had been free agents and everyone had hoped to sign them. Sony did well. The other big free agent on the market was Enrique Iglesias. Born in Spain but raised mostly in the United States, he had pursued a career very much on his own—keeping it a secret for as long as he could from his father, Julio—to avoid both riding on the coattails of his dad and being tied to him musically. After working with an independent label that produced his Spanish-language albums—earning him a meaningful international following—Enrique was ready to make his break into English-language and pop radio.

In 1999, right at this same time, we at Interscope were releasing the soundtrack for Will Smith's next movie, *Wild Wild West.* The music was mostly by hip-hop artists, but we were able to include a single on it by Enrique. Entitled "Bailamos," the song flew up to number one on the *Billboard* Hot 100, a full-fledged pop smash. This paved the way for us to sign Iglesias to a multi-album deal at Interscope and to go right into production for his first album for Interscope, *Enrique,* which landed another number one pop hit in "Be with You."

In 2001, the follow-up album, *Escape,* would be his most popular to date. It included the single "Hero," a beautiful song that happened to come out right at the same time as a Marc Anthony album, *Libre,* and its single release called "Tragedy." There was definitely a competition for which Latin artist's record of the moment would claim the greatest commercial success. Kind of dumb really, but that is the nature of an emerging art form that has to battle for legitimacy, I suppose. In any case, the contest was fierce. Marc Anthony, known as "the Voice" for being an unsurpassed male vocalist in the genre, was riding high. But then again, Enrique Iglesias, with his passion and multiple gifts as an artist, could connect to his audience with an electric current of emotion.

Then in the midst of all of us wondering whether "Hero" or "Tragedy" was going to steal the most thunder, it was September 11 and the competition was instantly forgotten. None of it mattered in the days and weeks and months that followed. Of course, "Tragedy" seemed fitting, even though it was a song about a love affair that might not have been what people needed to hear. "Hero" was also fitting and Enrique did sing it during the telethon fund-raiser that was broadcast on September 21, *America: A Tribute to Heroes*. Still, in that time when America really did try to come together as one nation, one complexion, to find our way through the darkness, charting record sales was the last thing on everyone's mind.

Once I got back to work, I was immersed in an ad campaign for Chrysler's new Jeep Liberty. They had named it that and had shot the commercial before 9/11 and, in what had come out of someone's imagination, included rousing images of the Jeep climbing up the side of the Statue of Liberty. Not sure at all about how the public was going to take this, I was very wary of a spot that featured the Statue of Liberty at a time when smoke was still coming up from Ground Zero.

And right as I was thinking about recommending that Chrysler scrap it, I had a stroke of inspiration. Two marketing challenges when taken separately were problems. But if you put them together—the Jeep Liberty commercial and the song "Hero"— the combination could be something redemptive for everyone in the very traumatic period we were going through. I went back to Interscope and worked with the head of new media, Courtney Holt, on setting the song to the commercial. When I took our rough version and presented it to everyone at GM, they loved it and went crazy, hoping that this could really solve their strategic problem.

There was a hitch. Since the publishing rates for the use of songs in commercials are typically very steep, we knew that Jeep would balk at going for a record already in release by a global superstar. But then it occurred to me there was a way around that issue. We approached Marty Bandier, EMI Music Publishing chairman, and said, "Marty, we're here to ask for six months." After a pause during which he said nothing, we proposed that if he would waive the publishing for six months, then Chrysler would be spending its assets—ten million—in media. And how was this good for the publisher? The argument from us was, "If you believe that ten million of media works, you know that we're gonna sell more albums and you're gonna make all that money in addition to making back the money you waived in giving the six months of the publishing."

The logic is clear today. But it made zero sense when we suggested it. The answer was initially, "Say what? Invest the publishing rights?" Nonetheless, I knew that it would tap a nerve, benefit the client, and sell albums like crazy. Sure enough, we put the commercial and the song together and debuted it during *Monday Night Football*. And that's how we began the launch of the campaign and how "Hero" cemented Enrique's place in the heart of America. As the result of the platform of *Monday Night Football*, radio stations put the record into heavy rotation. In turn, as it was played, the Jeep was successfully launched into the new millennium.

Many of these changes had been predicted in a groundbreaking book entitled *Future Shock,* written by Alvin Toffler in 1970. Toffler had predicted a state of future shock for generations that had already come of age and were not ready to deal with the rapid pace of changes in technology, globalization, and culture—changes that he believed future generations would be better equipped to handle. In an era that predated Microsoft and Apple, "TMI" was not yet in the vernacular—although Toffler saw the perils of "too much information" that would accompany those technologies and the challenges of coping with the resulting media onslaught. For those industries unable to remain "fluid," as he put it, the future didn't bode well. For those producers/ purveyors that could find a more direct way to link to their consumers, however, the shock of the future would be absorbed.

In the last of my days in the music business, some inklings of this paradigm shift were becoming clear to me. In fact, I had floated many of the elements that became known as "360 deals"— whereby a record company, for example, would invest in artists and become their partners in all avenues of entertainment, brand endorsement, merchandising, live performance, and so on, and participate in the revenues. Having everything under one roof, in the service of that artist, just made sense for all involved. But in 2001 when I was pitching the idea, pretty much everyone laughed.

Guess what? It took the demise, more or less, of the industry for everyone to realize that partnering in this way, working with advertising companies, was the future that had arrived. Record companies' marketing launches now needed to be subsidized and brands wanted in on that cool.

Again, there were old attitudes coming out of yesteryear, when the idea of artists and record companies aligning with marketing products was selling out to commercialism. Not to me, needless to say. The key, once more, was authenticity. How was it selling out if the product or project was authentic to an artist and to the audience aligned with the music already? If the uniform of country music stars was a pair of Levi's jeans, it was only natural that those artists should enjoy the rewards of keeping that brand, and whatever products they were already repping for free, current. The prime example is Bob Seger's "Like a Rock," which became synonymous with American rugged individualism by providing the slogan for Chevy trucks and led to more than a decade as the brand's advertising theme song.

Though my argument for forging partnerships between artists, record labels, and brands fell mostly on deaf ears in the early '00s, a decade later, it's a practice that's helping to resurrect the record business.

Be that as it may, at around this same period, on their own the properties of tanning were providing the more resilient brands with new means of connecting to consumers successfully— leading to a kind of future shock remix. So part of my job description as I got into the marketing world was to better understand and be able to translate these new tools, as well as the nuanced code our multilingual target consumers were speaking.

Meet the Millennials

In mid-'03, when I went to register and trademark the firm name, Translation, for my new marketing and consulting agency, I was very happy and frankly shocked that it was available. Now that I was opening up my own shop, I had decided to gain experience on the other side of the marketing fence by investing in a relatively new brand, Carol's Daughter, a line of hair and body products created by Brooklyn-bred entrepreneur Lisa Price.

Besides the beautiful, earthy, incredibly fragrant appeal of the products—luxurious body butters and rich hair pomades—I related to the brand values and to the story of natural beauty secrets that had been handed down through three generations of women and made with love and ingredients from nature. There was also something very cool about how Lisa had built her business through hand-selling that kept her in touch with her multicultural consumers, mostly women, who connected emotionally to her products.

In '04, when the doors to my marketing company, Translation, first opened, I brought those insights to the table when the team and I began major strategy sessions for a growing array of accounts. We quickly realized that if we were asking brand managers and corporate executives to drop their old categories for boxing consumers into demographics, we had to find ways to talk about the psychographics that were meaningful to their efforts. Instead of approaching this task in a more traditional way—that is, through data about where consumers live, what they earn, how they spend, if they belong to religious institutions, how or if they vote, what their educational levels are (all valid)—we wanted to explain our consumer target, also known as the millennials, in terms of their shared values and experiences. Broadly, millennials are seen as the generation born in the 1980s and 1990s.

While it is hard to pinpoint age, we were able to begin with a list of key virtues: a) Our consumer target is a mind-set, b) our consumer is urban, c) our consumer is savvy, and d) our consumer is in control. Elaborating on each of these virtues, we then went on to explain them in the context of the changes happening in the real world at the time—posing questions to get into the heart of our approach.

1. *What distinguishes the mind-set of the target consumer?* The mind-set of millennials is adaptive. Today as boundaries dissolve and information moves without restriction, demography tells us less about the "who" we want to engage. Within our general market consumer universe there exists this psychographic dimension that adapts and responds as a creative

collective—igniting pop culture trends, as well as propagating them into mainstream culture. The polyethnic consumers of this mind-set are inclined to make brands their own and within their diverse social networks leverage brands as creative new material in composing self-image and style.

2. *Where does our urban consumer live?* "Urban" evokes the images of New York City, Atlanta, Chicago, Houston, Seattle, San Francisco, Los Angeles, all cities or places where people live in close proximity to one another. In the '00s, "urban" is no longer confined to a literal definition or location. Urban consumers are movers who span urban/suburban/global. Urban consumers are confident and proud of their backgrounds and distinct cultural histories but would not be considered ethnocentric. Urban consumers are truly cross-cultural. They are exposed to, they understand, and they embody this mixing innately. The urban audience, millennially speaking, cannot be entreated in a superficial manner with style cues or compelled by inauthentic, prepackaged, or homogenized messaging. "What to have" and other status definers are all intertwined within the media they consume. The urban consumer is, in essence, the most exacting, precise consumer on the planet—influential not just individually or as a segment but as a megamovement. Their time is now.

3. *What kind of needs and wants define the savvy consumer?* With the ongoing debate as to who exactly comprises the hip-hop generation—whether it's late boomer adults who connected to the music and culture in the seventies and eighties or Gen X and Gen Y youth and adults who came of age in the late eighties and nineties, or the Now and Next teens coming of age—these savvy consumer millennials are marketing veterans. They have been marketed to—directly and indirectly—since birth and through their parents, giving rise to an extraordinarily aware and often cynical audience. Belief, therefore, is granted only by expe-

rience. They want attention and need a certain level of scarcity. Authenticity and aspiration remain critical for the savvy consumer, in both the need and want categories. They are fickle and can spot brands that feign understanding; they spot and shun brands that pretend to know them. The savvy millennial consumer wants to align with brands as badges of identity—as indicators of status. The need is for a much more meaningful relationship than simple utility. The savvy consumer wants to believe in brand properties that confer both instant and perpetual cool.

4. *What characteristics describe our consumer in control?* Above all, the consumer in control seeks out, takes pride in, and celebrates the unique expressions that define one's self. Consumers in control drive tastemaking forces behind consumption in a range of areas including fashion, technology, media, and entertainment. They are highly connected, infinitely mobile, literate, and empowered by technology. In the '00s, especially, the consumer in control goes beyond the mere functional use of technology to a self-motivated adoption, utilization, and creative expression.

What else? You'll have noticed by now that in describing the consumer target as a mind-set, as urban in their point of view, as savvy and in control, we haven't pinpointed age. Truthfully, the more we honor the psychographics, the less we can assert that there is an age range. Because we know that youth is a state of mind, not an age, we have identified a youth mind-set that complements the tan mental complexion—both of which are aspects of youth culture. While we already knew that those with a youth mind-set have a more profound relationship to technology than other consumers, we wanted to provide an overview of passion points for youth culture that were going to be valuable in our strategies. By no means comprehensive, the list includes: music, sports, entertainment, gaming, fashion/beauty, style/design, creativity and self-expression, social connections (real and virtual), the Internet, and, again, technology.

There was something else that we made sure to recognize going in and that is the fact that the remix of culture—which is exactly what hip-hop did from the start and continues to do— is the happy domain of the millennials. They know the history of what's been perpetually cool and they know absolutely what is over. This may explain why Betty White, Tony Bennett, and Jack Nicholson, each seen as having perpetual cool, have a youth following. Millennials like to identify cool and school other consumers. The millennials, raised on hip-hop as a fact of life, believe fundamentally in the power of authenticity. They keep demonstrating that the cool of technology isn't about the technology. It's about what we get to experience as a result of the technology.

Geeks, Gadgets, and Gangstas

To say that Silicon Valley produced more technology that changed America and the rest of the world than anywhere else is really just stating the obvious. But what we don't point out often enough is that it was those very brainy Silicon Valley guys like Bill Gates and Steve Jobs who made it cool to be a geek. And they started a movement of fellow cool geeks too—founders of search engines with funky names, social networking sites, and little garage tech start-ups that went on to sell for billions. Does it make them cool 'cause they got rich? Yes, being resourceful with whatever you've got definitely makes you cool. As far as I'm concerned, the boldness to be real and be different and even proclaim your geekdom is crazy cool. The first time I heard that the tech support team for Best Buy had started as a company that branded themselves the "Geek Squad"—those guys and gals that you invite into your home to solve technology problems—I wished that I'd thought of it!

Not surprisingly, brands that make and market technology live or die depending on their fluency with youth culture and on their proximity to cool. Let me provide some famous examples that may or may not be familiar. It's hard to remember that there was a point in time, not too long ago, when there was actually a wide-open race for what company would deliver the successor to the Sony Walkman when portable audio devices began their transition to digital. Why Sony didn't ultimately figure that out and failed at beating everyone else to the punch was not a competency problem. This was, after all, a corporation that owned music and film companies and technology companies—all the ingredients to make such a device.

Unfortunately, they were caught in the haywire of future shock remix and had a fluency breakdown. First of all, because of compartmentalization, executives in different divisions didn't talk to one another about integration of all these assets. Second, when they did research and development, they forgot about delivering to consumer needs—listening to younger-generation consumers before deciding what to build. Instead, they went forward and designed technology that was developed without regard for what the consumer wanted. Right here at the paradigm shift when marketing needed to depart from the approach of shoving products in front of consumers' faces, Sony missed the step.

The technology for Sony's Walkman MP3 player was actually excellent, even though the branding was confusing and emotionless—using model numbers, for example, instead of names to build on their former successes. Over at Apple, in contrast, when Macs were first vying for attention and being made in bright colors, the brand referred to the red computer by its color, "Ruby." What was more inviting—a Mac that went by the appealing name of a color like Ruby or Sage or Snow or a computer by whatever brand made it with a model number of X1256 that you had to remember, as a consumer, in order to get the one that was right for you? The disconnect that many technology brands had from the marketing aspects of delivering consumer needs was flagrant.

Reading some of these signs—around the same time that Apple was tinkering with its portable audio device and the online music delivery system it would develop, as Napster and its ilk ran roughshod—Sony developed a concept that would be an online platform for selling music called Sony Connect. I envisioned this would be the ultimate digital store as Sony already owned all the content—music/film/gaming/technology—and I had lined up a dream-come-true partner: McDonald's. Despite the initial enthusiasm from pretty much all the top Sony executives, at the last minute the divisions couldn't come together to embrace a new paradigm and take advantage of their own resources. This was terrain that Sony ought to have conquered that was rightfully theirs, but they were not even on the field. It dawned on me then that the main reason many larger corporations miss the boat when it's time to innovate is that executives are too busy protecting their jobs and not listening to the consumer. At that point, I understood the rule that says you can get anything done in most organizations as long as you're willing not to take credit for it.

I was disappointed that the company couldn't get their older, more vertical ways of doing business to be in sync with the new mode of horizontal alignment. Besides fear of taking a risk, executives who had been doing just fine up until that time were complacent. And complacency, time and again, is what ultimately leaves the consumer out of the conversation.

This was a cautionary tale that was being witnessed at a lot of companies in the '00s. Another portable audio device, the Dell DJ, the brand's cool-as-hell MP3 player, suffered from complacency when the company decided it would provide only a minimal budget for its launch. Their thinking was that if they put most of those resources into initiating a viral strategy to generate "cool" word of mouth, consumers would know a great thing when they learned of it. That was the problem. The whole power of viral is that it is spontaneous, authentic, and consumer driven. Dell's intended contact with the target consumer didn't happen. Then, after four weeks, all marketing support (traditional and online) for the Dell DJ stopped. Within days, blogs and community sites were up in arms over the contrived viral effort. Sales never took off and eventually the Dell DJ was discontinued, furthering overall negative brand repercussions. It was and remains a classic example of how cool cannot be concocted without dialogue that becomes megalogue, nor achieved by using strategies that don't involve a deep understanding of target consumers. The episode was also a reminder that without the ongoing consistent support of the brand at large, a new offering can't live long on a wing and a prayer.

Of course, Dell wasn't alone in being caught in the tangled web of future shock remix—in which reading trends without the correct cipher could sometimes be fatal. And they weren't the first or last brand to nail the technology but blow the marketing.

So who got it right? Who really understood where the music business was headed and what the delivery system of the near future turning rapidly into the now was going to look like? Well, it wasn't a brand with any experience, per se, in music. Why then did it turn out to be Apple, of all brands, that came seemingly out of nowhere and gave birth to a personal portable audio device that could well be declared the eighth wonder of the world? Unlikely though it appeared at the time, Apple was just doing what it always had done—finding a way to change the conversation.

The first tech company that had ever ventured into the realm of culture, the Apple team had long been paying attention to consumer cues. When they launched colored iMac desktops and named them with rich-sounding colors, they also showed the understanding that a home computer was décor—as much as they later understood that a laptop's color and design were aspects of personal fashion. Instead of talking about technology, Apple learned early in its history to shift the conversation and have it be about lifestyle, fun, individual expression, and ease of use. Those seductive elements that were woven into every aspect of design and marketing made for a very intimate relationship between consumers and the brand's products. To outsiders, loyal Apple customers appeared to border on being religious fanatics.

While this is what we know today, there is another story many have forgotten, about the October 2001 iPod launch that was, as they say, more fizzle than sizzle. No, the mixed reactions had nothing to do with the product. God no. Weighing in at a featherlight 6.5 ounces, the size of a deck of cards, its smooth eggshell-white plastic exterior looked futuristic. Besides the fact that it could store a thousand songs and fit in your pocket, plain and simple, it was sexy. The iPod responded to the touch—even the most subtle or suggestive. Seriously, the geeks in tech and design were hitting the bull's-eye of cool so far. And the other genius piece of the puzzle was that in a mere ten seconds, the contents of an entire CD could be downloaded. Paying attention to culture, the conversation wasn't about the mechanics of doing this but about how personal music collections could be portable, malleable, and preserved. Steve Jobs declared with certainty, "With the iPod, listening to music will never be the same again."

Glorious though it was, after nine months, Apple had sold only 150,000 iPods. How could that be? Though it's debatable, I don't think the issue holding the iPod back from its grand destiny was really its higher price. Asking $399 for a superior product was smart—even if other brands were selling for less. There were two stumbling blocks that prevented the launch from making history. First, there were compatibility concerns—or, at least, there was the perception by consumers who were PC-born-and-bred that they would have to convert to another operating system. Almost like changing their religion. As the visionary that he is, Steve Jobs took a peek into the future and came up with a way to solve the problem with the announcement that "hell froze over." By that he was referring to a former statement that not unless hell froze over would Apple's software be compatible with that of Microsoft's. So now that they had already released the iPod and were about to change their creed, the only way they could credibly assure the market that it could work on PCs was to blur the line in the sand and tell the public that hell freezing over wasn't going to be the end of the world. The message just took time to get out there.

The second, bigger problem was that there was no music industry infrastructure to market and promote the devices. That's why market analysts were so sure that Sony, with its music division, would eventually win this contest.

But as Alvin Toffler had warned in *Future Shock* about the lack of fluidity that would impair larger organizations, the rigidity of the corporate compartments at Sony got in the way. Aside from not maximizing the possibilities of Sony Connect, the marketing people never saw a way to take advantage of the richness of their music library or their stable of recording and movie superstars or their vast network of retail partners selling all their other world-class electronic products. The marketing divisions were not culturally attuned enough to see the big picture. Apple, meanwhile, was culturally attuned enough to realize that though they didn't have any of those assets, they had something in the shop that nobody else had.

It was called iTunes, an online music store with the potential to ultimately compete not only with Napster and the other music-downloading sites but also with actual music retail stores. In 1999, when it was in development, Steve Jobs had contacted Jimmy Iovine at Interscope/Geffen/A&M to tell him where they were with it and to get input, possibly to talk about collaboration. In those days—as we covered earlier—album sales, thanks to hip-hop and country music, were at their high-water mark. So the idea that there would come a time when record stores would be close to obsolete wasn't so pressing. The concept of iTunes as a way to charge for downloaded content and be able to pay record companies and artists was also a promising way to combat the scourge of illegal downloading. Still, for a record company to collaborate on such an endeavor—at that time— would have been a slippery slope.

But in 2003 that slope was starting to look a lot more appealing. The record business was in a dire slump, with one of the main culprits being the proliferation of Napster-type sites that allowed users to illegally share digital copies of recorded music. On top of that, those in-control, discerning, highly mobile urban youth consumers were buying fewer CDs in general—with popular trends rising and falling too fast for purchase consideration to get them into record stores. As we would point out at Translation, the influence of the savvy consumer was ratcheting up, not down, with increased exposure to media, brands, and diverse consumption choices—creating new, sophisticated sensitivities for timeliness and relevance.

Future shock remix had altered the shelf life of cultural

viability. As fast as a trendy phenomenon or a new artist, for example, could heat up, they could be gone. And what used to be durable was fleeting. Previously, it was known in the music business that if an artist was waning in popularity in the United States, he or she could still tour and sell CDs like hotcakes in Europe, the Far East, South America, you name it—because information about the artist's supposed lack of coolness hadn't hit yet and there was no way to fact-check the situation. Not anymore. The new consumers have so much connectivity that there was suddenly no delay in the export of culture. Same thing with consumers buying products. The new savvy consumer knew when a brand wasn't working or wasn't cool anymore because of instant access to cultural barometers from multiple media streams. Everything was becoming instantaneous—for better and for worse.

Leading up to this point, Jimmy Iovine had been looking to find a technology company to help stop the scourge of illegal music downloading that was killing the business. When he was explaining the dire straits to the chairman of Intel and underscoring what a spiritual wasteland the world would be without music and art, Jimmy was told, in essence, well, not all industries are meant to be forever. It was then that he began to discuss with Steve Jobs what a partnership between Interscope and Apple's iTunes would look like.

Even as the iPod was getting a slow start, Apple had adapted and had found a way—with this online music store—to change the conversation, again, away from technology toward a welcoming shopping experience. It was accessible even for consumers formerly intimidated or alienated by the impersonal aspects of making purchases without another human being there. The hardware and the software, or in this case the iPod and the iTunes content supply, were interconnected, each enhancing the other. The thrust had originally been that if consumers loved the iPod, since iTunes was designed to speak the same language and made downloading so easy, the online music store would be a hit too. Now the possibility existed that if consumers loved iTunes, they would naturally want to play their music on an iPod. Two paths to glory!

The partnership with Interscope supplied the marketing piece of the puzzle. In return for Apple underwriting video production for new releases, Interscope would provide product placement for Apple—boosting the business of both brands and eliminating costs to both corporations. A win-win. Plus, at that moment when the music industry was clinging to a cliff, Apple was offering everyone the means to fight digital piracy without spending resources on endless lawsuits.

In a variation on the wise practice of knowing what you don't know, Apple welcomed Jimmy Iovine's insight when he told them that the brand image they were using for iTunes, a picture of a guitar on a whiteboard, was wrong. He explained that the cultural drivers, the current generation, barely knew how iconic that guitar was. They had no connection to a guitar the way kids who grew up on the Beatles and the Rolling Stones did. The consumers who were going to connect to iTunes were all about the sound and the beats and the feeling of the music itself. From then on, the marketing for the iPod was developed to include the iconic silhouettes of individuals in cool active postures while listening to music on their iPods, with distinguishable earbud headphones connecting them to their devices. While there was no self-conscious effort to make the silhouettes appear to be specifically black, white, Hispanic, Asian, or any distinct ethnicity, the use of an understanding of tanning was striking—with silhouettes, male and female, sporting an assortment of hairstyles and urban, cool attire.

That was no accident. Using a diverse group of real people in silhouette was matched by using real music from a diverse group of artists—U2, Black Eyed Peas, Eminem, Mary J. Blige (all not coincidentally Jimmy Iovine's artists), all with different audiences yet each authentic and iconic. Artists' personal playlists were a very important part of the marketing plan, a very measured tactic to let consumers know what their favorite artist happened to have on his or her iPod. The universal connection to different kinds of music that wouldn't necessarily be predicted reconfirmed all the crossover that had happened as the result of tanning. I remember seeing Eminem's personal playlist the first time and being shocked that he had Jodeci on there. R&B and soul? Why not? Providing a sneak peek into what artists were downloading was yet another brilliant way that Steve Jobs saw fit to make the consumption at an online music store contagious.

The radical disruption came next. If it could be used the same way it had been employed in the marketing of "Nuthin' but a 'G' Thang," then all bets were on the iPod and iTunes becoming the new frontier. How were they going to pull it off? With a music video, of course. As it so happened, when the partnership between Apple and Interscope was coming together, the number one song and video was 50 Cent's "In Da Club." 50's album *Get Rich or Die Tryin',* on Interscope, was also at number one and he was getting ready to film the video for the next single, "P.I.M.P."

The video release was perfectly timed for a marketing bonanza for the iTunes store. And there was no subtlety in how Apple's coolest new gadget was featured at the opening of the star-studded, hilarious, sexy video—complete with 50 Cent in a swank bedroom, dressed in all-white, surrounded by beautiful women in white lace panties and bras, as the camera zooms in on his hands and he fingers the dial of his white iPod, clicking on a selection that reads "Playlist."

The single, album, and video downloads, exclusive on iTunes, blew the roof off. 50's G-Unit by RBK also received product placement and swiftly became the fastest-selling sneaker in the country. With a scene in the video that included a mafioso-style meeting—with Snoop Dogg at the head of the table—there was no violence, no guns, just P.I.M.P.in'. The video even featured a real pimp, Magic Don Juan out of Chicago, complete with headphones. Talk about art imitating life! It was gangsta remix, fun, outrageous, still in the hip-hop authentic lane where the gritty realities of the street meet the fantasy of limitless luxury. Not very many could afford the fantasy life, but they could afford the iPod. And some artists who could afford this life but had never really fixed the iPod on their radar all of a sudden were calling up Interscope and asking to get their hands on the devices. Once the iPod was in the hands of famous tastemakers, consumers gravitated en masse to Apple's offerings.

Within two years, Apple had sold over twenty-eight million

iPods and the company controlled 75 percent of the digital music player market, with its overall earnings having quadrupled as a result of this chapter of the company's growth. On a wide screen the story was, as we at Translation later liked to say, "It's not the iPod, it's the iProcess." That is to say that products are not what sells; an understanding of culture is what sells.

On another level, a case could be made that iTunes was the music version of what would happen if you legalized a street trade. After all, an illegal online business had gone legit, and Apple had figured out the mechanism for doing that and making sure everyone in the supply chain got a piece of the action.

There were and are still more challenges to confront with future shock remix. The music business had to adjust to the fact that consumers were now going to be buying a lot more singles than albums—which continues to test the resilience of the recording industry. Gone were the days of consumers paying $11.99 for a CD that probably only contained one song, which had been promoted to them and they liked. Oh, and then there was another form of online piracy and hijacking that had gone under the radar for years.

With music companies spending the money to make and promote videos online, the premise was that viewers would get excited and want to go download the music. What happened instead was that Web providers like Yahoo!, Microsoft, and YouTube were showing the promotional videos on their sites and then selling advertising based on all the traffic the music was attracting—not paying the record companies or the artists a penny from all the ad revenue!

One Saturday when Doug Morris, head of Universal Music Group, was at home, he went online to check out 50 Cent's "In Da Club" and noticed that before the video came on there was a Toyota commercial leading into it. Knowing something didn't feel right, he first checked with his chief operations officer to ask, "Did we get paid for this?"

Well, no, he learned, the video was promotional. This shouldn't have been surprising. After all, for almost twenty years the purpose of getting music videos played on TV was to promote sales of the music itself, not to generate revenue. Doug understood the importance of promotion, of course. His concern was, then, if the advertisers were paying the Internet companies for showing the videos, shouldn't the content creators participate in the revenues? This notion eventually led to Vevo, a video music hub that partners with Sony, UMG, EMI, and Google, and is at the time of this writing the number one streamed music video site in the world. Before any of that happened, the immediate consequence of Doug Morris's discovery was that every music video belonging to Universal's acts was pulled off Web sites until deals paying everyone on the record could be worked out. Initially, none of the Web providers wanted to pay for what they were used to getting for free. But after a short time, as they watched their sites lose traction quickly—with hits diminishing now that consumers weren't visiting to see the videos—deals were eventually reached. With other music companies following suit, rules and regulations were implemented that made the brave new world of the Internet a place where content could be protected to a greater extent and where revenue could be shared with the artists responsible for the video content. In the end, content is where the cool lies. The recording industry, thanks to that reality, lived to fight on another day—by being willing to change.

Thanks to the Interscope connection and Jimmy Iovine's perceptions and help, Apple successfully set a new standard in technology—by removing it from the equation so that the iPod found abundant life and that the prophecy of Steve Jobs that music "would never be the same again" came true.

Trends Are Perishable, Cool Is Forever

When Translation first opened, my initial partners, Charles Wright and John McBride, two of the most brilliant guys I've ever met, instigated a discussion between the three of us about the relevance of new technologies to urban youth culture. While this might seem like a statement of the obvious, we wanted to go deeper and to understand how technology was behaving in culture in a way that music had for years—especially in terms of bringing like-minded kids from different backgrounds together.

The three of us hadn't arrived at this discussion from the same route either. Charles Wright, African-American, had started with me at Interscope as a product manager. Originally from North Carolina, Charles had left home to seek his fortune and ended up in New York City, bringing with him great fashion sensibilities and an exacting feel for taste and style. Always impeccably put together, Charles thinks very much in the same way—developing concepts that are very, very neat and make total sense for everyone on board, yet touch on aesthetics that are irresistibly hip. John McBride, a white Midwesterner, traveled around the U.S. in his younger days, surfing and paying attention to cultural differences, and then got his professional education as a design engineer at Kodak. From design, he made the leap to strategy at Translation, bringing with him a razor-sharp understanding of marketing causes and effects, as well as his ability to look at aspects of packaging and product development in solving brand problems.

Like me, both Charles and John share an anthropological view of pop culture and they value a historical context for looking at trends. When we were starting out, I was the quarterback and they were my two touchdown-making wide receivers. The team spirit really was fired by a mutually held cultural curiosity.

So as we talked about the tanning force of technology—in so many words—we began to look at the generations and shared sensibilities reflected in the popularity of games, gadgets, online connections, social networking sites, etc. We thought it was interesting that though the entry points were different, there was a global affinity to the experience and the associations with having fun, hanging out, and spending a good percentage of leisure time connected to some form of technology and on a regular basis. My frame of reference takes me back to neighborhood bodegas where you could play for hours, going back and forth between the three or four video games installed in the back.

Charles and John noted they and others were first exposed to the same electronic entertainment in other kinds of venues not in urban America but dotted everywhere across the American landscape—in kid-friendly arcades, bars and taverns, honky-tonks, pool halls, and college pubs. There was no game that was marketed to one demographic over the other. Everybody loved Ms. Pac-Man, Donkey Kong, and Space Invaders and everyone wanted to go over to whoever's house had an Atari or ColecoVision game system. And from that point on, as the video game industry has exploded exponentially—expanding the consumer base from very little kids with handheld electronics to much older weekend warriors at home battling foes on their TV screens—the universal appeal has provided opportunities for further cultural exchanges. There has been as much exporting of culture as there has been importing of meaningful aspects of other cultures from around the globe. No racial barriers or demographic lines prevent any group of consumers around the world from loving Madden and Halo, as two favorite examples, any more or less than any other group. Just because the visual representations include, say, Japanese, Korean, or Russian lead players and accents, that doesn't make them any less heroic for the other nationalities playing the game. The playing field, virtual though it is, through electronic games made here and abroad, has only bolstered the growing polyethnic global population of youth culture. Gaming thus has become the same kind of unifying force as has music. Again, as Wright and McBride like to remind me, the main currency behind these forces of tanning is something primitive—the desire to have fun, to share in something cool.

At Translation, we came to the early conclusion that when we were being brought in to address issues for a long-established brand that was suffering in the marketplace, very often it was because they had landed on the wrong side of cool. And because they haven't adapted to the new rules of the new economy that require having the communication skills to speak with consumers of cool, brands who are faltering may not have any way of knowing where they fall on the bell curve of being cool, on the upslope, at the crest, or on the plunging far side, way past cool. As an example, we sometimes present brands with a diagram of that bell curve or hill to show where they fall in terms of pop culture relevance. If "not cool" precedes the slope and "cool" is at the crest of the hill and "over" is on the far side of it, they are asked to determine where they are and where they would like to be.

Many times when we meet brand managers who don't know what their marketing issues are, either they have no idea what their position is relative to cool or they'll admit they're pretty much in the "not cool" flats. A well-designed strategy can address the state of being "not cool" and is actually much easier to approach than being in the ugly state of "over."

In these days of future shock remix, the activation or reactivation of cool in a brand ultimately comes back to harnessing and leveraging the cultural influences and heat of the youth mind-set. To do that with companies that sell technology, as we've been talking about, requires not just a change in conversation but one that creates urgency. The emphasis isn't *If I don't take part in this brand's offering now, I won't be cool.* We prefer a conversation, as one suggestion, that leads to the discovery of a status definer, or something that acts as a badge. It doesn't just relate to price, although that's one aspect that can be cool. It may be a Swatch watch, as a classic example, that is a reflection of who you are. It says, *When I have X brand, people feel about me in Y way, and it shows my level of success.* Status definers can be badges that are descriptive of your personality, style, and what makes you stand out in a crowd. When the feeling connected to having the brand is meaningful to many, the coolness value fuels urgency and mass consumption.

A lack of urgency was one challenge that Hewlett-Packard had brought to us during a period of struggle for the brand. On the heels of the announcement from Apple that "hell froze over" a deal had been struck with HP to make good on the promise that the iPod would be compatible with the PC. In return for a minuscule piece of the profit, Hewlett-Packard was, in a sense, becoming the distributor and sales team of iPod for PC users—a great deal for Apple to get their technology into PC users' hands but of little lasting value to HP. There was nothing about the device that was unique to Hewlett-Packard, nothing that made them more than the reseller or would raise the level of cool about their brand by giving them proximity to a cool product. In fact, the device looked just like an iPod, and you had to read the small print or look at the logo on the back to even realize it was HP. So smart was Apple's deal that not only did HP distribute the iPod for Steve Jobs, but Hewlett-Packard was forbidden to make music for a certain period of time.

From a marketing standpoint, it was baffling that hell had frozen over and there was this revolutionary relationship between Apple and PC users with nothing to be gained for Hewlett-Packard. They couldn't even customize the color schemes because the deal required that it look exactly like the iPod at the time—all white.

As I pointed out to my team, "HP needs something proprietary around the iPod."

To that end, we came up with various ideas that were terrific but nothing really jumped. Then I had a breakthrough idea to do aftermarket customization and touch a pulse point of consumers—self-expression. We pitched the concept that if you wanted to print tattoo-style skins that would fit on your iPod, you could personalize them online with die-cut designs and then print them out with special paper that would transform your plain white iPod into something that was one of a kind and all the more cool. After I went to Interscope and asked if music icons would like to donate artwork, celebrities like Sting and Gwen Stefani contributed their personal designs that consumers could download and print out for their iPod skins— offering the choice of their own design or that of a famous artist. Besides the buzz this created, it went back to using and elevating one of HP's core competencies—which is printing. Hewlett-Packard now had something proprietary to promote around the iPod that in turn reminded consumers of the excellence of their other products related to printing—special papers and other printing materials, stickers, and photographic compatibility. We ran ads with directions in *Spin* and *Rolling Stone,* inserting the donated artwork with instructions as a free sample so that readers felt invited to this new way to wear your iPod by customizing the face. The immediate word of mouth was sensational. In coming up with a way for HP's deal with Apple to make any sense, we scored such a success that printable iPod skins became one of *Time* magazine's Top 10 Ideas of 2004.

The next challenge we took on for HP was to create opportunities for their proprietary technology and place it in culture. We noticed that while there were lots of brands that had cameras on the market, few had figured out how to engage with consumers with respect to the growing popularity of photography. This wasn't about fancy photographic equipment or printing technology but more about having a cool camera and sharing photos on social networking sites. The Flip camera, for instance, didn't make the best high-def video but it was fun and easy to use, and its videos could be posted quickly without a large learning curve.

With coolness and compatibility being of the moment, I proposed that HP release a limited-edition Gwen Stefani camera and got the thumbs-up. With her passion for Japanese design elements, it was called the Harajuku Lovers digital camera and it made taking photos as hot as the latest club dance.

In so many ways, Gwen Stefani was the visual profile of our consumer target—cross-cultural. A California suburban blonde with urban sensibilities, she could be hip-hop and rock, reminiscent of Blondie and Madonna but with her own twist. Likewise, the Harajuku Lovers camera was HP's offering to consumers to put their own twists on their images.

When we went to Las Vegas with Gwen for the annual consumer electronics show to unveil the camera—and the "Holaback Girl" video that was tied in to a commercial spot and happened to coincide with the release of Stefani's solo debut album—you would have thought that the merchandisers from around the world on hand to see it had died and gone to heaven. After the commercial aired, the limited run of Harajuku cameras we made, all five thousand of them, sold in a week. The cool was so potent that it packed an intergenerational wallop, making moms and female consumers not necessarily in the millennial age range part of the excitement.

In all of the HP marketing, what made the technology

appealing and what made it matter was that it was part of culture. With the iPod skins and the Harajuku camera we were starting our relationship with the brand by instigating *instant cool*. Such efforts are aimed at pushing a brand to the top of the cool hill, whereas the next phase of work aims at *perpetual cool,* and finally a third stage, to prolong activation forever and ever, is about *embodying cool.*

As we've seen at every stop of tanning, cool is not a given evolutionary principle but something that can happen instantly, with profound implications for brand success. And once you're there, you're there. That is, until they decide you are gone. Perpetual cool, therefore, requires long-term commitment—the kind that a brand such as Nike epitomizes. It's all about being vigilant in staving off the slide toward being "over," a constant fight against inertia. Perpetual cool demands focus, investment, and frequent refreshing via innovation. The strategy phase of embodying cool is about a full translation when a brand has successfully earned respect and loyalty from the consumer and has received permission to also be cool. It's all about understanding nuance. John McBride's position on embodying cool is for companies to "find the intersection where understanding those consumers can be translated to the hand of their brand, and then the brand can be taught to speak as if they're in the culture, and they can speak with a wink and a nod."

Brands sometimes want to skip steps in attaining levels of cool. What we hear most often from brands is that they want to be loved. The question comes up with every account—how can they become a loved brand? My first response to that is, well, maybe we should start with becoming a *liked* brand. Even before getting to the "like" stage, there is an approach we use that is akin to crawl/walk/run. The stages for consumer brand perception that span a relationship beginning as functional and evolving into emotional are Convenience, Consideration, Respect, Like, Love, in that particular order.

Convenience brands are those that offer rational product solutions and messaging without differentiation in a given category. Vizio, make of lower-cost home entertainment electronics, is an example of a convenience brand. Marketing of such brands is usually based on goals of short-term sales, rather than a long-term vision of brand building. Convenience brands do not innovate, nor do they contribute to wider culture or extend into people's lives. Customers for convenience brands won't intentionally "seek the brand out" or ask people within their community for advice about the brand. Convenience brands initiate a one-way dialogue with their consumers and rarely care what they think.

Consideration brands, in contrast, provide a rational alternative to respected brands. Consideration brands manage to transcend a sea of sameness through one-off products or communication. Take, for instance, the Kodak celebrity campaign with Drizzy, Trey, and Pit Bull, marketing that may manage to deliver short-term buzz but doesn't sustain momentum. Considered brands are normally in this category by virtue of their rational proposition versus an emotional connection—using Kia cars as an example. A considered brand is not seen as having a conviction beyond building market share.

Respected brands are those that have achieved trust from the consumer thanks to the delivery of a successful brand promise and as the result of long-term brand building efforts. A respected brand has a clear identity for both employees within the company and for customers, and typically follows wider cultural trends. A respected brand, say, like Samsung, enjoys customer loyalty and has a logo that inspires global recognition and trust. However, respected brands are invariably threatened by brands that deliver greater emotional appeal.

A liked brand is seen as having convictions that matter to its community and as caring more about the greater good than financial gain. Liked brands are often driven by outspoken founders or CEOs, say Richard Branson, who convey the brands' identity in personal ways. Liked brands are driven by the art and science of new media and technology, employing multiple approaches to communication with minimal messaging repetition. Like brands surprise and delight their fans through innovation and content yet work as hard at caring for existing customers as they do at attaining new ones—take the Soho House as a very much-liked brand. Liked brands have shared values and purposes with their user base. Their logo becomes a signifier that transcends race and geographical boundaries. Sony has achieved liked status for years.

Then we arrive at the characteristics that describe a loved brand. A brand that has a relationship with the needs and beliefs of communities of consumers, one that has evolved organically, can become a loved brand. This shared emotion can be so strong that consumers would genuinely feel their lives wouldn't be the same without the brand in question. In fact, loved brands benefit from these internal stakeholders who act as a wider marketing department. Loved brands regularly have a CEO who spearheads branding efforts for the company. Certainly Apple remains a leading example of a loved brand. Loved brands don't market to different cultures in different ways or stereotype people via their race. They utilize one narrative and allow cultural nuance to build emotional connections. Loved brands are culturally curious and look for advice from consumers, thus transcending a one-way conversation into a two-way dialogue and ultimately a megalogue that is advantageous to all.

How does the injection of instant cool affect a brand? Well, in the case of Hewlett-Packard, it set them on a direct course to being a liked brand. They then embarked on a journey to perpetual cool by next embodying cool—or that was the intention—with a campaign to reinvigorate the notion that the "PC is personal again." When Hewlett-Packard asked me to take a look at the campaign design—which was being helmed by Goodby, Silverstein & Partners, a masterful West Coast marketing company—I could see that the platform and the ideas were terrific. There was one problem. After all the work that had been done to gain instant cool, the new platform needed a better way to continue building on what it was that had come alive already. To launch marketing for the "PC Is Personal Again" campaign, they were going to use Robert Redford and Drew Barrymore. Both happen to be iconic actor/directors, both connected to film culture and global issues. But neither was right, in my view, to kick this big marketing idea out of the gate, coming from where it had already been, and for giving it some radical disruption with cool attached.

When I met with the marketing agency, I was blunt, saying, "If you start without a cultural context, I think you run the risk of losing the notion of cool that you're trying to build on. Why not start with artists who have a cool aspect to their own brand and who are not the most likely candidates?" The idea of having a shock or surprise element appealed to them when I mentioned Kanye West and Jay-Z, for starters. Then possibly after that we could go to less obvious choices. I proposed, "Once the platform has been launched you can then migrate to Redford and Barry-more."

My friend and partner, Jay-Z, once again trusted my instincts and loved the platform. The commercial was stupendous and aired the first time during the NBA finals. When it broke, not only did it drive awareness for HP—and it went on to win numerous advertising awards, including one at the Cannes Film Festival—but it enticed other celebrities from different fields to come on board, each embodying cool for different reasons. There was Olympic snowboarder Shaun White; entrepreneur/sports franchise owner Mark Cuban; Pharrell Williams; Mark Burnett, the creator/producer of the TV reality show *Survivor;* Serena Williams; and even Santa Claus (via the voice of Tim Allen from the popular film trilogy). In fact, when all was thrown into high gear, the marketers chose not to go back to Redford or Barrymore once the goals of embodying cool had been met.

In the process, HP had marched right into perpetual-cool territory belonging to competitors, claiming benefits ruled by others—the customization associated with Dell, the creativity of Apple, the dependability of IBM. By tapping into this broad range of consumer passion points at a time when no other competitor was on a message of why making the PC personal again mattered, HP's measure of coolness was reflected by seismic growth in its stock price. Marketing cool had allowed the brand to surpass Dell and become number one in worldwide PC market share.

There's often a confusion that I hear from brands about how far it is advisable to go in marketing into trends when trying to get the nuances right for embodying cool. Specifically, many corporations still view hip-hop culture as a trend at best and an anomaly at the least. Even as a marketing strategy, many brands visit the platform with some trepidation and hesitancy. The results in those cases tend to either fall flat with ads that have recycled concepts set to beats or are embarrassing because of inappropriate attempts to imitate cool—to try to use Ebonics or have people rolling their r's to promote Latino brands or force multicultural groupings that come off just as contrived as Dell DJ's effort to promote its own viral success.

For these reasons, one of my priorities with brands and with artists is to assure them that nothing in the pursuit of cool will put their core values at risk. The job of the translator, as a rule in the new economy, is to find the sweet spot between the brand's core values and the cultural cues. The good news is that our millennial generation is the most diverse in history. The more juxtaposed, the better. Differences no longer frighten. A fusion of tastes and styles is sought after. The tanning of and by this, the hip-hop generation, is diversity that celebrates individualism and the brand identification that marketing offers. This is why I've argued that tanning has done more to enrich brands and the economy at large than any cultural phenomenon like it.

Brands appeal to kids and young adults in this cross-culture who like to stand out but who also go with the crowd. With relevant, cool brands, they can meet their goals of being different and of being affiliated with networks. They use brands for code and shorthand to express where they're from, what team they love, what they're all about, and to "brandish" their status as a badge of honor.

What about turning off older consumers or those who aren't fans of urban culture? Interestingly enough, the marketing of cool has yet to turn off any core or older consumer in any case study or anecdote to my knowledge. On the contrary, a brand offering that is new, exciting, and stirring the hearts of the young and trend-savvy consistently provides the proverbial halo effect for the brand in general.

The millennials, as we've touched on briefly, really are

products of the branding age. Trends do matter to them. They want in. Moreover, they define themselves by their brands and expect their brands to keep up. Because of the blurring of the lines, marketing to one group has spillover to other groups—so it has to be accurate. Word travels fast. For brands that's big bang for bucks. By the same token, with ubiquitous connectivity, the shelf life of newness grows shorter and shorter.

Clothing designers, as an example, bemoan how quickly they can be embraced and then abandoned without warning. That leaves whoever came late to the trend holding the bag with unsold inventory. The key to trend survival, no surprise, is all about adaptation. There is nothing wrong with acknowledging a trend as part of the perception of nuance. There is nothing wrong with playing into a trend. But a word of warning to marketers: If you don't have control and you're not at the forefront of seeing the trend, you're in the back getting killed. Trend really can be a Ponzi scheme. When everyone moves on and you as the brand are the last guy to get the memo, you'll be chasing the last dollar and there won't be anything left.

As the Translation motto puts it, "Trends are perishable, cool is forever." Let that be the clarification of the rule that urban culture has bequeathed to the new economy. My take is that it goes back to being at that party or in the club. You don't want to be the last one to leave. That's uncool. So in the business of cool, you've got to leave money on the table when you're chasing trends. Like economies built on bubbles, brands built on trends have never had lasting power—but especially not in this time of the empowered millennial consumer. What happens is that when the trend dies, so do the brands attached to it. This is as true for those artists who are brands as it is for fields of industry, as it is for Fortune 500 fortress brands. Like Alvin Toffler said, you have to be fluid.

Back in 2004, Larry Light—the marketing visionary who had come to McDonald's and helped turn it around when it was losing consumer share—began to talk about that fluidity as a change in storytelling. Instead of having one catchy message or one simple idea to be hammered home like nails in the sensibilities of consumers, he argued that the time had come for a broader chronicle of many stories that spoke to why the brand mattered in the context of the times. He calls this approach "brand journalism."

As I would have the good fortune to get to know him and work with the talented team at McDonald's on launching their turnaround, I saw Larry's approach in action and became a fan of this philosophy and the strategies it inspires. Brand journalism suggests that there is a continual flow of news and information that is consumer generated and needs to be followed. In 2004, Larry's cautionary advice at a conference called AdWatch was that the timing marked the "end of brand positioning as we know it" and that "no single ad tells the whole story." Introducing the concept of brand journalism was his way of ringing the bell for new rules that mind the millennials. By using many stories to create a brand narrative, rather than looking for that clever hook to reach everyone, he wasn't trying to say that niche marketing needed to go further than it already had. That kind of thinking still ran the risk of overdoing trends instead of embodying cool and of overusing the demographic boxes. Larry Light's explanation was, "We don't need one big execution of a big idea. We need one big idea that can be used in a multidimensional, multilayered, and multifaceted way."

At AdWatch, he encouraged marketers to see these series of stories as context for authentically showing "what happens to a brand in the world" and to develop communications that follow the news of what culture cares about. During future shock remix, with increasing media fragmentation—providing opportunities and challenges—the narrative for the brand, not summarized in a single slogan or one ad, can be the mother ship of cool from which daring departures into new territory can be taken.

Clearly, survival of the fittest in our marketplace means you have to be ever evolving and always paying attention to cues. Branding and brand building, I often say, are like raising a child. You shouldn't do it if you don't have love to give. But once it grows up and learns to embody cool on its own, that brand—like hip-hop and the effect tanning—can have true, positive impact and make a real difference in the lives of human beings on this planet.

CHAPTER 8

SELLING MIND-SETS, NOT PRODUCTS

T he phenomenon of tanning as it emerged in the 2000s resulted in certain unexpected consequences. They seemed to come about in both natural and perverse (and hilarious) ways as people were melding, sharing values, and exchanging aspects of their respective cultures.

What really caught me by surprise was how much had changed from when I attended a mostly all-white high school in the mid to late 1980s—when big lips and a defined booty weren't traits necessarily viewed as attractive. There was a lot of joking that went on based on racial stereotypes; we all played into them in a fairly inoffensive way. The jokes about black people having big lips and black girls having big butts were pretty much standard fare. It never actually made sense that a female who had a flat stomach and small waist yet did have a plump derriere was considered fat. Even if she was a size 4, trim and in shape, how was it that having a body part bigger than her Caucasian peers' was not aesthetically pleasing?

As time passed, the tables turned in such dramatic fashion that several industries came along that were devoted to the cultivation of big lips and bigger butts for women not naturally endowed! True, bigger lips were seen as part of women's general pursuit of a more youthful appearance—with collagen injections to make them look more plump and voluptuous—but this was a trait that women of color already embodied. As for the enhancement of the derriere, I thought that I'd heard of everything— from infomercials selling exercise techniques to tapes and manuals, as well as injections and cosmetic surgery—until not long ago when I saw a commercial for Booty Pops. For girls and ladies with flat or skinny bottoms, the claim with this product, like a padded bra for the bosom, is that it offers the lift and definition described as a "pop." And then there are the two sneakers in 2010 vying for the number one bestselling spot in America— Reebok's EasyTones and Sketchers' Shape-ups. With the claim that wearing the sneakers can help tone the entire body, where the real firming happens is with women's hamstrings, with a motion that has been proven to develop the muscle that goes up to the butt. What a switch for an aspect of the body to become redefined and seen as more desirable, when twenty years ago it was regarded as fat and a source of embarrassment.

Certainly tanning has happened in reverse too. We also see more black and Latina women putting golden and platinum weaves in their hair—going for the unapologetic "blonde hair" look. Since the 1970s, skin lighteners have been widely used by consumers with darker skin—revealing the fact that in the minds of many, black wasn't necessarily beautiful yet. However, as the journey of cultural tanning has taken off and the beauty image of appearing more ethnic and exotic has spread, the fade creams and skin lighteners have increasingly been rejected as inauthentic and harmful.

With these trends reflecting the simultaneous darkening and lightening, the tanning and coming together, of the mental complexion of America, I think they also include, by the way, an acceptance of the right to feel and look sexy. By 2003, the bathing beauty on the cover of *Sports Illustrated,* deemed by many the most beautiful woman in the world (the same artist who would rank as the top-earning music entrepreneur of the first decade

of the new millennium), was Beyoncé Knowles. The very singer who delivered the term "bootylicious" epitomizes the new definition of beauty—and is coming at you with hips, butt, lips, and an attitude of cool, sexy, and confident that other women are empowered to adopt too.

The next thing we all knew, J. Lo's butt and body became cultural news. When Fergie of the Black-eyed Peas performed the song "My Humps," which praised the power of her derriere and her breasts ("lovely lady lumps") to draw luxury-brand gifts and attention galore, the code implied that it was a shared value, no color line dividing it. Today it's Kim Kardashian and Jessica Biel as prime examples.

This aspect of tanning, I believe, has been a healthy change allowing women from diverse cultures to come to a place where they can meet and match and have common aesthetics. What I hear while listening to female consumers is that whatever makes you feel good about yourself is optimal and truly freeing as long as you can choose for yourself—*Oh, that's the hair I want, that's the body, I want some meat on my bones and hips and lips.* Or not. Those borrowed and then shared traits of women who are African-American, white, Hispanic, Asian, Native American, Indian, you name it—and from cultural beauty standards and style borrowed from other countries—all come together to create a very feminine, womanly, self-loving aesthetic.

It has been a source of pride for me to know that urban culture has been one of the prime movers and carriers of these tanning changes that have taken place over the last twenty years. Likewise, it has been affirming to watch the far-reaching influence of the urban mind-set when it comes to defining what makes a man attractive, stylishly groomed, and well presented.

At first glance, the uninformed marketer might assume that these aesthetics were and are being adopted on an anything-goes, "whatever hip-hop says is cool today" basis. But in fact, as per the belief system that spread tanning, there are attitudes and reasons behind why a look or a trend is endowed with the power of cool—and why it isn't. Understanding those reasons and the stories behind them, as we now know, is critical.

Cool Is . . .

In early 2003, the Associated Press put out a release that captured headlines in sports and business pages all across the
nation. "Retro jerseys all the rage" was a snapshot in time of how
forcefully hip-hop-fueled tastes were driving consumption of an
item known for its dated popularity: throwback jerseys.

Though the trend extended to various sports, the main
action was in basketball—where a retro jersey might run anywhere from $250 to $400. The press release noted, "Some of the
retro buffs couldn't care less about the history on their shoulders: they just want to look old school—or keep up with their
friend down the block." Stories of kids picking up, for example,
a Celtics jersey and not recognizing Larry Bird's name were all
over the place. Because of throwbacks, one apparel company
reported annual revenues jumping from $2.8 million to $23 million in just two years (even in what was then considered a down
economy); another sports clothing manufacturer had seen a 300
percent rise in its fortunes in half that time. An explanation for
the craze came from Isiah Thomas when he observed, "It goes
back to the first principle of fashion—what's old is new." Others suggested that maybe it was the longing for a different era
of sports—when legends like Magic Johnson and Kareem Abdul-
Jabbar were in their prime.

Sports jerseys in general had been in high demand for years
and the throwbacks added a new element of scarcity. Just as in
the days when we had to befriend the manager at Foot Locker
to get our Air Force 1s, in Philly at a store called Mitchell and
Ness that had the best collection of the rarest vintage throwbacks there was a guy named Reuben whom you had to know
and who would alert you when goods came in. When that happened, insiders would race from NYC to Philly hoping to be the
first to pay the four to five hundred dollars for the obscure Brett
Favre numbered jersey that nobody else had.

In hindsight, I would say that rather than being about a longing for another era, the throwbacks were a last act of the sports
jersey heyday that had begun in the late eighties and was now

finally coming full circle with a grand finale. Why do I say that? Because eight months after that press release proclaimed athletic retro as the new cool, pumping the sales of throwbacks even more and further enriching league coffers (like the NBA's annual $3 billion in receipts), Jay-Z released a record that signaled it was time for a new look. Simply entitled "Change Clothes," Jay-Z (featuring Pharrell) talked about the need not to get stuck in a rut, not to become a prisoner of the trappings of success or the uniform of cool, not to forget where you started, and never to lose the aspiration to keep on moving. Literally what he said was *"but y'all n***as acting way too tough / throw on a suit get it tapered up and let's just change clothes and go."* In the story of a guy telling his girl that's all they needed to do to stay fresh and go to the "top of the globe" the song was also empowering. Wow.

Just when you thought that urban style had gone as far as possibilities allowed, so much so that it had to go get something old from the closet and call it new again with throwbacks, the time for a reinvention had been announced. Because of the millions who were now part of urban culture, the minute Jay-Z said it and replaced his old look with a button-down collared and tailored shirt in the video, the legions followed suit.

The funniest thing happened next, something that opened my eyes to the ambivalence toward hip-hop still felt by many brands and organizations representing the status quo. It came up for me when NBA commissioner David Stern—noticing the steep decline in sales of licensed sports apparel—asked me, "Maybe you could ask Jay-Z if he would change clothes back again?" He was serious. And it's hard not to love David Stern, who really does want the best for all the teams. However, Stern had been the one to first institute a dress code for players when not in uniform and to strongly discourage cornrows and tattoos, until he couldn't do anything about them anymore, and to openly admit to feeling that the rap thing was always in danger of getting out of hand. All of a sudden, he's asking me to tell Jay-Z to change clothes back again!

At that point in my career in marketing, it highlighted a generation gap that certainly could be expected. But it also prepared me to deal with brands and corporate executives who wanted the profitability of urban culture but didn't always have the under-standing of why it was bringing (or could be bringing) them in money hand over fist—and didn't understand the motivations of the army of consumers who were paying the money.

What was getting lost in translation (phrase intended) was that defining what's cool is less about the specific style of shirt and more about how wearing the style of shirt makes you feel. When hip-hop changed from a saggy-baggy, antiestablishment attitude to a more cultivated hipster haberdashery kind of feel-ing, it was very much like an overdue celebration of having done well and having earned the right to party. And as much as Jay-Z was the guy who put out the invitation to go there, the person throwing the party—literally, as an individual and an entrepre-neur and as a brand unto himself—was Sean "Puffy" and/or "P. Diddy" Combs.

There's no doubt as to what an important global driver of cul-ture Puffy had been over the years. How about keeping everyone on their toes by taking over Broadway as an actor in the Sidney Poitier role in a revival of *A Raisin in the Sun* and, in spite of mixed reviews for his acting, helping rake in more money than any non-musical production in years? How about then going off to Paris and suddenly becoming the toast of that town? Even knowing all that and remembering the days when P. Diddy had climbed all the mountains first—the first young African-American entrepre-neur who could walk into a club and happen to mention he had just gotten a check for $40 million—the moment when I really saw how far he had taken tanning was during Estée Lauder's launch of the Sean John fragrance line.

John Demsey had known Puffy since the nineties and de-scribed him then as "a pretty glamorous figure around New York City. He was dating everybody and was in his J. Lo phase." Those were the breakout years of Sean's lavish affairs out in the Hamp-tons where everyone came dressed in all white and when he threw fantasy birthday parties for himself with guest lists ranging from rappers to Donald Trump and Oprah to foreign heads of state.

The reason Demsey approached Puffy to do a men's fragrance line for Estée Lauder was, as he later noted, "One thing about beauty, especially fragrance, is you're selling aspiration. You're selling a lifestyle. And that's one of the reasons that I think Sean has been more successful than a lot of people—because of the lifestyle and swagger he has." John Demsey described Puffy as having an uncanny ability to make suburban kids want to be him and at the same time connect to kids in the urban neighborhoods where he grew up. In the '00s with the millennial consumers, a celebrity who came out of hip-hop music was all the more powerful. How so? According to John, "Everyone defines themselves by the music they grew up with. It doesn't matter who you are or what you are. If you grew up in 1995 and you looked at seven of the top ten singles, you were defined by hip-hop. And that's it, that's your reference point."

Launching the Sean John fragrance on the heels of Puffy's Sean John clothing line, which was doing phenomenally well, was not a leap either. But in Demsey's assessment, the most compelling reason for working with Puffy was that he was at the leading edge of the paradigm shift—the Thinnest Slice—of moving niche to pop culture all the way. Sean Combs had the advantage of being perceived as an entertainer, though he is so much more, in Demsey's eyes, "a businessmen and impresario who had transcended brand, personality, and lifestyle." When my Translation partners and I consulted with Demsey and his team at Estée Lauder, they made it clear that they were marketing a lifestyle mind-set that was Sean John Combs–esqe, and not a product.

What was the mind-set? It was cool that made you feel infinitely confident. Puffy, as Demsey put it, being the archetypal "guy who knows how to work a room," exuded that drawing power, that ability to know what is press-worthy, how to harness the uses of media—to gain optimal exposure, creating controversy, and still maintain some scarcity. Moreover, Puff knows how to recover from missteps. John Demsey's overview was this: "Just when you think you can count Combs out he reinvents himself. He went from Biggie Smalls and the whole West Coast/East Coast stuff, and completely transcended himself into the king of the Rat Pack. He rebooted himself. And successfully. The brand is him. It is completely driven by personality muscle." Just when you thought he was not going to change his name again, he was back to Sean "Diddy" Combs and everyone had to write about that.

All of that thinking and decoding went into the understanding of why a stand-alone brand—Sean John—would work well for a holding company that offers distribution and marketing like Estée Lauder. It was the thinking that went into the naming of the two fragrances, Unforgivable by Sean John, and later, I Am King by Sean John. On the whole, men's products were a small part of Lauder's business. They had previously had great success with Tommy as a designer fragrance (with Tommy Hilfiger) but until the Sean John brand, there had been no attempt to go after New Generation male consumers.

Where was the competition in terms of younger-mind-set marketing? On the super high end, there was Creed, an independent perfumer based in Paris, started in 1760, that prided itself on having been the private fragrance designers for ten royal families— and six generations later was experiencing a surge in demand thanks to hip-hop and Hollywood royalty. For young teens, there was Axe—which was in drugstore distribution that put it on the end of the spectrum that lacked aspiration. Then there was nothing else—other than "let me wear my dad's cologne," i.e. fragrances from established brands and designers such as Ralph Lauren, Calvin Klein, Hugo Boss, and Giorgio Armani.

In 2005, the marketing challenge wasn't in proving how cool Unforgivable by Sean John really was. And it wasn't in getting Estée Lauder to understand the mind-set of their target consumer. Clearly, they were paying attention. The obstacle they faced was setting up communication channels and creating a community that didn't exist for their new offering, and that's why the brand valued our input. Because the community wasn't primed to be excited about a designer men's fragrance that could be meaningful to their lives, there was going to be a learning curve for the consumer target. Therefore, some "edutainment" was in order. Without having to do full-on radical disruption, where you reinvent the wheel, we treated it like a movie launch—with the tag line "Life without passion is unforgivable." Nor was it a shotgun approach, where you go as broad and big as you can and hope to hit as many consumers as you can. We were strategic and targeted in the building of community that was made up of different demographics but had a like-mindedness that came from being raised on the music that would have Puffy on its radar.

John Demsey gave us the power to really think differently about the intersection of consumers and their product, and really trusted my instincts—much as Paul Fireman had with sneakers—to do things that weren't in their regular distribution channels. On radio, we marketed the fragrance as if it was a new record getting ready to drop and had DJs doing shout-outs and running contests with hot giveaways. Our media plan was to buy airtime not just when we knew our audience would be watching but, rather, when they would be *intently focused,* the watchwords for our campaign. Most advertisers usually just buy big media—playoff sporting events like the Super Bowl or the NBA championship. Those are usually great times to be noticed but I wanted to go a step farther. Instead of just buying a sporting event with X amount of millions watching, I wanted to go where the consumer target would be tuning in with excitement to watch their heroes—LeBron James going up against Dwight Howard or Kobe Bryant dueling Dwayne Wade. I wanted to buy those particular events that I knew the core consumer would be intently watching; I was confident that this way we couldn't miss. And that's how we ran the media. By targeting the media in a manner that specific, we hit multiple home runs with media buys.

As we saw with this campaign, the savings for spending advertising dollars this way is monumental. Instead of buying inventory that's useless—when you're just buying empty eyeballs (as most companies do)—you're buying focus and passion from the audience. When I argued this point against the traditional approach, I started calling it a departure from "empty eyeballs." When advertising companies recommend media buys all too often they are drawing from data that tells how many viewers their commercial is going to reach—when, in fact, those are empty eyeballs. None of those statistics provide a measure of how many people are actually paying attention. Digital campaigns are mounted on claims that a site gets millions/billions of hits. But how many coming to that site are paying attention and how often does that translate into sales? As I would later tell clients, by buying focus, we can avoid being in the empty-eyeball business.

During the discovery of this phenomenon with the Unforgivable launch, all I knew was that buying NBA alone wasn't meaningful; I wanted to pay for what mattered. Because we knew what mattered, we could save a lot of money—buying local games and then using the rest of the money to buy more media that mattered. Avoiding empty eyeballs let us save money we could then spend on more targeted media *and* it got us a much better ROI than if we had tried to be in all places.

With that thinking for our TV commercial buys, we went directly to where our consumers were going to be watching intently with marketing worthy of their focus that aligned the Sean John aspiration with that of the athletes. How? With fun, risqué story lines in nonconventional formatting. One tactic came from Puffy's idea to shoot behind-the-scenes footage of the different romantic settings used for the commercial and making that into a short film—showing him and two women in a ménage à trois and a flash of nipple, making it much too controversial for television. Next thing we knew the film had gone viral online and had become our ready-made digital campaign!

As obvious as this might sound, believe it or not, a lot of brand executives and advertisers don't see the value in targeting a core community. The attitude is, *Why would we speak to an audience that's already made up their minds about what's cool and what isn't?* As a case in point, I can recall a conversation with a very upset marketing executive for a major beauty line who wasn't seeing traction after going through most of a multimillion-dollar budget on a fragrance being endorsed by none other than Beyoncé Knowles. After my advice was solicited about how to best use what was left of the budget, I had to ask what they had spent most of the money on so far. That's when it became clear they had put everything into high-end beauty and glamour placement, but that wasn't focused on her core audience.

In addition to producing a stunningly beautiful commercial, they had bought lavish spreads in *Vogue* and glamorous movie starts—ads shown on massive screens in movie theaters right before the beginning of the movie. But why hadn't they targeted media where Beyoncé's fans would be engaged?

Upon hearing the question, the brand executive shrugged and then said, "Give me an example."

"I just listened to everything that you did," I replied, and went for the example of low-hanging fruit by asking, "Why didn't you run the commercial, let's say, on BET?"

And the brand executive asked, "What's a BET?" After I explained, the executive's follow-up was, "She's big on BET?" Unfortunately, there wasn't a lot to do at that stage of the game. It was a situation in which not understanding her core audience held back a terrific product from reaching its potential.

Working with John Demsey in a hands-on capacity with Unforgivable, we knew that mistake wouldn't be made. But you know what? John would be the first to say that many of the executives at his own company were skeptical about investment in a consumer group that had no track record at driving purchase consideration of a men's fragrance—let alone a new fragrance associated with a hip-hop luminary.

Then again, true to Puffy's personality muscle, we made sure that the community we were building would fan out in all directions. There was the Brinks truck delivery of an exclusive, limited edition of the fragrance to Saks—with heavy security and tons of press. There was a New York Stock Exchange bell-ringing and samples delivered to downtown offices in the thousands, and P. Diddy antics on all the talk shows, including a Sean John and David Letterman battle with the two spraying Unforgivable in each other's mouths.

Imagine the skeptics and their flabbergasted reactions when tanning forces ricocheted from a core to a global mainstream embrace, making it the number-one-selling men's fragrance in no time, with an estimated $35 million in sales the first year. The campaign was named the best-executed launch strategy of the year by a leading beauty marketing association, among numerous other awards. Sean John's follow-up fragrance, I Am King, was released within the year and topped that act. By 2009, even with a troubled economy and consumer spending down, both fragrances were in the top ten. I Am King was at number two, doing more business than Ralph Lauren and Calvin Klein.

How was that possible? Again, because the messages of life without passion being unforgivable and having the audacity to say you are king—of whatever it is that is your arena—are so much more cool and valuable than just smelling good.

And herein lies the ongoing challenge to marketers who know, on the one hand, that it is not advisable to dictate to consumers how they should define cool, and who, on the other hand, want their brand to be considered any time a consumer is asked to complete this phrase: "Cool is . . ."

There is a strategy that helps balance those two concerns. But for it to work, first brands have to believe in their own intrinsic coolness, no matter what their bottom line or the desirability of their products at the time.

Cool Isn't *What* You Have; It's *Where* You Got It

Whenever I ponder why "Change Clothes" caused social habits to change en masse or why the launch of Sean John fragrances for men struck the chord that it did (or why for a few years throwbacks were the coolest consumption items on the market), I think back to a time when being in the know about what was cool and where to go get it was all that mattered.

Don't get me wrong. Of course it was exciting to witness the success of people who came from the same place as you and who were showing up in the latest fashions, driving expensive cars, wearing flashy jewelry—or, even cooler, when they had those items customized! To have something that was one of a kind or that only an exclusive few could ever attain, well, that meant you had more than money—you had access. And there was a mystique and intrigue attached to wherever it was that gave you access. With real success you had a pass anywhere. You could go to places with exotic, foreign-sounding names that you had no idea where they even were.

Throughout the eighties and nineties, there were a couple of illustrious destinations right in New York City that were the equivalent of traveling to those distant ports of call—the Shangri-las of style and luxury. They were attached to so much status that the only advertising ever required was word of mouth. You had to know someone who could even tell you where such destinations were. One of these was the boutique design shop known as Dapper Dan's on Harlem's historic 125th Street—where Dan Jenkins, couturier extraordinaire, kept an endless and secret supply of logo-emblazoned fabrics like Louis Vuitton, Gucci, MCM, and Chanel, which he magically transformed into sundry custom designs, from clothes to hats to auto upholstery.

Dapper Dan played an extremely important role in introducing the founding hip-hop generation to couture brands. What's more, he translated those elements of haute couture into applications that were understandable to young, hip aspirational tastemakers. At the time, Gucci would never have made, as Dapper Dan did, sweat suits. They would never have upholstered a car interior. They wouldn't have understood. But Dapper Dan understood the aspiration, and he put it into silhouettes that were cool and street and influenced a generation's idea of what was high style. Because of Dan, I believe, an appreciation of specific couture brands became inbred in hip-hop culture. For consumers growing up in the culture, whenever we looked at our heroes and their album covers—at the ones who were having an impact on style and fashion—they were all wearing Dapper Dan's clothing. Later, designers like Marc Jacobs would specialize in making couture hip-hop accessible. But back in Dan's time, there was nowhere else to get oversized Louis Vuitton anything. He did it by customizing it, probably with fabric he secretly knew how to get on Canal Street, enabling his clientele to walk around adorned in scarce, aspirational looks, brands, and materials that no one else had. Catering to everyone from high-rolling street patrons to athletes like Mike Tyson to the some of the earliest rap artists like Big Daddy Kane and Salt-n-Pepa, Dapper Dan's was mythical—earning as many name-checks in rap lyrics as Barneys and Saks put together.

And then there was Jacob the Jeweler. Today Jacob & Co.

is headquartered at the most prestigious of addresses, at East Fifty-seventh Street and Park Avenue, across the street from the Four Seasons. It's a far cry from the tiny shop in the Diamond District that was first opened by then twenty-one-year-old Jacob Arabo, an immigrant from Uzbekistan, so he could put food on the table for his family. As time went on, he became known as the diamond jeweler of choice for pop culture figures through-out the big bang of bling.

Besides his ability to unapologetically customize any piece of jewelry with the most bedazzling encrustation of the fin-est of diamonds, Jacob was an infectiously likeable character. With his Eastern European accent and slicked-back black hair, he brought flair to the game—he'd come to your office with his jewelry or meet you at a hot spot for drinks and let you see his latest. Customer service, baby! People would take him their already expensive watches, and he'd remove the bezel and bling them out. He treated his clientele like family. Oh, yeah, there were the street guys who paid in cash, no questions asked. But the mainstay of his business was pop culture celebrities either already famous or on their way—and Jacob cornered the record industry. He understood the value of bling. He understood the culture, the reason why pushing the limits of ostentation was a form of expression that was important at the time. And he also knew that a lot of his musician clients had business managers and record companies cutting their checks and that they were busy too. So instead of making highly valued customers wait for their jewelry, he would let them have the goods and then pay when they got paid. Basically, he gave credit. Not only that, but Jacob would freely loan pieces for award shows, as well as for media and video shoots.

In the beginning Jacob the Jeweler was such a well-kept secret that it took a lot of legwork to find out that he had a pri-vate space on Forty-seventh Street. He used to put up headshots of celebrities you could see through the window to let custom-ers looking for him know they were in the right place. Getting on that wall was a rite of passage. Those photos ran from Biggie to Bono. Puffy may have gotten up there early, and so did Mary J. Blige. Soon it was everyone—Jennifer Lopez, Elton John, Britney

Spears, Justin Timberlake, Mayor Rudy Giuliani, David Beckham. Before long, because of his customized offerings of huge "iced"- out crosses, Stars of David, chains, and his gift for adding after- market designs to Rolexes and Cartiers and Audemarses, you had to make appointments. Jacob became so big that he had to start quarantining different customers in two private offices—in case there were rival rappers or warring record labels or execu- tives who didn't like each other but happened to be there at the same time. With his larger-than-life personality, Jacob the Jew- eler managed it quite well—inspiring his own legend that grew and grew, earning shout-outs in more than seventy-five major hip-hop releases over the years since 1999.

My marketing revelation was in thinking about how some- one who wasn't even a brand was getting so much word-of- mouth advertising that the world knew about him. That's when I realized that it wasn't about what you got, but where you got it. You got it from Jacob. He became that big. Then the question for me became, *How does Jacob the Jeweler become a brand?* Well, naturally he needed a product. In other marketing challenges, as we've discussed, marketing is sometimes done in product creation. This was the reverse—he had built-in marketing that was already spreading his name but neither a brand as a com- pany nor a product line. Amazingly, however, Jacob already had the ability to sell a lifestyle mind-set, to speak to the values of aspiration like nobody else. He already represented the "top of the globe" for pop culture—the farthest destination you could ever imagine being able to go to. He had authenticity, credibility, and so much proximity to the top hip-hop artists that they were name-checking him in every other song.

When I set out to develop the foundation for a physical prod- uct that would define a brand right out of the gate—an ambi- tious undertaking—I knew one thing above all, that whatever it was had to have a name on it. Crosses and chains and earrings— the bulk of the products he sold—didn't work well because they didn't lend themselves to names. Watches were a different story. As a matter of fact, as I mulled it over, the realization hit me that a luxury-brand watch was all about the pull-up value. Wear- ing a Rolex had nothing to do with the fine inner workings of

Swiss timepieces. It was about the equivalent of pulling up at the curb, pulling up your sleeve, and showing what's on your wrist. The pull-up begs the question, *How does this look as you notice it?* Since everyone was going to Jacob for aftermarket diamonds to add to their watches, I thought coming up with a Jacob-branded watch made the most marketing sense. Besides, watches were ideal for displaying brand names even with as many diamonds as possible. That seemed to be the way to go to place Jacob the Jeweler in the hierarchy to which he belonged, or so I felt, to make him the Harry Winston of the new generation. He even looked the part.

But talking to Jacob about the power of branding was way too abstract. Then we started talking about doing a watch and what ultimately gave us direction for the idea was his story as the international symbol of success—a rags-to-riches journey just like the one many of his famous clients had taken that embodied the American dream for an immigrant. It was in the tanning DNA. By 2003 his global reputation reached so far that his family of clients around the world was in five time zones. Why not design into that mind-set? Jacob knew that nobody needs to know what time it is in five time zones at a glance, but he also understood why that was the cultural story of the times. With that thinking, we competed with a watch from Audemars Piguet, this one-of-a-kind urban myth that retails for a million dollars and is so blindingly diamonded out, you can't even believe what you've beheld with your own eyes. The sickest watch in the world.

Jacob the Jeweler took that watch face idea, staying with over-the-top bling but adding a leather strap, along with color and to-die-for touches that allowed you to customize the watch by taking off the bezel and showing the diamonds or screwing it back on and wearing it plain. It was fun, sophisticated, and diamonded out, all at the same time.

One of the highlights of the experience working with Jacob came when I made a trip to Paris to show the prototype to style arbiters whose opinions would be important for marketing to a very exclusive consumer. On that trip, I was able to arrange for a meeting with Karl Lagerfeld. When the appointed time came, I was practically pinching myself as I walked into the House of

Chanel—where I met Lagerfeld and placed the watch on his wrist. And he loved it. Lagerfeld loved the size of it; he loved the audacity of it. He wasn't concerned at all with a brand name he didn't know; it didn't matter. He didn't care about that. All that mattered was that it was a big-ass, blinged-out watch, and the pull-up value was the same. Besides loving it and letting me put it on his wrist, he allowed me to take a photograph of it on him. This, yet again, was a moment like others that let me know this was all tanning. He liked bling as much as the hip-hop industry did.

It was that moment when I gave it to him and Lagerfeld's eyes got big as he looked at it—as if to say, *"Damn!"*—that I realized those six degrees of separation are really more like two. What is the separation? The difference is between those who aspire and those who don't.

Needless to say, I returned to New York ready to take the world by storm. We seeded the watch in music videos and not only did it go absolutely crazy after that, but a brand was born. And for the next several years, the line went insane—everything built on superb design, the highest quality, and the fact that where you got it was from Jacob & Co.

Escalade: Arrivals and Departures

When I first got to know the executives at GM in the early days of my marketing career, I was incredibly relieved. For one thing, my fear had been that with corporate America and Madison Avenue now discovering the hip-hop impact, they would want to go out and do things that had nothing to do with their brand—like sponsor rap battles. Thankfully, GM was too culturally sensitive to try to force proximity that way. The other source of my relief—and frankly excitement—was hearing how the GM team drew from mind-set marketing to rekindle the cool of a classic brand: Cadillac.

Kim Brink, a former GM exec, recalled where things stood in the late 1990s, when she came on board, moving over to Cadillac from Chevrolet—where she had gained a strong background in marketing trucks. The image of Cadillac in the luxury automobile universe at the time, Kim acknowledged, was weak. "It was known for white people from Florida," she said, citing research, "snowbirds, traditional, country clubs, comfort, older generation."

Like many established brands caught in the all-too-familiar trap of needing to innovate and connect with younger consumers without losing core customers, Cadillac had been going through an identity crisis for some time. Finally, enlightened GM executives came up with the inspiration for the Cadillac Escalade—a luxury utility vehicle that was going to be designed for the urban landscape.

My question to Kim was whether they were aware from the start that it would appeal to urban consumers of luxury cars— enough for it to receive its cool credentials, which would then influence a suburban mom in Bloomington, Indiana, to purchase the reinvented Cadillac.

Though she wished they could say that they knew a plan to target urban culture would lead to broader success, Kim didn't remember everyone having that kind of clear insight. From her perspective, coming from the truck side of the business, "You saw a kind of escapism, on the mountain, everything four-wheel drive." Now they were mixing that powerful road-dominating message into the Cadillac code. She and the rest of the team asked themselves, "Okay, we're bringing a luxury utility to market, what can we do to completely differentiate it from the category— disrupt the norms, the conventions going on in the category?" That's when they started tracking other luxury brands and seeing how once the urban market adopted a brand, its popularity spread dramatically from there. And the idea that suburban moms would eventually be driving an Escalade to pick up their kids at prep school, of course, could then become a reality.

Mike Bentley, a GM marketing executive who worked with Kim when I got to know him, went so far as to describe the importance of the Escalade and the positioning of it within the urban market by saying that if it hadn't happened that way, "Cadillac might not be around with us now."

Born and raised in England, but a passionate devotee of American cars, music, and culture, Mike told me, "Escalade fits the code of what Cadillac is. None of the other models did. I came to see that Escalade, and what it stood for, kept Cadillac alive. One of the reasons: It plugged into hip-hop culture."

Mike drew parallels between the badges of success valued by the urban mind-set and the fact that the Cadillac has been a potent symbol of success from the moment of its creation over a century ago. Deep within the code, he explained, Cadillac represented "arrival." When a focus group was conducted with people from a mix of backgrounds and cultures, they were asked to reveal their first emotional impression of a Cadillac. The group had first taken time to vent about negative experiences with car dealers or rising gas prices and then had done a relaxation exercise to connect to their true feelings. So when the question was asked of them, Mike recalled, "stories came pouring out. We analyzed those stories for plots and themes. One interesting thing about Cadillac—literally all the stories start with the Cadillac arriving and someone successful getting out of it. To us, those stories say, 'I have arrived. I am here.' Nearly always it's a successful male—just the guy who lives on the block who is a little notch above the rest. White, black, Hispanic, and Asian people write that story."

Interestingly enough, Mike Bentley said that similar questions asked about Ford as a brand and emotional impressions of it "started with a story of a group of people getting in the car and going off together on an adventure."

Not all companies, large or small, are willing to delve into these deeper strands of meaning so important to marketing strategies—and so clearly revealed from conducting this kind of pop culture anthropological study. Ford, I should add, had clear insights over the years in recognizing that departures were key to their code. Think of the names of their SUV models—Ford Explorer and Ford Expedition. In the luxury utility category, the competitor to the Escalade is the Lincoln Navigator, also reflective of a departure into new or different terrain. Even the model Ford used to launch its entry into hybrid technology speaks to departures—the Escape.

Following in the Cadillac tradition of being about arrivals, Escalade was now also veering into the terrain of departures.

The name itself embodied arrival and upward mobility, yet also being undeterred in the expansion toward all those destinations that sound slightly foreign—yes, global—places that might have previously been unreachable. Pure aspiration. Taking a word not in common usage like "escalade"—which summons the idea of force and speed, as in *escalation;* has Latin, Spanish, Italian, and French in its DNA; and was first used in the late 1500s—was a marketing stroke of brilliance. Touching on the power of making the old new, here are definitions from a 1913 edition of *Webster's Dictionary,* both as a noun and a verb:

> 1) \es'ca*lade"\, n. [F., Sp. escalada (cf. It. scalata),
> fr. Sp. escalar to scale, LL. scalare, fr. L. scala ladder]
>
> (military) furious attack made by troops on a fortified
> place, in which ladders are used to pass a ditch or mount
> a rampart.
>
> 2) \Es'ca*lade"\, v. t. [imp. & p. p. {Escaladed}; p. pr. &
> vb. n. {Escalading}.] (Mil.)
>
> To mount and pass or enter by means of ladders; to scale;
> as to escalade a wall.

Kim Brink pointed out that by doing this archetypal work and taking a word that once referred to how warriors conquered castles but had evolved to mean a form of ascending, climbing, moving up, mounting a campaign, or going up with steady progress, the internal positioning came through all the more coherently. "The positioning in our internal strategy," she explained, "was invincibility. *I'm invincible. I'm invincible as a person and this sport utility vehicle makes me invincible on the road.*"

So the theme of having arrived and being in a place of success where departures were possible too led to mind-set marketing strategies and was also woven into design elements distinct to the Escalade. Kim said that the target consumer was the psychographic that would relate to that feeling, aligned with invincibility.

GM also didn't want to lose the importance of the past and all the stories of arrivals and emotional first impressions of Cadillacs. She said that when participants spoke about what was the essence of the brand, what made it cool, "color was a huge deal—pink Cadillac, black. It was always a color associated with it. So that drove some of our naming strategies. In the catalog, instead of calling it 'green' we called it 'Green Envy.'" Some of the stories that included important historical events having to do with Cadillacs did add another layer to the code. These touched on a particular kind of departure as a passage from one place to the next. Many recalled that Kennedy was shot when he was riding in a Cadillac, even though it was actually a Lincoln. Some associate the ornate styling of a hearse with that of a Cadillac—a potent symbol of a departure.

The other major association to Cadillacs, of course, is the chrome. Kim gave examples such as "big expressive tail fins" and "big chrome bumpers." "If you look at the design of Escalade, chrome is everywhere. Chrome rims, chrome badges, chrome door handles."

Mike Bentley added that the word "shiny" was in most every story and memory having to do with a Cadillac. Again it related to the announcement of arrival—"you show up like you paid attention to your appearance." Yukon, also made by GM, and Escalade share the same footprint, as Mike confirmed. But because of the added chrome, Escalade looks bigger, more invincible. He elaborated, "The other thing about setting it in the urban environment is that Escalade has hyper-potentiality. It represents more power than you'll ever need. But isn't it nice to have that excess of power in the urban environment? It emphasizes how much power you have. You are clashing two codes together: SUV off-road is clashing with urban." This kind of juxtaposition when you merge two things that are naturally conflicting in cultural meaning, Mike felt, speaks to something very powerful in our human wiring when that merger works.

This was the process that Cadillac had undertaken to connect to its intrinsic soul of cool. To my knowledge, GM was the first automaker to study the booming aftermarket industry that had been supported by urban culture for some time and to design into it with the Escalade.

The aftermarket work wasn't just for systems that could prove how loud a car was or how fast it could go. That was version 1.0 aftermarket work. But when hip-hop superstars, athletes, and other high-profile urban culture figures started putting in spoiler kits, getting their luxury cars tricked out so they could raise and lower them to music, putting bigger rims on the car that let them stick out past the fender, adding all-chrome exhausts, changing out the grills, putting DVD-player screens in the headrests, and adding signal beams, that was version 2.0.

Kim Brink explained how these kinds of aftermarket features were incorporated early on, saying, "We did a lot of things with the product, whether it was hot technology with a DVD player or OnStar navigation, that appealed to that market, that made the driver feel invincible in trendsetting and in technological advances." They paid special attention to urban culture to drive innovation and customization.

The eventual assumption—and it was correct—was that by including the customized elements into cars rolling off the line they would make those assets infinitely desirable in suburbia.

While all of those cues were incorporated in ongoing design and special advertising, there was also an effort not to be too heavy-handed in designing what GM thought was urban. Mike Bentley said that his colleague Susan Dockerly set the tone on that. She could have called up every hip-hop record label and offered them a fleet of Escalades. Instead, when the calls started coming in, they were able to cultivate relationships with musicians and athletes.

"If you push it," Mike said, "you are brokering the conversation the wrong way. Marketing has to be conscious of that. Marketing is about facilitating the conversation. We wouldn't want to be seen sponsoring a hip-hop festival and having Escalade all over it and then inviting people from the suburbs. It's about authentically having things happen." Seeding Cadillac into top music videos, for instance, became a much more authentic strategy without hitting consumers over the head or being phony.

Is this conversation between marketer and consumer— via the strobe of pop culture—about a product or a mind-set?

Indeed, it's about both. But without the respect and willingness to honor the mind-set and to really see where culture is going, the product and its symbolism become seriously diminished.

When I asked Mike Bentley where he saw this tan mind-set going and what he predicted for the future of hip-hop/urban culture's impact on commerce, he expounded on ideas that were certainly in my understanding. Mike observed, "Urban culture is blending with digital culture." In fact, he went on, "Digital culture is going to be the next phase of urban culture. Digital enables a guy living anywhere to feel a sense of connectivity. Hip-hop has gone from being a local indigenous culture to being the first global culture." Mike saw the escalation of how hip-hop/urban is being driven by digital culture (in all media, but mainly social networks like Twitter and Facebook) as further killing off the demographic boxes describing types of culture. This was the conquering of castle walls separating populations. Bentley's prediction? "I think it's going to become 'culture' rather than 'urban culture.' It's going to lose the word 'urban.' It will be the new normal."

How, you may well ask, does this translate into marketing strategies? Well, that's where you take out the cards up your sleeve and play with the possibilities of tanning and reverse engineering.

McDonald's: Unbranding and Recoding

In 2003, when I first went to Oak Brook, Illinois, to meet the McDonald's marketing team, they didn't have to tell me that the brand was in trouble. The global fast-food chain had maintained market dominance for decades by continuously building on their core story—tying back to the late fifties and early sixties, when a mind-set of reinvention had put the golden arches on the map and made them the successful symbol of founder Ray Kroc's refusal to bet the odds. With the crazy belief that he could take the template of the local success of one hamburger joint in San Bernardino, California, owned by the McDonald brothers, and turn it into a national phenomenon, Kroc—who was a marketing guy, an independent sales rep, and had never built a franchise even in his dreams—did just that. And the brand had never abandoned his four keys for organizational success: quality, value, service, and cleanliness. To reaffirm an earlier section we covered, Kroc also famously said, "We're not in the burger business, we're in show business."

However, by the early '00s the global powerhouse that McDonald's had become was no longer fresh and new and running off the energy of innovation that had first made it a mass-market success. The brand was now entrenched in the realm of the Happy Meal, PlayPlace, mothers, young children, and families. And as the kids who grew up on that were becoming young adults, they were not staying loyal to the golden arches. Instead, competitors like Subway, KFC, and Taco Bell had been keeping up with the times and becoming more popular among hip young adults— urban/suburban/global.

Mickey D's problem was more loaded than having lost proximity to cool. It was possible that in adopting family-friendly marketing, the brand had unwittingly taken on baggage that was repelling the young adult target. A reinvention or brand extension or radical disruption would be tough because it wouldn't be authentic. Plus, any reboot focused on appealing to a hipper mind-set would risk compromising their core consumer base, comprised mostly of moms and young kids.

With those concerns, we came up with a series of revolutionary strategies that together would honor the essential brand values and respect core consumers while decoding and reinterpreting the same values in a way that would speak to global youth culture. It was about storytelling and revealing what had been cool all along. Where there were important changes and innovations to be made, the storytelling would be about the fun variety of new multicultural flavors and choices at McDonald's, and about loving a healthy, active lifestyle.

Reverse engineering helps tell the story and make it credible— by first putting it in a pop culture form that isn't connected in any way to the brand. Why do that? Because of the glut of product placement in various pop culture platforms, our savvy urban consumer is not as impressed anymore. On the other hand, the framing of fresh ideas and trends that are seeded into the consumption of pop culture and then can later reverse back to the brand is a much more invitational approach. Specifically, for McDonald's we were going to tell their story to the audience of teens and adults who were the most important market spending force for all the combined industries of entertainment—through music, the most powerful pop culture medium of all.

The team at McDonald's was hesitant. My point that our consumer target might be turned off by traditional means—that they were no longer compelled by seeing a celebrity holding a product and saying, "Buy this because I do"—made sense to them. When I made my pitch for music, they assumed I meant that we would have a celebrity doing the usual canned jingle.

Not exactly. There was another approach we could take: commission a song to be performed by an iconic artist; promote it months before McDonald's campaign; and at the same time start promoting the marketing slogan. We would follow the example of marketing movies and television shows. We agreed that if the song did well in the marketplace and the slogan hit the right chords, both would serve as a backdrop for a worldwide ad campaign that pulled out every stop.

The initiative was big, and so was the gamble. With Larry Light, the brand's chief marketing officer, championing these strategies that reflected his ideas about brand journalism, as I mentioned earlier, along with the support of then chief marketing officer of North America, Bill Lamar, and Marlena Peleo-Lazar, chief creative officer, everyone took a leap of faith that I know Ray Kroc would have applauded. For the first time ever, McDonald's would launch a campaign simultaneously throughout the world with a narrative that could translate into every market. The one artist I was certain could carry that weight on his shoulders and make it look like a stroll in the park was Justin Timberlake.

Many of my marketing and recording industry peers were shocked. To reach a global, multicultural, hip-hop-consuming audience, why not have an artist more aligned with the accepted understanding of urban sensibilities? Some looked at the brand values and wondered if a white kid from Tennessee who had risen to fame as the multiplatinum top-selling lead singer of the pop vocal group N'SYNC was the guy who could pull this off. Yeah, Justin Timberlake, who had blown us all out of the water just the previous year with his debut solo album, which had vivid hip-hop influences—and went on to sell seven million copies. Besides being a gifted singer, dancer, and actor, his cross-cultural appeal as a personality, with his self-effacing sense of humor and cool, smart attitude, was exactly what we wanted. He was the personification of the tan mind-set, appealing to a multicultural music audience, and, frankly, someone that McDonald's moms and children would love too.

The brand was used to celebrities being much more product friendly—like holding the burger and eating the fries. Meanwhile, Justin wanted an organic relationship and didn't think that overdoing the product angle would be necessary for consumers to realize that he was down with McDonald's. We had some give-and-take in the negotiations that followed that was somewhat nerve-wracking, but a marriage was made. I knew that Justin Timberlake was the right one to carry what McDonald's wanted to portray as their welcoming lifestyle.

For the team to produce the song that was going to make or break the strategy, we went with the Neptunes—a.k.a. Pharrell Williams and Chad Hugo—who had already produced tracks for Justin on his debut album. Music being the great equalizer that it is, the team was likewise tan: Timberlake, a white southerner now known for his soulful sound; Williams, African-American, a hip-hop artist, writer, designer, and producer; and Hugo, a Filipino-American who is a saxophonist, pianist, and guitarist. Both Williams and Hugo had been members of the funk/rock band known as NERD. A tasty recipe, I'd say.

In August 2003, the history-making collaboration was released by Jive Records and it shot up the charts instantly, propelled by an unforgettable five-note song mnemonic:

"I'm lovin' it, dah-dah-dah-dah-dah. I'm lovin' it, dah-dah-dah-dah-dah."

DDB Germany, a phenomenal advertising firm, was responsible

for coming up with the overall concept and the inimitable slogan while I handled the music part of the campaign. Drawing from my background in the record business, I can attest to the fact that no stone was left unturned in the relentless pursuit of airplay—on urban, rock, and Top 40 radio platforms. As the song grew in popularity, so too did the adoption of the catch-phrase "I'm lovin' it."

Even before we went to the next phase of the marketing, where the reverse engineering would hopefully do its magic, it was astonishing in the best of all ways to hear the saying come up in common everyday exchanges—an expression of approval, of enjoyment, an answer to the question of how you felt about something that raised your vibrational, emotional status.

Adding to the appeal was the music video, which used camera work done in a "run and gun" guerilla style of shooting, capturing a documentary feeling with footage of real reactions from fans as they saw Justin Timberlake, an international superstar, just walking the streets of New York. Even before the video made its premiere on MTV's *Total Request Live,* the buzz began on the Internet—not only that this was cool footage but also, breaking news, that there was a possibility, according to rumors, that the song and video would be the next marketing campaign for McDonald's.

Did this bring everything to a grinding halt? Not at all. The story dominated entertainment news. The syndicated television show *Access Hollywood* confirmed the rumors hours before the premiere and got exclusive behind-the-scenes footage of the making of the video. How were we liking that? We were lovin' it! Once the video debuted, it shot up the chart on MTV, eventually peaking at number two on *Total Request Live.* In 2003 the cultural connection with the MTV audience was a marketing coup. Not only were youths receiving McDonald's new message, they were the ones propelling it forward!

Within days of the video release, McDonald's made two global announcements. First and foremost, the brand would be the presenting sponsor for Justin Timberlake's European tour, called "Justified and Lovin' It." Additionally, the company officially announced that it had indeed entered into a partnership with

Timberlake to use the title of his song as McDonald's new world-wide brand tagline. Because this was the first global campaign in the fifty-year history of McDonald's, the news was announced and covered in most of the 118 countries where the brand does business. The media attention was beyond anything we could have dreamed possible.

With the television advertising that followed, another team came in to do the spots that maintained the theme of mind-set over product, showing vignettes that appealed to hipper families and youthful adult consumers. No focus on burgers, we were selling lifestyles—just different faces and attitudes. Between the song, the video, and the follow-up commercials, a gathering of community was created that spoke to over forty-seven million customers around the world—speaking different languages and living in different environments. The tanning effect had gone global with the idea of a shared mental complexion, a like-mindedness that celebrated differences and connection. All had the same aspirations. The world was all hip and cool. The world was many colors, one mind-set. And, of course, we all loved McDonald's.

Continuing the momentum, McDonald's sent out street teams to distribute fun branded merchandise with Timberlake's name and their own—showing up in heavily trafficked neighborhoods of the company's largest ten markets: the United States, Brazil, China, Japan, France, Germany, Spain, the United Kingdom, Australia, and Canada.

McDonald's used street teams to extend the message and maintain an ongoing conversation with its customers, in a manner that was authentic to consumers. Justin Timberlake more than did his part, making key appearances at events and at select McDonald's restaurants. He walked the fine line of coming off cool and real, yet at the same time not offending or harming McDonald's investor base or its reputation.

The "I'm Lovin' It" lifestyle campaign had broken so many rules and had been so successful that I'm sure there were many at McDonald's who doubted if it could ever be topped. When they approached Translation in 2004 about how they could re-create the excitement of Justin Timberlake's launch, we switched the approach and aligned the brand with Destiny's Child—with

Beyoncé Knowles, then the lead singer of the three-girl group that had already sold forty million records worldwide and were seen as iconic in the worlds of entertainment, fashion, and music.

McDonald's thus became the sponsor of Destiny's Child's upcoming worldwide tour, which was aptly entitled "Destiny Fulfilled and Lovin' It." The group was enlisted to serve as the global ambassadors of McDonald's annual fund-raiser, World Children's Day. When the album, *Destiny Fulfilled,* was released in November 2004, there had been rumors that it would be the trio's final release and fans rushed to purchase it; eventually six million copies were sold worldwide. With rave reviews as well, by the time that the tour started in the spring of 2005, the concert tickets were among the most coveted in recent years.

The "I'm Lovin' It" lifestyle and mind-set, alive and well at this writing, secured McDonald's position as a brand and industry leader—because executives were brave enough to lead with ethnic insights and embrace the rich psychographics of a tanner America. The inclusive thinking allowed urban youth culture to come back to the cool that had been there from the start, and McDonald's to offer new menu choices, with more diverse flavors and healthier options (smoothies, salads, snack wraps), while keeping core consumers feeling better about healthy, more active lifestyles for themselves and their children.

Some of these changes came about, rightfully so, in response to the negative reports from health organizations about rampant youth obesity plus widespread criticism of fast food in general and McDonald's in particular, especially with the films *Super Size Me* (2004) and *Food, Inc.* (2008). Given those dynamics, we weren't sure what kind of fiscal read there would be to show how effective the marketing had been for the "I'm Lovin' It" campaign. Lo and behold, in 2008 McDonald's stock hit $67 a share, a 198 percent improvement from the $22.45 that it was trading at five years earlier.

Meanwhile, one of the ongoing changes being discussed that was near and dear to my heart came from the stories that I heard when we interviewed McDonald's employees who lived in urban neighborhoods. I was convinced that if the brand really wanted to align itself meaningfully to the lives of millennials and remain aspirational, they had to do something about the outdated, conservative uniforms. Kids told me in interview after interview that the outfits were an embarrassment. They were so ashamed, in fact, they would change out of their uniform to walk home. No one wanted to be seen in their neighborhood in clothes like that—for fear of being teased, bullied, or worse. Addressing the dire issue, I asked executives, "Why not dress employees in the kind of apparel that would make them proud to come to work and that would appeal to the consumers we're trying to attract?" When I presented recommendations of people to design the new uniforms, I showed sketches from the same creative designers behind the Sean John clothing line and Russell Simmons's Phat Farm apparel label.

As the McDonald's executives were debating, the media predicted that Translation had really pushed the envelope too far this time. The July 4, 2005, issue of *Advertising Age* had a Ronald McDonald dressed in sweat pants, with a baseball cap turned sideways and a huge gold dollar sign hanging around his neck. The headline read: PHAT FEEDER DOWN WITH DIDDY.

And in the nationally syndicated cartoon *The Boondocks*, cartoonist Aaron McGruder drew his two main characters, Huey and Riley, engaged in the following exchange:

Huey: "Steve Stoute says McDonald's is a lifestyle brand."

Riley: "Sounds like somebody might be smoking a little McCrack."

Hey, you know that you're working in the business of culture when you start becoming noticed by culture. My behind-the-scenes cover was clearly blown.

And pretty soon the uniforms were updated. These experiences validated what I knew about the scope and power—and pitfalls—of tanning that had proven itself to the world. Cool is . . . getting to say, *Yeah, we have arrived.*

Fully activated, feeling invincible, the millennial generation with the shared mental complexion was also ready for a departure—to flex its muscle not just in the marketplace but in the voting booth.

PART THREE

THE FUTURE OF THE TAN WORLD

(nav·i·gā·tion)
[*nav*-ih-**gey**-shuhn]

a) theory, practice and technology of charting a course for
a ship, aircraft or spaceship b) a channel

CHAPTER 9

1520 SEDGWICK AVENUE–
1600 PENNSYLVANIA AVENUE

In May 2007 a group of South Bronx residents, concerned about the fact that rents were being raised in their poorly maintained hundred-unit building, made a startling discovery. Thanks to various search engines they'd been using to learn more about the company that owned the building—and its predatory practices—every time one of them plugged in their address, 1520 Sedgwick Avenue, countless hits referred to the building as "the birthplace of hip-hop." Until they decided to reach out for help from affordable-housing advocates and do the research, none of them would have had any idea that right there in their very own rec room, still in the building—although unusable because of needed repairs—DJ Kool Herc, a.k.a. Clive Campbell, had started the party that turned into a global phenomenon.

Advocates and residents then teamed up to try to make the building a national landmark in the hopes of gaining attention from city officials as well as from prominent hip-hop figures. At issue in 2007 was the fear that the owners of the building—who had opted out of a city-wide program that helped subsidize rent-controlled apartments for low-income families—would let conditions get worse and then sell to the highest bidder, who, in turn, would fix up the building but kick out tenants who couldn't afford the exorbitantly higher rents. Actually, the following year, the building was sold and, true to the pattern, living conditions worsened. There were complaints of rats and roaches everywhere, floorboards missing, and unpassable stairwells. In spite of all the attention, progress was slow. But then, finally, in September 2010, through the efforts of city, state, and federal housing authorities, it was announced that the building would be purchased and refurbished as the centerpiece of a new partnership between public and private concerns to provide decent, affordable housing to poor and middle-income families across the five boroughs of New York City.

Early in the coverage of this story, I had been shocked that a cultural landmark, one that had played such an important role in many of our lives, could have been so easily overlooked and forgotten. At the same time, when word of the tenants' plight surfaced in 2007, and *The New York Times* and other media were reporting about hip-hop as an institution with a vibrant, influential history, it was uplifting to see how many people felt connected and proud to belong to the diverse worldwide congregation. The idea that our culture even had its own monument, despite its disrepair, was a clarion call to everyone and anyone who had aligned with the movement at any time in their lives, past or present. Suddenly, 1520 Sedgwick Avenue—and the August night in 1973 when the first party rocked the building—became a touchstone for just how far the diverse global hip-hop community had come.

I also learned something very interesting when I was reading the stories that came out in these recent years. While I knew that Cindy Campbell (Herc's sister) had been involved in helping organize and market the first house party, I did not know the real reason that she—not her brother—came up with the idea. As Cindy told *The New York Times* in 2007, the venture was something she "dreamed up as a way for her to get some extra money for back-to-school clothes." But not just to look cool and fit in.

Cindy Campbell explained, "I didn't want to go to Fordham Road to buy clothes because you'd go to school and see everybody with the same thing on. . . . I wanted to go to Delancey Street and get something unusual."

That one comment speaks volumes about why the music that came out of those parties mattered so much, why it had practical relevance in the lives of the teens who were part of making it happen. Cindy Campbell didn't want to stay put. She wanted the means to challenge the assigned demographics and get down to lower Manhattan.

Today that might not sound so revolutionary. But almost forty years ago, it was definitely going against the grain. It's a reminder that, as much as aspiration drives culture, it is oppression that breeds resourcefulness—which in turn breeds empowerment, economic, social, and political.

Hip-hop, let us then acknowledge, came about to serve a higher purpose, to be a cultural bridge to the promised land of what America's founders dreamed. I believe it did as much for civil rights as any other force since Dr. Martin Luther King Jr. And the bridge wasn't just for people of color, for the impoverished and the oppressed. As DJ Kool Herc said about his first party and the mix of music that was played, "It wasn't a black thing. It was a 'we' thing." Truly, hip-hop was marked as a color-blind space.

Tanning is also a "we" thing—the same "we" that could look back and say, "Yes We Did," when it came to electing a president. For that reason, I like to think of all the groundbreaking done in the early years and of 1520 Sedgwick Avenue as both the birthplace of hip-hop and where the road to 1600 Pennsylvania Avenue for our forty-fourth president of the United States took an auspicious turn.

While much has been said and written about the historic campaign that helped put Barack Obama in the White House, a few lessons from a cultural perspective are worth revisiting—for both their marketing insights and, hopefully, their most cherished American values.

The Rule of Three

On the evening of November 7, 2000, at 9:04 P.M. Eastern Time, Reuters News Service published the headline BLACK VOTERS KEY TO GORE WIN IN FLORIDA. Al Gore had earned a stunning 94 percent of the African-American vote in Florida, as well as a majority of the Hispanic vote. For the nearly 60 million Americans who would be counted as having voted for Al Gore (48.38 percent of the popular vote versus 47.87 percent for George W. Bush), triumph was short-lived.

Strange and sinister things suddenly began to happen—including the denial of requests for legal recounts amid evidence of as many as eighty-five thousand black and minority names being scrubbed from voter rolls for alleged felony convictions (95 percent of which turned out to be speeding tickets or fabrications). Thirty-six thousand newly registered Democratic voters who had signed up at the DMV never made it onto the rolls. And when a recount was attempted, the GOP hired busloads (as confirmed by ABC News) of young operatives to stop the process.

In a later legal review of the facts by Spencer Overton of Florida State University, who addressed the issue of race in the election, these points were established:

> In the 2000 presidential election, African Americans made up only 16% of the voting population in Florida but cast 54% of the ballots rejected in automatic machine counts ("machine-rejected ballots"). Across the state, automatic machines rejected 14.4% of the ballots cast by African Americans, but only 1.6% of the ballots cast by others.

Later studies conducted by the likes of the Massachusetts Institute of Technology as to how these patterns manifested in other states around the country suggested that extreme irregularities produced as many as two to six million uncounted votes.

While many of these details were lost in the shuffle, most everyone got the memo as to what happened on December 12 when, by a five-to-four decision, the Supreme Court of the United States of America found in favor of George W. Bush's argument that a complete recount would violate the equal protection clause of the Fourteenth Amendment. A vast majority of legal scholars protested the decision and its tortured logic, as well as political bias. But the Florida recount was immediately stopped—an act without precedent in American justice—and the presidency was effectively given to George W. Bush.

Whatever this meant politically was yet to come. But culturally the ground shifted immediately. On that December day when the verdict was handed down, it caused an instantaneous mental tanning moment for a significant percentage of the sixty million Americans who had just been disenfranchised by having their votes not counted. For a lot of white nonminority voters, the feeling that I heard being expressed was *Oh yeah, now I get it, now I know what discrimination is.*

Who was going to right this wrong? For urban youth culture and leading hip-hop voices, that question was a call to action. In the past, part of what had defined the movement was less about political activism and more about using lyrics to speak "truth to power." There were exceptions. Rock the Vote, a nonpartisan organization founded in the early nineties, had been reaching out through artists from across the musical spectrum, who had helped add significant numbers of young voters for both parties. Russell Simmons, an early activist who believed in the importance of young people engaging in the political process, had organized Rap the Vote prior to the 2000 election.

At colleges and universities in the early nineties there were on-campus hip-hop communities and student organizations that had, in fact, been instrumental in helping bring South African apartheid to an end by working to mobilize unions, municipal pension funds, and American corporations to pull out their investments in the regime—until political change was accomplished.

Yet for all its influence culturally and in the marketplace, hip-hop's countercultural stance—and its innate distrust of political institutions—made the idea of organizing around a system that appeared to be unjust anyway, more or less, a fool's errand. Why not seek power in the boardroom and through economic means rather than the community-organizing route, as some might say? Others, like Russell Simmons, again, and Sean "Puffy" Combs, didn't agree. What's more, the dissatisfaction with George W. Bush was coming up in a lot of the rap songs that reflected what was going on in people's lives. Rather than giving in and letting 2000 happen all over again, 2004 became a landmark election in terms of rallying the youth vote. Between Russell's Hip-Hop Summit Action Network and concerts headlined by Kanye West and 50 Cent, a viral video about the importance of registering to vote with Eminem, along with Puffy's "Vote or Die" efforts with Citizen Change, voters between the ages of twenty-one and thirty went to the polls close to twenty-one million strong. The increase was 4.6 million additional young voters—up 18.4 percent.

In 2000 young voters had broken 48 percent for Gore and 46 percent for Bush. By 2004 the gap was 55 percent of millennial voters casting their ballots for John Kerry versus 45 percent for George W. Bush. In terms of tanning, this was proof that the cultural shift was having political reverberations. More than half of the new young voters, as a matter of fact, were African-American and Hispanic.

To the dismay of Puffy and Russell, a lot of the mainstream media used John Kerry's loss in the '04 election as proof that youth in general weren't showing up and that hip-hop was not the rallying force it was supposed to have been. Both were quoted in the press crying foul. Puffy was accused of being defensive and claiming there was a conspiracy in the media. It bothered him so much that there was no applause for the increase in young voter turnout that he was quoted as saying, "This generation gets knocked down so much for being irresponsible, that this generation doesn't care, that this generation isn't interested in things that are serious. Then, something like this happens—four million or so more votes! Young black and Latino kids are voting for the first time, and what are folks saying? I'm not being defensive. I know the truth."

According to media analysts, the reason that the youth turnout didn't deliver the vote for John Kerry had to do with the higher-percentage turnouts in all the other demographics as well. Of course, these percentages were based on exit polls and estimates that made certain assumptions. Some of the same voting irregularities that were seen in 2000 were alleged to have happened in 2004—leaving lingering questions.

Even with the disappointment of Kerry's loss and the dispute over the impact of the youth vote, there was one question that had been answered. Over the past two elections, focused efforts in turning out the youth vote were producing meaningful results. And for those youth and younger adult voters who hadn't forgotten the disenfranchisement of 2000, the results were gaining ground on behalf of Democrats.

Then, in August 2005, Hurricane Katrina sent the floodwaters over the levees in New Orleans, submerging most of the city, causing $85 billion in devastation, killing thousands, many of whom were never found, and stranding those who couldn't get out of the city in time, most of them people of color, poor and without resources. The federal government's shockingly delayed response was not only ineffectual, it was criminal.

In spite of the reluctance of the media to initially embrace such an assertion, it would be painfully revealed as events unfolded that were hard to spin. Why? Because a) the public was witnessing them happen in real time with their own eyes and ears, and b) the on-the-ground reporting was based in facts that were incontrovertible. The administration's later claim that they never could have imagined the ultimate devastation that took place, and George W. Bush's statement, "I don't think anyone could have anticipated the breach of the levees," were simply lies.

As early as Friday, August 26, when Governor Kathleen Blanco declared a state of emergency in Louisiana and when governors of all the gulf states convened a joint task force requesting assistance from the Pentagon, every worst case scenario was outlined. At five A.M. Saturday morning when Katrina was upgraded to a Category 3 hurricane and Governor Blanco announced, "I have determined that this incident is of such severity and magnitude that effective response is beyond the capabilities of the state and affected local governments," there was no ambiguity. This was even echoed in the statement from the White House that it was designating FEMA, specifically, as "authorized to identify, mobilize, and provide at its discretion, equipment and resources necessary to alleviate the impacts of the emergency."

On Sunday, August 28, when Katrina was upgraded to Category 4 at two A.M. and then to Category 5 at seven A.M., President Bush was specifically warned of possible levee failure by the National Hurricane Center Director, Dr. Max Mayfield. That afternoon, the National Weather Service's special warning described the nightmare that would follow a dead-on hit from a Category 4 or 5 hurricane, saying that most of the area would be uninhabitable for weeks or longer, that homes would be destroyed or severely damaged, that power outages would last weeks, and that "water shortages [would] make human suffering incredible by most modern standards." Meanwhile, the media ran headlines alerting the entire nation of forecasters' fears that storm waters would top the levees after the hurricane had come through. With a massive evacuation under way, New Orleans Mayor Nagin said, "We're facing the storm most of us have feared." In no uncertain terms, he emphasized that it would be an unprecedented event.

After the National Guard requested seven hundred buses from FEMA, only one hundred were sent. Of those left behind— most of them people of color, poor, families with children, elderly, and disabled—some stayed in their homes to ride out the storm while the Superdome filled up with thirty thousand evacuees and only a day and a half's worth of food and supplies for all of them.

As a Category 4 hurricane, Katrina made landfall at seven A.M. on Monday, August 29, and though the media exhaled for a second with the news that the city had dodged a bullet, within a half hour that relief was canceled by the announcement that the levees had been breached. The Associated Press reported that the Bush administration was notified of the realization of this worst case scenario; the White House acknowledged it along with twenty-eight various other government agencies. With harrowing stories of floodwaters rapidly rising, pump stations breaking down, and accounts published of concerns voiced to President Bush (then on vacation at his ranch in Crawford, Texas)—by none other than the guy with no experience heading up FEMA, Michael Brown—it seemed the commander-in-chief had other priorities. Announcing that he had put the matter in the hands of Homeland Security, President Bush told reporters that he was getting on Air Force One to go discuss immigration with John McCain. Before noon, he was posing for a photo-op with McCain and his birthday cake. The president's next stops included resorts in Arizona and California to promote the new Medicare prescription bill he had just signed and that night a commitment to go early to bed—without a word about the American city that was in the process of drowning.

Although Brown had ordered one thousand National Guard troops to the region, he had given them two days to get there. In spite of what was seen next through horrific images of people stranded on rooftops, snakes and alligators devouring people, countless missing persons, and the loss of people's pets, plus violence erupting amid the chaos, the response on Tuesday from the Pentagon was that there were adequate units in the gulf region to handle any problems. As for the USS *Bataan* that was sitting offshore ready to serve with the ability to make up to one hundred thousand gallons of water a day, its own hospital operating rooms, doctors, food, and beds for six hundred, it was left at sea and empty. Seemingly oblivious, President Bush on Tuesday afternoon was playing guitar with a popular country-western musician.

On Wednesday, August 31, after FEMA workers warned Brown that people were dying at the Superdome, he was unable to respond because, his press secretary noted, he needed more time for his restaurant meal. The *Los Angeles Times* described conditions that day, with thousands still trapped at the Superdome, as if out of a horror movie. With no sanitation, the smell was said to be "overwhelming." Walls had bloodstains on them, bathrooms were littered with crack vials, and people had no choice but to urinate on the floor. Among those who had died was a man who had leapt to his death unable to live with what he had seen. Children were reported to be among rape victims.

Eighty thousand men, women, kids, and babies were estimated to be stranded in New Orleans, as Reuters reported. Wednesday afternoon, George W. Bush flew over the city in Air Force One, at the same time that Homeland Security issued a statement praising the federal government's response to the disaster.

On Thursday, the administration put its energies into damage control, asserting that they never knew the levees could be breached and, in the case of Michael Brown, that no one had told him about the violence and about people dying in the Superdome. The following day, White House activity was focused on blaming local officials for the bungled response. Karl Rove was in charge of this PR, yes, but it was the president of the United States who two days later told *The Washington Post* that Governor Blanco had never declared a state of emergency.

Five days after the levees broke Bush flew to the Mississippi Gulf Coast and famously congratulated "Brownie" for doing a "heckuva job," staging photos with workers and appearing to cheer them on.

And so, while watching what looked like the end of the world unfolding, the final straw for me was when the White House released a statement from Bush that he had visited with Senator Trent Lott, who had lost his house and was determined to rebuild. The president added, "And I'm looking forward to sitting on the porch." This must have been the last straw for a lot of the media too. *Time* said that the comments were "astonishingly tone-deaf to the homeless black citizens still trapped in the postapocalyptic water world of New Orleans."

These were the events that preceded a telethon held on Saturday, September 3, that featured a most diverse group of artists—in tanning terms they were polyethnic, multigenerational, and from across the musical spectrum—all of whom wanted to lend their talents to the effort to raise money for the victims. After six days of witnessing unacceptable images showing people of color poor or without resources, left and abandoned by the federal government, when comedian Mike Myers of *Austin Powers* fame and Kanye West came out to speak, Kanye was moved to go off script and say what was on a lot of people's minds—"George Bush doesn't care about black people."

The moment those words came out of Kanye's mouth it was, for lack of a better phrase, the shot heard round the world. He wasn't voicing a minority opinion. There was a clear lack of concern for humanity. Overwhelmingly, much of the public—white, black, and other—couldn't have agreed more. All at once a majority of Americans of good conscience, regardless of political persuasion, knew that a change needed to come and had to come—that this was not America. The tanning, it turned out, was in the shared grief, shared outrage.

It was the following November 2006, during the midterm elections, that the political climate change took many pundits by surprise. With Democrats regaining control of both the House of Representatives and the Senate, the elections were interpreted as an expression of discontent with Bush and the war in Iraq. But they were also historic in terms of how many voters under the age of thirty had voted, compared to the previous midterms—two million more. And what no one could disregard this time was the fact that they voted more emphatically Democratic than ever before—voting for Democrats by a 22 percent margin over Republicans.

By 2007, with the Democratic presidential field wide-open, I started hearing the political marketing principle known as the rule of three—meaning that if an unaffiliated voting cohort consistently votes for one party over the other for three successive elections, they could be counted on for life.

Though I have no certain knowledge of how Barack Obama considered the rule of three when he was debating over whether to run or not, I just have the feeling it played into his decision making. Did he expect that in the primary contest he would win 60 percent of young voters versus 40 percent for Hillary Clinton? Probably not. But I think he knew that once they were in his corner and had his back, he was going all the way.

Subtext Matters

One of these days, I'd like to play cards with Wolf Blitzer. I'd clean up. The man cannot keep a poker face. I'll never forget hurrying over to Jay-Z's place to watch the returns of the 2008 presidential race on CNN with him and his wife and other friends and sharing the experience of seeing history unfold—history our generation had helped make happen! Wolf very clearly knew how things were trending in Obama's favor from the exit polling but wasn't allowed to say anything. Still, he was practically telegraphing the results. Great, I thought, one of the most exciting moments in many of our lifetimes, and Wolf Blitzer is making it anticlimactic! Well, almost. The truth is that none of us could forget what happened in 2000 and I certainly wasn't going to have that glass of champagne until it had been declared Obama had won by a landslide.

Waiting for those results, I thought back over the important roles that hip-hop and the tan mind-set had played in changing culture over the years and in helping shape the environment in which Barack Obama could be a legitimate candidate. I also thought about one of the aspects that made Obama a transformative candidate, and that was how culturally curious and conversant he was with people from all kinds of backgrounds and age groups.

The truth is that he wasn't aligned with one culture over the other, but rather showed a respect for all. Such evidence was on display during a moment on the campaign trail after he got roughed up in one of the tougher primary battles. On that occasion, Obama had reassured his supporters with a gesture of confidence that needed no translation—taking his hand to his shoulder and flicking imaginary dirt off it. If you had never seen that bit of nonverbal urban slang, perhaps when an athlete did it or when a hip-hop artist employed it as a gesture, you would still get it. It's about being confident without being arrogant—which, by the way, is the perfect pitch subtext for every and any marketing campaign ever mounted.

So that brings up another question that I pondered on election night as the results were coming in. If the cultural mixing of tanning, as we have seen, was being successfully harnessed by the marketing world, to what extent did the brilliance of the Obama campaign draw from the same principles?

Offering a partial answer to that question, a few weeks earlier, on October 17, 2008, *Advertising Age* had published a potentially premature headline that read OBAMA WINS! They did not mean the presidential election. They were talking about *Ad Age*'s vote for Marketer of the Year. As determined by the hundreds of votes by advertising executives and leading brand-builders from companies large and small, Obama and his campaign team had "edged out runners-up Apple and Zappos.com" as well as "mega-brand Nike, turnaround story Coors and Mr. Obama's rival, Senator John McCain."

For starters, there was a degree of disbelief in how swiftly the campaign had made a leading presidential candidate out of an Illinois senator previously best known as a "skinny kid with a funny name," as he referred to himself in his 2004 Democratic Convention speech for John Kerry, and for his outspoken opposition to the Iraq War before the invasion. Many marketers noted that the campaign would be studied for years to come, particularly the use of social networking and the organizing tools that had been created for engaging volunteers and voters. Journalists quoted in the article, like Jon Fine of *BusinessWeek,* who said in amazement, "It's the f**kin' Web 2.0 thing," recognized that everything achieved in total for the campaign was groundbreaking.

The fact that a presidential campaign had won that year over Apple was very telling. Apple's marketing genius, after all, can be seen in its consistency, a brand attribute conveyed in subtext in all their advertising. And Zappos, the dark horse that surprised a lot of experts by coming in third after Apple, had taken mind-set marketing to a new level by weaving the idea of "delivering happiness" into an online shoe business. Moreover, its name played well with agency executives hip to the power of Hispanic and multicultural consumers.

Obviously, an understanding of culture had been important to all of those brands and certainly was vital to the Obama campaign. But that was only scratching the surface. Looking more closely at the strategies that were used, however, revealed a more direct linkage to youth culture and the properties of tanning. That was apparent when I revisited the speech Obama had delivered at the 2004 Democratic Convention and looked at the main theme that first put the spotlight of history on him. It was the thesis of a like-mindedness, about celebrating differences and connection, about sharing the same mental complexion while coming together and caring for one another:

It is that fundamental belief—I am my brother's keeper, I am my sister's keeper—that makes this country work. It's what allows us to pursue our individual dreams and yet still come together as one American family.

E pluribus unum: "Out of many, one."

Now even as we speak, there are those who are preparing to divide us—the spin masters, the negative ad peddlers who embrace the politics of "anything goes." Well, I say to them tonight, there is not a liberal America and a conservative America—there is the United States of America. There is not a black America and a white America and Latino America and Asian America— there's the United States of America.

Woven into the speech were other themes that resurfaced in his own presidential run: Obama's story and the idea of an American dream in need of rescue. There was a mention of the audacity of hope and a call to vote for change. But the real subtext of that speech and of his eventual campaign for president, if you were paying attention, was empowerment. That was a new marketing message, a new call to action, not to be a passive citizenry but to become involved in solving the problems of the day.

That was the message the young generation had been waiting to hear and that must have struck those who heard him in 2004 with the same dog-whistle effect that happened hearing hip-hop for the first time. He represented something different and not even political. He was authentic, believable, smart, cool, and aspirational. And young. And because he had spoken out against the invasion of Iraq at a time when it was not politically expedient to do so, he had some counterculture credibility too. Suddenly, as early as the spring of 2005, kids started showing up at rallies protesting the war or at Earth Day celebrations or at cultural events—in cities and suburbs alike—bearing home-made signs reading OBAMA '08.

Grassroots organizing, in its earliest stages, had begun even before the candidate had formed an exploratory committee. Like hip-hop, it was not a case of a leader founding a movement; rather it was about people creating a movement and summoning a leader. This then became fodder for media speculation that in turn handed marketing opportunities to the campaign when it prepared to launch.

From the coverage of how Team Obama evolved and how strategies were developed, including *The Audacity to Win* by campaign manager David Plouffe, I could see other lessons drawn from the manner in which a culture that started in a central location proliferated so rapidly. What the South Bronx was to hip-hop culture, the ground game the campaign built in Iowa would be to Obama's presidency. Plouffe writes about why so much energy was poured into that radical disruption phase, explaining, "From the get-go, it was clear we could not win if the caucus universe was the same as it was in 2004. . . . To win, we would have to attain the holy grail of politics—a fundamentally altered electorate." In going up against an odds-on favorite like Hillary Clinton or a popular figure like John Edwards, there was a comparison to the marketing world, as Plouffe described: "Say you are a business trying to expand your percent of market share against an established brand-name product. Your competitor's customers have been buying their products for decades and are unlikely to sample something new. How do you outsell that competitor without converting their customers? You have to recruit new buyers."

With that, Team Obama had the inspiration to grow the electorate with outreach to younger voters, more minorities, more independents, and Republicans who were open to the messages that an outsider candidate could offer. Basing the campaign in Chicago, in Obama's hometown, rather than in Washington, D.C., also provided important subtext to communicate to the public about a candidate who was taking a stance against the status quo. Much of the structure could then be built on community.

Volunteers—much like the street teams sharing mix tapes in the spread of hip-hop culture and street marketing teams representing brands interacting with consumers—were to become the fertilizer for the grassroots movement. What was being sold? Not a candidate but a mind-set—the belief that engagement in civic life worked to the betterment of all citizens. Volunteers not only helped organize communities in different locations in organic ways, like the spread of culture, but also grew the numbers rapidly, which naturally led to smaller-donor-base fund-raising and offered a person-to-person endorsement of the candidate. The campaign was careful not to create inauthentic messages or talking points for volunteers but instead encouraged them to speak from their hearts about how they had become involved.

In the past, architects of political campaigns had kept pop culture figures at arm's length—much in the same way that brands were once hesitant to align themselves with hip-hop figures. There was no such distancing for Obama, who not only understood the culture but met with those artists who wanted to do more and who had insights on multicultural outreach. The Obama team recognized that music, in particular, was, is, and will always be the barometer for marketing's impact because it's so immediate, such a touchstone for the audience. Not much can come close to the cultural immediacy of music unless it is presented as rooted in truth and emotion. Obama knew that, felt that, and honored it. Even before Obama had decided to run for office, he had met with community leaders and hip-hop figures to find the truth of what was happening in the inner cities.

Individuals like actress Kerry Washington, Mary J. Blige, Jay-Z, and Puffy played active roles in getting out the vote—at some points going to three cities a day to warm up the crowds at youth rallies and on college campuses. Kevin Liles, the music industry executive who had risen up through the ranks to become the head of Def Jam Records before going on to a senior position with Warner Music Group, was also extremely important as a bridge between younger voters and the campaign. Besides being someone who is passionate about political involvement, Kevin is someone who takes time to understand issues and their relevance to voters—keeping in mind the greater good.

Of course, the campaign's technological infrastructure and harnessing of it by and for volunteers was to evolve in creative ways from the start to the end of the campaign. No one had ever amassed a database of millions upon millions of e-mail addresses or cell phone numbers to be texted messages about when and where to go vote.

One of the most important elements of the planning, as David Plouffe pointed out, was not necessarily strategic—but it did project loud and clear as a welcoming invitation to all ages and backgrounds to come join in. And that was the intention: to make sure to have fun. The subtext had to do with the positive power of involvement for everyone. It also projected an important value for a future president who understood the tough times people were going through and would continue to face.

The tone of the campaign, as articulated by the candidate and by everyone on the team, especially chief strategist David Axelrod, was one of respect and calm. The "no-drama Obama" attitude had the subtext of what the country needed in a time of crisis. There was enough drama in real life such that political gamesmanship wasn't appealing. Toward the end of the primary season leading up to the convention there was unavoidable drama when the schism between Obama and Clinton voters began to take its toll on the party. The fact that the convention allowed the healing to take place in such a real, emotional, and public fashion—with Hillary Clinton's speech—was absolutely important for bridging the generational divide and to reassure those within the general electorate. The theme of unity was not strictly about the party but was the healing message for the nation. And then the roar of the crowd in its standing ovation before Bill Clinton's speech, which went on and on until he had to say, "I love this, but . . . ," reminded everyone, without hitting it on the head, that he really had been the first black president and played a significant role in the tanning of America. The truth is, there is only one person that you can name as someone without whom there would be no President Obama. And that is President Bill Clinton.

I could go on, of course, and talk about how visionaries like will.i.am took an Obama speech and did a remix on video with artists from all walks of culture, expressing the belief in possibilities. I could talk about how visual artists tapped deep into our psyches with logos and bumper stickers and portraiture that was so cool the Obama gear it inspired became enduring fashion. I could talk about the value of the tanning that paved the way for Obama's legitimacy as a candidate from people like Oprah Winfrey, Will Smith, and General Colin Powell. I could talk even more about how Bill Cosby and his all-American family on television that just happened to be black attuned the sensibilities of white, mainstream America to feel comfortable seeing an African-American family in the White House.

These kinds of tanning influences were important not only for helping Americans feel more accepting of a black presidential candidate but also for helping voters from different backgrounds to feel more accepting of each other. Certainly, they were meaningful in enabling African-Americans to believe that someone who looked like them could be president—and to see that voters who didn't look like them would agree.

Later on a study would look at how positive images had contributed to growth in overall feelings of happiness in the African-American community. Reported in *The New York Times*, it would show that in spite of terrible economic stagnation and an income gap—with blacks earning 35 percent less than whites (compared with three decades ago when they earned 40 percent less)—there was a marked improvement in happiness. Why this was the case wasn't clear, although the inference was that it reflected a significant reduction in the daily indignities of racism. At the same time, the happiness of people of color was associated with seeing images of themselves as aspirational and as being celebrated on television, rightfully so, for collective successes.

In 2008, the dynamic was there—that after years of seeing these images on television, or in movie scripts and commercial vignettes, that reflected what was going on in your own household, your imagination and visualization of possibilities were stimulated. This turned out to be the case for African-Americans, Caucasians, Latinos, Asians, and other groups, and more importantly for the growing numbers of individuals seeing themselves in multicultural polyethnic terms and of blended, mixed heritage. The timing was such that as the black community came into its own as a psychographically successful collective, a candidate stepped forward and also represented the reality and possibilities for other groups. Hispanic-Americans, the majority minority, are probably next in line.

Visible success for members of a minority group had been

necessary to open up the conversation for a serious minority candidate running for the most powerful office in the land. At the least, I think hip-hop helped create the open-minded relationship between individuals of different backgrounds that had a lot to do with white young Americans saying, *You know what? I don't have a problem and I'll vote for a black president.* Granted, it was not as shocking to the youth as it was to older generations. And there was some shock value for a lot of people, let's be frank. How so? a) It was shocking that he was a black guy, but b) forget that it was a black guy; older generations were shocked that youth were voting, regardless of color. They were used to their assumption that younger people didn't care.

Not too long after the election I would speak with a teacher who had some interesting observations about teenagers, both white and black, and their reactions to the fact that America was in a position to finally elect a black president. She was taken aback at first by the way that her students didn't think this was so earth-shattering. But then it struck her that previous generations had laid the cultural groundwork so well that thinking had truly changed and teenagers had the right to feel matter-of-fact, like—*why shouldn't this happen?* When I heard this teacher's insights, it confirmed for me that we really have done a very good job driving the culture forward and making it possible for popular thought to be in this tan state.

If the reaction of youth came as a surprise, so too did the level of engagement that young voters invested in bringing about political change. Did the general public expect those voters to think about the images they saw during Katrina and find them unacceptable? I don't think so. Thirty-five years earlier, it wouldn't have been noticed that a mostly black and poor city was allowed to drown. George W. Bush's mishandling of the crisis pulled the trigger for an uprising and set the wheels into motion for a transformative, healing leader to emerge. And with the youth vote, it was never that younger voters didn't have preferences in terms of candidates or their politics; the resistance to voting came from feeling your vote wasn't going to have an impact or that it couldn't change your circumstances. And now suddenly through a campaign of hope and empowerment that involved cultural heroes and popular artists there was a chance to effect change and control your destiny by getting involved. Ironically, the expansive thinking here in America that made Obama's candidacy real and possible was, in some countries, considered late. If they were shocked, it was in how long it had taken us. As much as we export culture and open up other minds and change habits elsewhere, as much as we are the *United* States, the youth generation was and is still needed to break down walls here. Obama was history's answer to where we needed to go next, a symbol of the tanning of America as much as the evidence of it.

No, we were not all arriving at this place of open- and like-mindedness together. And I think many boomers, white, black, and other, worried about that, maybe for justifiable reasons. Then, in the midst of the campaign, history was made when Barack Obama courageously looked at a nation and opened the floor for us to begin a conversation about race—because as painful and prolonged as it might be, not having the conversation was hurting us even more.

On the night of the election, it wasn't as if that conversation had been concluded. In fact, a year and a half into Obama's presidency—at this writing—there are times when it seems the intolerance has become more vocal and the conversation less civil. Not long ago, a right-wing talk radio host went on a crazy tirade using the "n" word repeatedly, later blaming it on rappers. Instead of apologizing and seeking help, the radio host ended a lengthy broadcast career, bitterly complaining about not having freedom of speech, totally insensitive to people of color in the audience that supported that career for years.

It's ironic to me that culture can be so threatening to certain political and media forces here in this country that they would seek to limit or demean anyone different from themselves. After all, America's number one export, the one thing we make right here in this country that nobody in the world can do better or take away from us, is our popular culture. We are powerful and enriched because of our diversity, because of what it produces: our music, our television, our movies, our design, our style, our technology, our sports, our games, our celebrities, our brands, and our unparalleled abundance of ingenuity, creativity, and resilience.

The other irony about racial and cultural differences and how we ultimately get beyond the divisions is that there is a generation that has already moved on, that stopped seeing color, ethnicity, religious persuasion, or sexual orientation as a determination in identity a while ago—if they ever did.

When polls closed on the West Coast and Wolf Blitzer could finally exhale and announce that Barack Obama had been elected the forty-fourth president of the United States, and then we watched the diverse gathering of a hundred thousand people in Chicago's Grant Park, it was the most beautiful sight to behold—people who were old, young, middle-aged, happy, serious, tearful, tired, exuberant, proud, and humble all at the same time.

The youth vote had given Obama a two-to-one victory over McCain, 66 percent to 34 percent. Analysts Michael Hais and Morley Winograd described the contribution of millennials as demonstrating the "political emergence of a new, large, and dynamic generation and the realignment of American politics for the next forty years." Unprecedented. Also noted about the youth vote was the diversity. Among young African-American voters, 95 percent supported Obama, as did 76 percent of young Latino voters and 54 percent of the white youth vote. Hais and Winograd stated, "Millennials cast ballots in larger numbers than young voters had in any recent presidential election." Out of the nearly five and a half million more voters that had been added since 2004, almost two-thirds were under thirty. "Young voters accounted for about seven million of Obama's almost nine million national popular vote margin over John McCain," they noted.

The final point made by the analysts was that while many were considering the vote of millennials for Obama as a one-time phenomenon, they had shown themselves to be as solidly behind progressive platforms, policies, and other progressive candidates as they were Barack Obama. No matter what any marketer's politics might be, or what subsequent elections have and will show, these '08 numbers should be heeded. This is the generation whose time has come. Without a doubt, economic changes mean they are being sorely tested for the first time in their lives. But they are also taking their destinies into their own hands, being resourceful, throwing their own parties, pushing past boundaries, summoning their own leaders—never betting the odds.

CHAPTER 10

TAN IS THE NEW COOL

In June 2010, *Rolling Stone* magazine featured Jay-Z on its cover with the headline right over his name reading KING OF AMERICA. The article included photos of him with his early mentor Jaz-O in 1989, one with LeBron James on the court, and another shot with Beyoncé at Coachella. Earlier in the year, when Jay had headlined Coachella—the international concert in Indio, California, a premier music festival for leading and indie rock bands—Beyoncé had graced the stage to do a duet with him on "Young Forever." If you've ever listened to the melody and paid attention to the words, maybe you would agree that it perfectly captures the spirit of wanting to hold on to the fleeting moment that is now—in a way that is both timeless and timely. There is a sadness within the celebration that acknowledges how hard life is and how suddenly it can all end—but of wanting to become embedded forever in a time when, to paraphrase, nobody grows old, the champagne is always cold, the music is good, and pretty girls stop by the 'hood. How does that not translate everywhere, anywhere?

Besides raves calling that number the highlight of the festival, the two connected just as meaningfully to the audience and the other acts by sticking around and offering raves in return. The crowd was mixed, nobody wearing their demographic badges or their musical preference badges. Some of the bands were older, some new and edgy as hell. The next time I talked to Jay-Z after that, his language was fresh and full of nuance that came from the indie rock world. More code-sharing and boundary-pushing, more ground on which to find common values.

Three years earlier the news of hip-hop colliding with indie rock in this way would have been groundbreaking. But that was then and this is now. Jay had paved the road already, doing hugely successful mash-ups like his duet with Linkin Park and his gripping live performance the previous year on the Grammys with Coldplay. Now, as Mike Bentley from GM had said, the labels are so ill fitting that it is time to start calling the rich output that is happening everywhere around the world with millennials and adjacent generations simply "culture."

When I followed up with Mike and asked him to elaborate, he described the brush of tanning as having shifted the balance in America, creating the urban mind-set for a growing percentage of the public, regardless of age. In addition to that he pointed out, "The majority of the population now lives in an urban environment rather than suburban and rural. We've become urbanized." In his industry, with what we were all seeing—especially given economic and energy crises shifting the focus to *need* marketing versus the *want* marketing of the past—it was easy to predict where values were headed. Urbanization and lives lived in closer proximity to one another were shaping the landscape for European-style smaller cars to dominate the streets. Adaptation. However, Mike noted that marketing the cool of brands, as always, would still look to culture to provide cues. And toward that end, he believed that hip-hop was going to continue to be that truth-telling force able to hold a mirror up to real needs in consumers' lives.

As we discussed this further, it was clear that cultural globalization—the counterpart to economic flattening—was giving rise to hip-hop music bubbling up in developed and developing nations, thus creating a global tanning effect in other nations. The countercultural voices coming from the poetry were being empowered to challenge color and class lines, in some countries, that had been in place for much longer than America has even been a country.

"The thing that gives me a lot of confidence," Mike Bentley said emphatically, "is that young people don't see it as white culture, African-American culture, or, in the UK, Caribbean culture or West Indian culture." Again, it's seen as just culture. "That is the future of hip-hop and urban culture—that's where it's going. Its influence has to grow," Mike said, and he admitted that it would be exciting to see another new form, another paradigm, come into being. Remembering "Rapper's Delight," he went on, "There haven't been new breakthroughs since 1979. What's the next thing that's coming along? Hip-hop seems remarkably enduring. I was listening to it in my twenties. My daughter's listening to it now." Other than rock music, which has a multigenerational following, Mike asked, "Can you think of another genre that's done that?"

Yeah, he's right, I can't. On the other hand, there are some generational language gaps connected to culture that still need better translating.

Jay-Z told me an interesting story about a visit to the home of an elected head of state when he was in Europe—French president Nicolas Sarkozy. Mr. Sarkozy invited Jay and his beautiful wife to his home for a delicious, elaborate luncheon with spectacular wine and wonderful chocolates. As the group moved from the table to the sitting room to enjoy cigars and more conversation, the president's twenty-three-year-old son joined them. As he walked into the room, the father apologized for his son's "french" braids. Apparently, Sarkozy's son was an avid fan of Allen Iverson and wore his hair in cornrows to embody the same youthful rebellion as his pop culture basketball-playing hero.

President Sarkozy didn't get the look. "Oh," he said, "why do you wear those dreadlocks?" Then the president proceeded to talk about how he had taken his son out to a fancy restaurant and had told him that people would be offended by an inappropriate hairstyle and would stare at him.

"And that is what happened," the president insisted. He described how there were stares from many of the diners in the fine restaurant. Then, turning to his son, he reminded him, "Yes, I was right, they did look at you differently."

At that point, Sarkozy's son smiled and said, "Dad, you've told that story before but you never tell the part at the end when I'm the one who gets with the beautiful waitress." Or words to that effect.

In the middle of all that elegant culture, there was nothing to do but laugh. Generations mixing with one another, like cultures intermingling, and like brands with consumers, just need to have dialogues and megalogues and get to the common intersection of understanding.

Fortunately, nothing about that punch line went over anyone's head. They continued storytelling and joking, smoked the rest of their cigars, and agreed that certain rites of passage never really change. Perhaps that's why global youth culture has made hip-hop so enduring.

Hard Knock Life Remix

There was a time not very long ago when I seriously wondered if the end of my generation's story would be about how we created an art form, built it from nothing to become one of the most influential forces on the face of the planet, had it all, and then gave it away. That is what happens to relevant cultural forces when they become so popular that they're not rooted to their origins or to the real and the true anymore—to the needs and the wants that summoned them into being in the first place. In fact, Nas wrote a song some years back called "Hip Hop Is Dead." Later he spoke about what he meant in Michael Eric Dyson's far-reaching book *Know What I Mean?* and went on to say that there were many who came forward to agree and disagree with him. His point was, "Although the voices may have clashed, the one constant in the clamor was that all of these people out there felt that hip-hop was worth fighting over and fighting for."

The solution that Nas recommended was, "We need to be able to learn from our history if we are going to take control of our future."

In fact, that's exactly what's happening at many of the country's top universities that now offer hundreds of classes in hip-hop studies. Howard University offers an interdisciplinary minor in hip-hop history and culture. Boston's Berklee School of Music offers a course in writing rap lyrics and creating beats. At UC Berkeley, political and legal scholars are writing doctoral theses on how urban culture has influenced law enforcement and the judicial system. A class at Columbia University taught by a leading cultural historian analyzes the poetry of hip-hop's prominent voices. NYU's music school 2011 schedule offers a class in The Business of Jay-Z. Courses across the nation cover aspects of hip-hop culture taught from the perspective of anthropology, ethnography, philosophy, linguistics, ethnomusicology, music history, poetry, literature, and more. The formal study of street dance now includes classes in everything from uprock and break-dancing to popping and locking.

As Nas can attest, learning from the past to understand the future also means staying connected to the scene—which he does by touring and using his stature as a headliner to feature some of the young voices on the local level as opening acts for him. In the process, his own work becomes all the more relevant and informed by what kids are going through.

It's true that what they're going through today may not be as apocalyptic as was the crack cocaine epidemic—the catalyst that accelerated the music's journey into becoming a culture and a creed for survival, with its code for language and behavior that made it possible for a community to keep from becoming collectively insane and provided aspiration to move forward. But without a doubt these millennials are going through their version of hard knock life remix. Many of them have never had to face the challenges they're experiencing now. I don't just mean economic woes but also with everything coming to a head that has needed fixing in our country for a long time. Then they are dealing with issues that other generations never had to confront in their youth. Many millennials lived through 9/11 in the same way that earlier generations witnessed Kennedy's assassination or that their parents got the news of Pearl Harbor—or whatever their equivalents are in other countries. Many in this group know better than other generations that climate change is real, that energy resources are dwindling, and that life on earth, if not valued, is not as forever as it once seemed.

Let me quickly add, however, that I know every generation has had its own existential/economic crises and crossroads that have caused values to be recalibrated. This isn't exclusive to now. The eighties had corporate excesses that led to a crash. In the nineties we had a dot-com boom that was bigger than the gold rush until it went bust as we entered the 2000s. Now we're confronting the lawlessness on Wall Street that got out of control in the first years of the new millennium and emptied coffers across a lot of industries. With CEOs' pay now being restricted and the opulence of earlier eras being scrutinized with a finer eye, questions arise about a culture of excess—*Is that cool or is it too much?* And those are cues brands should acknowledge as people's values are reset.

Millennials have adapted well to the shift from *want* marketing to *need* marketing—and that you should get what you can afford, not all that other stuff that's not within your means. Cheap credit was everyone's crack and it dried up. In some ways, it's been easier for this more adaptive generation. You can hear it, in fact, in the values of music, which are shifting too. In rap, talking about how much money you have is still part of the code, but it's starting to be downplayed or put into the context of other realities. Aspiration remains, first and foremost. How do you quantify the aspiration, connect it to authentic challenges of the present, and make it lyrical? Those are the questions that millennials are answering in their art today.

With all the raw material coming out of life, hip-hop is humming as a music form, localizing and globalizing simultaneously, with a vibrant and diverse cultural scene that is as varied as the people who are increasingly being drawn into it. This rich diversity is a healthy outgrowth of tanning often overlooked in all the coverage of the death of the record industry.

And just how bad is the music business? Well, the numbers ain't pretty. In 2009, sales of CDs for all genres were down by 52 percent from where they were in 2000. Physical units of CD sales were the biggest decline, with an impressive 1.16 billion downloaded singles for the year. Digital, accounting for 40 percent of all purchased music, wasn't going anywhere.

All of this makes it clear that for millennials, the scene today is very much an online affair—with posted music and videos shared in a variety of networking sites that serve as the mix tapes of now.

On MySpace alone, there are 1.8 million rock bands, 1.6 million R&B artists, and 4.9 million hip-hop/rap artists. As a result, the equivalent of yesterday's underground counterculture is mainly Internet-type rappers who have developed followings with postings of their latest content, sometimes without monetizing it, and who don't necessarily have local followings or many opportunities to perform live. Edgy music blog sites, such as Nah Right, post new songs, samplers, and videos daily, driving traffic and promoting greater circulation with listeners. There are also entertainment and fashion-news blogs with music too, like YBF.com and hypebeast.com, that provide connection for global youth culture.

The question from brands that we often hear is, *Where are the emerging youth markets for music and culture?* The real question should be, *Where* aren't *they?*

Whenever I check in with Fab Five Freddy—who has his finger on the creative underground pulse as much as anyone—he reports on the latest new crew he has discovered in Brazil or in South Africa. Recent break-dance champions have come from places like Korea and Russia. Fab has also confirmed that here and abroad, it is an art form open to everybody: black, white, brown, yellow, red, male, female. As polyethnic as it has ever been. From younger artists, the talk that I hear says many of the MCs making names for themselves in local scenes still happen to be male and African-American, but there are increasingly exceptions, with more females, more artists coming up the ranks who are Latino, white, and Asian, crowds that are more multicultural and multiracial. The story of *8 Mile* remains in the code in that when kids from different backgrounds connect, ethnic/racial differences pale once someone proves they can rhyme or shows their moves are real. Timeless and timely.

Around the world, we're seeing style moving as fast as information, sometimes driven by leading American artists and sometimes by local groups before being adopted elsewhere. This is another reason that I maintain that American culture and entertainment continue to represent out most profitable export. James Lassiter, who rose up from the grass roots of hip-hop as Will Smith's manager, to become his business partner and now film producing partner at Overbrook Entertainment, has not only watched the evolution of the tanning effect in developed countries everywhere but is seeing it in the developing nations. Not long ago, he and Will came back from Tanzania and reported seeing huge painted likenesses of hip-hop and pop culture icons on the different buses and the barbershops. Instead of even having business names, the barbershops are simply known by whoever's likeness graces the front window—like Ice Cube or Snoop Dog barbershop. James and Will saw a bus go by and that was Beyoncé's bus. James said, "Tupac is omnipresent." So you could go to Tupac's barbershop or travel on Tupac's bus route, seeing his face everywhere. Of course, in bigger cities, like in Kenya, they have similar iconography, only the pictures are real photographs, as James said, "High tech."

None of this should have surprised Will Smith or James Lassiter, given their respective journeys. In his own way, James had been a pioneer for a new generation of entertainment industry executives to follow nontraditional paths to success. He once told me about the amazed reaction he got from Howard Stringer, the CEO, president, and chairman of Sony Entertainment Corporation, who hadn't realized until then what a significant role that hip-hop had played in James's career. Unlike most black executives who go to Wharton or get their MBAs at Harvard or degrees at law school so they can compete at the highest levels, James had taken his own route to the top through hip-hop—but without the ten-year delay. He recalled to me that "had I done those other things and then had to work my way up through the corporation, it would have been that much more difficult because it's not easy to be the third man in the room with Howard Stringer." But coming in with the expertise and experience that managing a hip-hop duo had given him, James was able to walk through any room and sit at any board table with any chairman and hold his own, at twenty-two years old. How? Mostly, James remembered, it was because "I was smart enough just to listen and not talk my way out of those rooms."

As hip-hop expands its reach and germinates in different cultures and economies around the world, we're seeing others follow similar routes—with young entrepreneurs coming out of music and entertainment to be influential business leaders. The millennial path to success has been redefined and repurposed—as have the signifiers of style and status.

After Jay-Z wrote "Change Clothes" and the retro jersey days were left behind, there was actually a swing in the other direction toward more tailored shirts, tight-fitting apparel, and skinny jeans that briefly became a cross-cultural millennial uniform. That soon went the way of the baggies and has now settled into looser but better-fitting silhouettes. Reflecting the economy, millennials seem to be searching for classic, dependable brands that have quality and some scarcity—or for the latest find that isn't overpriced but has been anointed with a level of cultural cool. In some circles that sustains demand for Louis Vuitton and most high-end brands or helps down-to-earth brands like Converse, while within other circles it's harder to find names like Diamond Supply Company and the Supra sneaker line, which are a couple of the hot sellers at this writing.

One of the coolest things I see about this tan generation and the scene they're cultivating now is that there is no uniformity and that's a style unto itself. The unapologetic attitude of today draws from that permission to lead and to be different. That's in the DNA.

As for the language being spoken in this culture by young America today, I think that Mike Bentley had it right when he talked about the evolution of urban culture into digital culture. Read any texts or posts online by the under-thirty set and you will pick up an intonation that can only be described as tan—it's a cultural mash-up of code. Madison Avenue loves to drop in on this language or pick up the latest street slang and turn it into advertising. Again, that runs the risk of losing its shelf life of cool faster than you can shoot the commercial.

What I try to say diplomatically, whenever the occasion allows, is that, first, you can't visit the topic and expect to become conversant with how to speak to young America, or it becomes a situation of going to Paris and seeing the Eiffel Tower and then coming home. You didn't experience Paris. The executives try to have the Cliffs Notes to culture, as if having a Facebook page, owning an iPad, and listening to Lady Gaga is enough, when they are really skipping the process. Besides the problem that too many executives are stuck in their boardrooms, not going out and immersing themselves in culture, the act of simply *listening* to the consumer is so much more important than trying to pick up the lingo.

By the way, the language of cool right now is so amorphous,

trying to jump in on that group megalogue in the middle of it can really be, as they say, *awkward*. There are numerous hip-hop slang books and even pretty funny flash cards that break down old-school and new-school expressions. But they too are only as relevant as the date on which they were printed. It is, therefore, a misconception that at any given time there exists certain slang that is universal to urban youth culture as a mind-set. Language is and has always been a very regional thing. Variances show up between cities and even neighborhoods.

This diversity has only enhanced the musical storytelling. Not only that, but as Fab puts it, "The resources for creativity for young artists today are unlimited, especially with everyone having equal or similar access to technology." For instance, the availability of beat-making software and downloadable beats has given rise to waves of new young rappers—who can become producers with little money invested in equipment. In 2009, SoundScan reported a record-high sale of vinyl records, leaving no doubt that the format is in the midst of the biggest revival since Berry Gordy invited Detroit teenagers in to listen to the latest vinyl pressing of a Temptations hit, "My Girl," and asked them the question "If you were hungry and broke and only had enough money for this record or a hot dog, what would you buy?"

At one point, not long after Jimmy Iovine had to make the argument to iTunes that most kids didn't even know to associate guitars with music, I heard that the international chain Guitar Center was actually selling more electronic turntables than guitars. DJs have all kinds of new tools and technology for mixing—including a very cool HP console that Translation helped develop and market in its early stages. There are also programs like Serato that will let anyone with a turntable that hooks up to their computer mix any song on their hard drive as if it was literally on vinyl—basically allowing you to scratch a computerized "blank" of the record and mix it for repeated usages.

Fab Five Freddy went so far as to say, "There's no excuse not to be creative with the resources available." The climate now, he feels, has close parallels to the early days when the scene and the music achieved liftoff on extremely limited resources.

With all this resilience and resourcefulness in the music

scene today there is one dramatic difference that had bothered Jimmy Iovine for years. Whenever he and I used to talk—
catching up on this and that, as well as projects we had in the
works together—he would happen to mention how frustrated he
was becoming with the dismal quality of the sound that kids
today were getting from listening to music on their laptops and
with cheap earbuds. Remember those beloved speakers of his
that he always used to discern whether a record had transformative powers? After all these years, the importance of the sound
experience was still an obsession.

And there is a deep-seated reason why he is right. The
globe-shaking and mind-changing power of music, the force that
draws together people from all kinds of different backgrounds
and weaves them into communities, lies purely in the emotion
that is carried by sound. When Carlos Santana said that music
has the capacity to rearrange the molecules in the psyches of
listeners, he was referring to the emotional relationship between
music and audience that comes from the sound. The magic happens in the feeling.

Experts disagree about how the shift from analog to digital
has impacted recorded music's sound. Some feel that the computerized and digitized sound, not unlike high-def video, has helped
to refine and perfect all the parts of the whole—creating as close
to a live and in-person experience as possible. Others say the
opposite is true. They argue that technological improvements
have blurred the raw and gritty emotional components that were
captured more truly on vinyl and in vintage recording studios.
Such is the thinking that has to do, in part, with vinyl's resurgence. Where everyone agrees, however, is that with most music
being heard through laptop or low-quality computer speakers or
through inexpensive earbuds, the sound is hugely diminished.

That is the backdrop to a revelation that happened one day,
back during the time when 50 Cent was blasting off with his
G-Unit sneakers and Jimmy was shooting the sh*t with Dr. Dre—
who was half-joking about how he wished there was a sneaker he
could promote. All of sudden, Iovine got an idea. "Forget sneakers," he told Dre, "we're going to do speakers."

With that, the two of them started working with engineers to develop state-of-the-art headphones as a product line that was perfect for Dr. Dre—perhaps the most iconic music producer of our time. During this development process Jimmy learned of a study that showed them what they were up against. The question posed by a team of researchers to different age groups was whether they could tell the difference between music played on the most state-of-the-art speakers that cost $100,000 versus a similar-looking set of speakers that cost $1,000. With the 40-to-50-year-olds, 85 percent could identify the better speakers. With the group of 30-to-40-year-olds, about 80 percent could also tell the difference and identify the higher quality. When they got to the younger group of 15-to-30-year-olds, only 25 percent could tell the difference and identify correctly which were the $100,000 speakers and which were the $1,000 ones.

These findings alerted Jimmy and Dre and their partners at Monster Cable that they were veering into uncharted waters. Would their target consumer—millennials—have a need for headphones retailing for over three hundred dollars and would they even care about the improved technology? Well, what they were betting on was the idea that it's not about the technology but about what it allows you to experience. And that was the story that needed to be told, with a fashion and style component that made them cool. Very simply, authentically, Monster Beats by Dr. Dre arrived after two years in development with a statement from Dre that explained his passion, why this product filled a need—because "people aren't hearing all the music." Who has greater credibility on that point than Dre? No one to my knowledge. Dre's statement went on, "With Beats, people are going to hear what the artists hear, and listen to the music the way they should, the way I do."

Oh, yeah. The truth sells. You might not be able to be a legendary music producer, but you could share the experience with professional-quality earphones for consumers that delivered sound as it was meant to be heard. Plus, they looked as cool as they fit. And when they hit the market, the sound experience more than exceeded expectations. By leveraging Interscope's stable of iconic artists, along with innovative partnerships with HP and Best Buy—not to mention superb marketing that included the likes of LeBron James in what became a must-see commercial with him sitting in his locker room with his Beats by Dr. Dre on and singing along (off-key) to Cyndi Lauper's "Time After Time"—a sea change in awareness about the importance of sound followed next. The reception was so robust that a short time later Beats by Dr. Dre put out headphones with a Lady Gaga signature and high-quality earbuds for Sean "Diddy" Combs. When *AdAge* named Beats by Dr. Dre one of the hottest brands of 2010, Jimmy Iovine reported 1.3 million pairs sold for the year. He also announced that he and Dre's next collaboration with Hewlett-Packard was HP Beats Audio inside PCs and that five million units were readying for release.

Miraculous as it must seem to develop a high-priced product in the midst of the worst recession in modern times and have it turn out to serve a cultural need such that multiple industries are supported and enriched by it, I can attest that it's not brain surgery. It's problem-solving.

Such is the focus, I believe, that gives us a navigational compass reading for where millennials and brands, together, can move forward in this remix of economy, culture, and values. The solutions, just as in the past, will come from anyone and everyone with innovation and passion, anyone willing to take risks and to seek comfort in discomfort.

The Thinnest Slice

When Translation first opened its doors, we began to describe a phenomenon that we felt was going to be key to our work and that we also saw was being acutely overlooked by Madison Avenue, corporate America, and many of our competitors in the arena of branded entertainment marketing. It had to do, in part, with a language gap that was less between the iconic brand and the consumer—or the celebrity icon and the audience—and more between the brand and itself or between the artist and his/her medium. It also had to do with a tanner public that wanted to have both dialogue and megalogue, as we've noted, but particularly didn't want brands speaking to their communities one way and to other communities another way. But most of all, the faltering of blue-chip brands and entertainers once deemed immortal has to do with the trap of their own success.

In my observation of this phenomenon, I've come to conclude that there's a point of saturation in which one's success and celebrity cross the line into backlash, apathy, and boredom by the consumer. What happens next is that consumers become rejecters of the core value proposition. In other words, all that work that was done to market into customers' core values goes out the window. It turns into the "can't win for trying" syndrome. This happens when there is a lack of credibility, be it a celebrity, a clothing line, a shoe company, or automaker. Suddenly, the mismatch of the "success attained" versus the "success maintained" becomes transparent to all.

What are the causes for that perilous crossing of the line and loss of credibility? At Translation we've identified three main culprits:

Lack of true depth. When a brand or an icon exhibits the inability to really deliver the goods time and again, they become exposed as not having truth or depth or both. Sometimes brands that do deliver in terms of sales still lack true depth. In music the classic example of lack of depth is the "one-hit wonder" ("Mambo Number 5").

Lack of true understanding. Here's how a lack of true understanding of tanning can be problematic. It's important to understand and look at the world through the eyes of cultural producers on the street, in the malls, in neighborhoods, and to arrive there at the moment to witness what is now counterculture but will soon become culture. Generally, where there is understanding those who are pioneering and daring enough to forge ahead and *accept* the changes usually succeed, while those who keep their heads in the sand fail. With political brands, you can observe how lack of understanding worked in 2008 for Republicans versus Democrats.

Lack of innovation. When change is ongoing or imminent, icons and brands can tumble from not knowing how to innovate against what is coming and from not being able to embrace a culture of rebirth and reinvention. Probably the best case in point is Windows versus Mac.

Earlier we touched on a few aspects of the Thinnest Slice as it relates to artists in culture. What is it then? Simply put, it's where a person, object, or concept is so authentic that it becomes popular because of this authentic truth. It becomes so popular that it occupies the closest distance possible to being "mass culture" but it doesn't cross that line; rather it manages to maintain living in that space. This space is defined as the Thinnest Slice. At Translation we wanted to pay closer attention to this balancing act and its relevance in a changing, tanning global marketplace as a way of addressing different brand challenges. So, we concluded, the point where you can walk that daring line—standing on the bleeding edge between enduring success on one side and, on the other side, consumer apathy and rejection—is the precise location of the Thinnest Slice. The strategies required in the balancing are not easily managed and demand equal parts prescience and science, restraint and courting the masses.

The willingness to take a marketing position that goes to the Thinnest Slice is by itself a bold start. Next it's a programming challenge that involves careful planning and ongoing support—all the while staying authentic and true to the brand's original story, but continually refreshing and updating it to stay within the tide of the times. There is no formula or guarantee. But there are those who are better at finessing the Thinnest Slice than others. Before Tiger Woods fell from grace, he had been a good example of an athlete as a brand unto himself who raised the level of the field and brought continuity, another important trait for those who can reside at the Thinnest Slice. Charles Wright rightfully pointed out that Tiger had entered the game as a phenom and maintained that by constantly excelling at the sport. Before Tiger Woods was known to golf fans, Charles observed, "there were different leaders different weeks, a different face atop the leader board." Once Tiger was in the game, Charles went

on, "there was someone to follow—a consistency that drew followers and fans. There was an expectation that either paid off
(he won) or didn't (he lost), but within the expectation that he
would win we were programmed to follow, and thus Tiger Woods
lived at the Thinnest Slice." To illustrate just how fragile and thin
the line is, Tiger's marital infidelities and his divorce and incon-
sistent performance once he did return to the game show what
happens when an icon steps onto the wrong side of that line.

But sometimes the reason for the fall is much less sensational. Sometimes it's an annoyance as trivial as ubiquity that
can hurt brands, or as routine as becoming overexposed for
entertainers. Sometimes it's complacency, as we've seen, and
occasionally it's the effort to be cool when that's not what the
brand needs to be doing. Sometimes being too cool kills opportunities afforded to those at the Thinnest Slice.

In many cases, a solution can be found in the DNA, in the original code—which may require deconstructing the brand to find
out what buried treasure lies beneath that has gone overlooked.
When Translation worked with Wrigley this process revealed
a highly important principle for the wary brand manager, particularly at iconic brands. It's the "permission to own real and
permission to lead" rule. It goes back to our recurring theme
that millennial culture is unapologetic. Brands that have earned
iconic stature are granted unique permission to be unapologetically real and to lead.

Wrigley knew it was time for "refreshment" of their brand. They
also understood that new packaging—a fine strategy—might sell
a couple more sticks of chewing gum, but that was not going to
solve their stagnancy. To contemporize the brand we needed radical disruption that also drew from their past and that came with
a wow factor too. With the goal of making news out of their evolution (as opposed to reinvention or reincarnation), our mutual aim
was to enhance the use and enjoyment of Wrigley-brand products without diminishing what generations have come to know
and love as distinctively and definitively Wrigley.

Using reverse engineering, tried and true, we brought on not
one, not two, but three different artists to express their affection for the values imbuing the brand with three authentic songs

to be promoted through normal entertainment channels and then incorporated into the marketing for Wrigley. From Ne-yo there was a song that referenced Big Red with "*kiss a little longer*" and from Julianne Hough, famous for *Dancing with the Stars,* there was her Juicy Fruit homage with "*the taste is gonna move you.*" The biggest hit, which became a number one smash around the world, was the setup for Doublemint with Chris Brown's "Forever," which had the lines "*double your pleasure / double your fun*" and that later turned into advertising that brought back the classic appeal of the Doublemint twins.

Why did it not matter to the public, after the fact, that these were embedded marketing messages? Because the brand had the permission to lead, to come into our house, so to speak, and remind us of our shared history—our associations with chewing gum, the values of refreshment and dependability, how familiar the brand already was in the DNA of pop culture, where the chewing gum flavors lived in our collective landscape and in our memories.

Wrigley needed to call attention to their own brand assets, to proclaim that, no, we're not the coolest or the most extreme with taste that pops your eyes out of your head, but yes, we are a true American icon. Could the brand be uncool but in a really cool way? Of course. That's the permission afforded to the iconic, and as such, it implies that we are not static but ever-evolving.

"Ever-evolving" is marketing code that I have found most helpful in other campaigns. "Ever" represents enduring, the promise that the brand is going to always be there, moving forward, remaining true to its essence. It too encompasses timelessness and timeliness. "Evolving" references dynamism, improvement, adaptation. So "ever-evolving," when it comes to the Thinnest Slice, summons the spirit of a keen sensitivity, of knowing what to change, how, and when.

As an ever-evolving American icon, Wrigley is granted permission to own real and proudly share the values associated with their chewing gum. In the code was the idea of being the real deal, having an independent spirit and an industrious nature, brand values that are American values. Permission to lead comes from being over 110 years old as a brand and an originator of all that is loved about gum. With that status, there is no reason to doubt or second-guess the brand's standing in consumers' minds.

What other brands earn that kind of permission? Some that come to mind for me are Coca-Cola, Tide, Converse, Budweiser, Harley-Davidson, and Swatch, to name a few. And they too live at the Thinnest Slice.

This leads me, finally, to the paradigm that we see going forward for pop culture, for marketing, and for values that I believe we all share in wanting a robust, buoyant economy in which all ships rise. The new rule, written by the next chapter of ever-evolving hip-hop, comes from the understanding of cross-culturalism. The new total-market approach is an outgrowth of research with consumers, analysts, anthropologists, and economists. Johnson & Johnson has a study in the works based on research that predicts 2020 as the first year in which the majority of babies born in America won't be white. The other prediction we've seen well publicized is that by 2050 whites in this country will no longer be the racial majority. We should be asking how these trends will impact all of us and how society is shaping itself to prepare us for what's to come. How will they influence the way we look at each other and respect each other? What do the numbers predict in terms of racial biases and racial tensions? What do they mean in terms of putting people in boxes? How will this play out for those generations that hold on to the old labels and compartmentalizing of culture? The information is only now beginning to be processed as the 2010 census continues to be examined. At the date of this writing, we are only starting to see the numbers of multiracial families being announced state by state. Everyone should be paying attention to staggering changes.

Will we adapt? How will we repurpose and reinvent new marketing rules? Take, for instance, the products that dominate our shelves—the fact that we have a black beauty aisle or ethnic beauty aisle for women, say, for African-American women looking for hair and skin products. What does it do to these boxes as the new realities start coming out? Are these companies going to sit around and fall victim to the changes, like those companies that didn't recognize that the digital age was coming? Will brands adapt to cross-cultural thinking and pool resources to respond to

consumers' needs—as to forces in radio that didn't care about television and network TV powerbrokers indifferent to the movie business? Will the new shared mental complexion and the actual ethnic
sharing remind all of us how these changes affect one another? Will
it be remembered what has already happened in all kinds of industries because no one wanted to recognize change? Well, hopefully
so, because culture's speaking and a change is coming.

We have a chance, me and my generation—all of us watching
this metamorphosis of cultural diversity and shared values—to
prepare and lead this change. This is what Martin Luther King
was speaking about when he had his dream, now a reality as
people come together from all backgrounds. One in seven mar-
riages in America is between people of different cultures, different races, proving the power to choose outside the boxes and
to be with the love of their lives, someone with whom to spend
their life and raise a family, someone with whom they share true
values but not racial or cultural demographics.

The faces of this mixed-race, tan America are not just on college campuses, but they dominate politics, business, and sports.
The ethnically ambiguous are especially ubiquitous in movies
and television shows, advertisements, and news, joining with one
another in social networks, dating Web sites, and even mixed-race
film festivals.

Cultural curiosity is alive and well too.

In studies done of the 2010 census, we observed an emerging
like-minded community around music coming from Latin culture
and with it an abundance of exciting cross-cultural marketing
opportunities. From the earliest days of ragtime music, minorities
in this country have created the majority of pop music consumed
by the general population. This reality has unleashed the development of a deeper way of reaching the general market based on
multicultural insights. Stay tuned.

Cross-culturalism is the next phase of tanning and is not
about homogenizing or mixing cultures to the point of dilut-
ing the elements that make them distinct in the first place. It's
about loving one another, the last critical point I would like to
add to our conversation about rules for the new economy, which
I hope has only just begun. Very simply, the credibility in pop

culture movements, as in brands, that is required for sustaining loyal followers and consumers as much as it is for attracting new ones is built on love.

The marketing rule, as Procter & Gamble's Jim Stengel told an interviewer at *Fortune* magazine not too long ago, is that "businesses and brands that are breaking records are those that inspire trust and affection and loyalty by being authentic, by not being arrogant, and by being empathetic to those they serve."

Let me hone in on the affection part of the dynamic for the economy. As long as brands and companies are showing the love, they're almost always forgiven for missteps and miscues. Love is rarely discussed in boardrooms or in marketing meetings. Love is a seriously undervalued commodity. Though it should be obvious, consumers do not want "wham bam thank you, ma'am" from marketers. That's why culture serves appropriately as a conduit for showing the love between companies and consumers.

It's easy to survey the current landscape and pick up on the extremism and the hate that is out there. There is unfortunately a reactionary backlash against the epic forward motion of a change election that was buoyed by a generation unafraid of going off into the unknown; it has been inflamed, frankly, by a fear of the tanning of America. The hate has volume, it's extreme, and it's fed by propaganda and people in media who make a ton of money from stoking the flames. They are hate profiteers, and outside their own industries, they are just bad for business. Besides, they are not cool and never have been. The war against culture hates the fact that tan is the new cool, that they are losing the weapons of mass distraction they use to separate us because of our differences.

Love, on the other hand, is timeless and is the universal currency, the common tongue, the language we all know. To speak of it, to talk of our love for one another, our love for products, for the emotion we feel when we hear music, the love that allows us to fulfill our human purpose, to come together with all of our differences, not to be like each other but to live peacefully with each other, sounds corny. I know. But it's true and it is what builds economies, helps culture grow and flourish, and keeps us in spirit "young forever."

CODA:

CULTURE'S NEXT
IN-CAR-NĀ·TION

So it's a Sunday morning at the end of January 2011 and I am seriously past deadline on turning in these final thoughts. They're not just about where tanning is taking us next but also about how we can all use cultural insights, in practical ways, for the betterment of everyone. The problem wasn't so much putting down *what* I wanted to say and who I was going to ask to expand on some of the key points but simply—where to begin?

Then, lo and behold, I wake up and have the answer delivered to my front door. It's a featured series in *The New York Times* entitled "Race Remixed" with the subtitle reading, "Black? White? Asian? More Young Americans Choose All of the Above."

First of all, what a validation it was of the value dear to my heart that I've embraced for most of my career—both as a record industry veteran and then moving on to the advertising business. It validated the lessons that I had been fortunate to witness up close and personal, as I speak about early in the book, while watching how culture happened in response to the offerings from the record business that in turn had to be very, very honest. It was amazing to watch the influence of radio stations and their need to play music that was ethnically and culturally relevant on the local level because those local stations were in the front lines of culture. The rule was clear: If they didn't play the music that the people in that zip code or area code or band-width reacted to, they were out of business. Just as amazing, but to my despair, was how far away from the cultural pulse were too many in the advertising, film, and television industries—and how their business models didn't encourage them to replicate what was happening on the front lines. That distance has been mind-boggling to me.

So, for starters, to wake up on a Sunday morning and see a powerful analysis of culture and where it's headed on the front page of the Sunday *Times* honestly put a twinkle in my eye! I called my girlfriend, I called my friends and colleagues, and I was jumping up and down. What I really loved about the article, and what made me feel so inspired, was its declaration that the term "mulatto," so long employed to describe someone of mixed race, was no longer enough. Mulatto doesn't apply to an individual, say, who's Portuguese, African-American, and Haitian. It doesn't apply to someone who can check off the boxes that are "Black" and "White" but also "Polish." Mulatto doesn't apply. Nor should it.

We have a lot of old history to overcome. Back in the 1930s, the Census Bureau had a standing rule that if you had any trace of African-American in you, you were considered African-American, and they had to put you in that box—the "one-drop rule." Then they decided to open up the conversation, and by the 1970s there were more choices. Sort of. The article states, "Americans were expected to designate themselves as members of one official recognized racial group." You could select any of the following: Black, White, American Indian, Japanese, Chinese, Filipino, Hawaiian, Korean, or Other; with that "Other" box intended for Hispanics, because they were viewed as an ethnicity and not specifically a race. It wasn't until 2000 that the Census permitted responders to mark more than one race. When seven million people did so that year, about 2.4 percent of the population, it led for the first time to a category understood as multiracial. The Census Bureau now estimates that within ten years the percentage of the population considered mixed-race has exploded to 35 percent!

Just how far and wide this phenomenon has spread was underscored in yet another installment of the "Race Remixed" series in *The New York Times*. This one was on racial intermarriage and looked at census data from the Deep South, a region historically hostile to mixed-race couples, and revealed that a dramatic shift in attitude is well under way. Love, it turns out, is as powerful in changing the mind-set of America as the marketplace.

When I started using the term polyethnic to speak to marketers about the races coming together, we were asking them to look literally at society and see how different ethnicities look, overlap, and touch. Tanning, even though we use it broadly at times, is something much different. Tanning speaks about how the cultures come together, where the cultures touch. The article was backed up with facts about how polyethnicity is coloring society—where one in seven Americans are marrying outside of their "race"—on top of the digital acceleration of cultural tanning that is happening with shared information. The reality is dramatic, given that somebody can go online and listen and watch and pick up other cultures quickly; for example, that a four-year-old from Newark, New Jersey, is learning skateboarding at the exact same time a four-year-old would learn it in Venice Beach, California, where skateboarding culture is dominant. With music, culture sharing continues unabated, amplified by youth culture and college students on social networks. Nobody's sticking in their labeled box culturally or even ethnically.

We have more bridges to cross, although I, for one, am excited about seeing the commingling of different cultures that has inspired me all along. One of the meaningful barometers I love to study is the American edition of *Vogue* magazine and everything it stands for. I was speaking to a particular artist of prominence who pointed out that no matter how many icons of color have come to epitomize beauty and style, there may have been a very small number that after many YEARS of hard work had the privilege to grace this most prestigious cover—some of whom include Michelle Obama, Halle Berry, and Naomi Campbell. A newcomer who happens to be white, like Blake Lively from *Gossip Girl,* gets on the cover after two years of her rise to prominence, while it took superstar Beyoncé ten years of world-wide success and sixteen Grammys to receive this privilege. Good for Blake Lively. But the fact that the media specifically puts people in these boxes and decides what category can go on the cover—because of some traditional measurement that no longer reflects the way people feel today—is something that I see as needing to fall by the wayside, that I hope this book will propel. Again, it always confused me that only in America do you still see that women of color have a special aisle called the Ethnic Beauty aisle. Does that mean Caucasian or Asian women who see Rihanna grace a magazine and love her hair need to go down the "Ethnic Beauty aisle" to find those products? This cat-egorization needs to stop. (Amazingly, not long before we went to print on this book, most of an *Allure* magazine was devoted to the subject of multiethnic beauty, demonstrating how the chang-ing cultural attitudes brought about by tanning have already created a new cross-cultural aesthetic.)

To know where we're going next, I hope that telling the jour-ney of how we got here can point out the way, a shared cultural heritage that has and will continue to provide us with opportu-nities to speak across the generational and social divides. The polyethnic and multicultural megalogue has developed organi-cally and against the odds.

In the entertainment business, as an example, it was artists like Eminem who had to make music for all cultures—African-Americans and Hispanics and Asian-Americans and others—that they could understand, rock with, and connect to his POV. The cultural collision with commerce happened because multi-cultural audiences in mass wanted to duplicate the way he dressed and spoke, or duplicate the way Jay-Z spoke and what LL Cool J and Puff Daddy and Lil Wayne and all the artists who have galvanized culture did.

Just as "Race Remixed" tells us, the specifics of our racial DNA do not define who we are as individuals or as a cultural group. Race doesn't define how you choose to dress or how you choose to act or what you decide to purchase. The beauty of this time and how we move forward is that I think the boxes are ready for the dustbin of history. The Census Bureau, along with the advertising businesses and media companies, are starting to see the memo. Finally, culture is in the driver's seat.

The future of tanning is the option to look at all the boxes and mark off the one that reads "All of the above." By choosing "All of the above," I mean in the sense of spirit, in the sense of shared humanity. Isn't that what we are all about? Aren't we all about tasting different foods, tasting and borrowing each other's culture to understand one another better and to provide insight about ourselves? Sure, we grew up into a race and into a household that had certain understandings around religion, certain understandings around tradition of that race in particular. But it doesn't set us up or prepare us for when all these things come together and they're shared, and it cannot work within the confines of the boxes when we should embrace our shared connections as Americans.

One of those connections, obviously, is in the marketplace. How will culture help us reenergize and remix the power of our shared economic interests? What are the new rules?

Let's face it—the only rule that really matters in the new twenty-first-century economy is that thinking in terms of rules has limited marketplace value. That said, I would hope that if we've learned anything from observing the economic, social benefits of tanning, it would be the truth that our distinctly polyethnic American culture is our greatest, most valuable, and most underused national resource. And based on that premise—call it Rule One—I'd like to offer some final recommendations as to how all of us can learn from tanning's powerful properties and apply the lessons we've seen so far in new, repurposed ways.

As a prime example, we can look as far back as the early house party days when a movement was born out of an MC's need to extend an invite to as many people as possible; the goal was to get them to show up to a countercultural event that simultaneously marketed inclusivity and exclusivity. This created the DNA for today's social networks, using the party-rocking capacities that have created the multibillion-dollar successes out of the likes of Facebook.

I point out the comparison as a reminder of how one of

the most impoverished, marginalized, underserved segments of society was able to transform its economy, starting with nothing but beats and rhymes, and why there is no reason that we shouldn't be borrowing lessons learned for the creation of new industries—which in turn will create jobs and revenues for the enrichment of all.

To help me in this discussion, I wanted to talk to someone who I didn't have a chance to interview earlier in the book but who generously sat down to answer questions about his experiences and his cross-cultural point of view, and about some of the following themes that we've been speaking about all along: Aspiration, Authenticity, Risk (finding comfort in discomfort), Cultural Curiosity, Tanning in Culture and Commerce, Relevancy in the Marketplace, Revitalized Storytelling, the New Code of Cool, and Tanning Economic RX.

My conversation with Eminem began on the subject of his film *8 Mile* and the comments over the years that I've gotten from people who changed their thinking on race, culture, and the generation gaps from seeing that film. This was another instance of how music/culture/commerce fuel aspiration and act as a powerful goodwill ambassador and economic stimulant.

STOUTE: People have said that *8 Mile* is responsible for teaching people the history of hip-hop.

EMINEM: I don't know how much *8 Mile* teaches people about the history of hip-hop, but I did have some random older folks coming up to me after the film saying things like "I saw your movie. I think I understand rap now!" If the film had that unintended effect of making people respect or understand the music more, that's great.

STOUTE: Marshall, let's start with the subject of aspiration. What hip-hop artist first inspired you to rap and when did you realize you had that gift for storytelling?

EMINEM: Ice-T was one of the first rappers that I ever really heard, when I was ten or eleven. My uncle brought me over cassettes of Ice-T and the *Breakin'* soundtrack had "Reckless" on there. That's when I started to get into it. And then, I got turned on to Run-DMC, and got put up on the Fat Boys and then the Beastie Boys came out. And the Beastie Boys kind of got my thought process going that maybe it could be possible. Then LL probably made me actually want to do this. As a kid, I wanted to be LL. Like I literally thought I was LL, and that's when I would start writing raps and they sounded like him. I may have said this before, but that's who really made me start dabbling and made me really think, Wow, I can put some words together, they sound like him, but I'm able to rhyme these words and make these sentences and say them in a rhythm similar to him. But as I started to get just a little bit older, around fifteen, as far as storytelling, I remember taking a beat from Doug E. Fresh from "Play This Only at Night."

STOUTE: Right, that was fitting. Because in those days if you wanted to hear rap on the radio the only thing you could do was listen and tape records at two in the morning. You would listen to underground hip-hop in the middle of the night because that was the only time the records would get played. And some people would go to sleep and leave the tape player on all night recording.

EMINEM: Yeah, I was one of those kids. And the Doug E. Fresh record was from one of those nights when I fell asleep while I was recording. I would always go back the next day and listen to what I had recorded. Because in those days in Detroit The Wizard was on WJLB and he used to play all these great records, crazy ones that I'd never heard of before. And this was when I was first getting into hip-hop and it was—oh, my God, I've never heard this record! So, I'd fall asleep recording the radio and wake up in the morning to see what I'd taped and that's how I first heard "Play This Only at Night." There was something about that beat that made me want to tell a story over it. There was an open verse with a loop that went on for a long time so I made my own homemade loop. . . .

STOUTE: Storytelling began with the beats. When did you know that there was something you wanted to talk about? Or did that happen from a particular experience or actual story?

EMINEM: There's a true story that happened when I was living on the east side of Detroit in a house with my mother, where I grew up pretty much all my teenage years. There was a neighbor on one side of us that apparently caught his best friend with his girlfriend, and he was beating her ass. My upstairs window was level with their's and the shades were open and you could see everything. He beat up the dude and then started smacking her—I'm not sure how it all ended up playing out, except that my mother called the police. The next night, and I'm not making this up, on the opposite side of the house, the couple who lived there did the very same thing.

STOUTE: Everyone lived upstairs, houses close to each other, everyone on the same level?

EMINEM: Right. And I'm looking through the window and damn if they aren't doing the exact same thing. But they're *both* naked. And he's beating her ass all the way out of the house into the middle of the street. Somebody called the cops and he goes to jail and that's how that played out. So I made a story up based on that. But this story might have even been an early version of "Love the Way You Lie" in some way because of the subject matter—me obviously not knowing it back then—but instead here I became the hero at the end. I talked about "I went downstairs in a rage, ran to the closet, grabbed the twelve gauge." My mom had a shotgun in the closet and I pretended it was mine in the rap. In the story, I ended up shooting the dude to protect the girl and saved the day. I rapped about seeing those things happening, a story from top to bottom, and becoming a hero. That really was the first time I realized that I could rhyme words and tell a story at the same time.

STOUTE: And you didn't look back after that. So how do you stay relevant? You've been doing this for twelve years and what's important for you to do to not lose your relevance?

EMINEM: The main way that I stay relevant is I study the game, I watch what's going on, . . . I watch what other artists are doing. . . .

Why? For one, to stay current and sound current; and two, to make sure that I don't sound like anyone else or anything else that's out. So I kind of get a feel for the pulse for what's out there; I just watch and listen. And also, I think that just trying to stay competitive with myself and trying to compete with what else is out there keeps me relevant. And, most of all, by just being part of it—because I just love hip-hop.

STOUTE: There was a moment when you first really got everyone's eyebrows raised, when you did the Biggie "Dead Wrong" remix, and everybody was "Wow, this guy is incredible." How did that feel?

EMINEM: I remember the response that I got off that record and I remember not understanding it, because some rhymes take longer to write than others and that one in particular just kinda came out quick. It didn't take that long to write it—it was something about the beat and getting on there and being excited about being on a track with B.I.G., so it didn't take any time. I didn't understand why the rhymes that would really take time to craft didn't get notice but this one did. Not that I was ever mad that it got the attention or the acceptance.

STOUTE: That's when hip-hop just went crazy.

EMINEM: That was definitely a crazy time in rap.

STOUTE: When you did that, I felt that was when the hip-hop underground, core rap guys looked at you and said, Yo, this guy is nuts. And so I wonder how important it was to you getting to that point not to be considered another "white rapper" like Vanilla Ice or MC Serch. What did you have to do to make sure that you weren't put in their category?

EMINEM: For one, I really like MC Serch a lot. . . . I love 3rd Bass, first and foremost. I couldn't figure out who I liked better: Pete Nice or Serch. There was something about Serch's voice and delivery that I really liked. They both had their own thing. But anyways, even though I thought they were both dope as f*ck, I felt, for one, I don't want to sound like nobody, let alone any other white rapper. I just want to do me and be the best me I can be and go absolutely as hard as I can. And you know, back in the day, by me being competitive and going out and battling other rappers and doing that kind of thing—being on the battle scene—helped at being me a lot. Certainly, it helped for credibility matters, and it helped me to develop as a rapper.

STOUTE: Did you ever feel reverse racism? Did you ever feel that because you're white, this is a black man's thing? Was that a real thing you felt coming up?

EMINEM: Coming up there was always a bit of that. You had people who were going to say what they wanted to say—you shouldn't do it, just because you're this color or because you look like this or whatever. But I also had my crew of people and my crew of supporters, with Proof being the biggest one. At that time, if I ever got discouraged, they were there for me and would tell me to just keep going.

STOUTE: When did you feel you were crossing over, that black kids liked you and white kids like you, and when did you realize that you were crossing all demographics? You had made a lot of records where you commented about not being a wigger who made records and you brought up Elvis Presley. It feels that you were conscious of that, maybe that you had the responsibility not to repeat that history.

EMINEM: Well, obviously, I knew that people were going to make jokes and say what they were going to say. I felt that "crossing over" even on a smaller scale, before Dre or any of the fame or anything like that, just locally when I would do shows at places like the Hip-Hop Shop—when I would rap or freestyle or battle there and was the only white kid and started to get acceptance. . . . And just going up in there and getting acceptance from my peers back then was like, Wow, this actually could be possible. I was starting to gain respect from people who actually did hip-hop.

STOUTE: These were mostly black kids or maybe a few white kids now and then. But when you started really bringing different audiences together, did you realize that you were doing that? It seems to me that you felt your experience—being poor and white, coming from nothing, what I call the impoverished mind-set—was the same experience of kids of color growing up in the inner city. Were you aware that you were creating this common ground, that you were bringing like-minded kids together?

EMINEM: Well, I'd love to be able to say I had a plan for all this in the beginning. But I certainly didn't ever know it would amount to that or be like that. I remember saying to people around me, even early on before we got signed to Dre, man, if I could have a gold record and just be respected by other MCs—for the craft—that would be a dream for me. And make enough money to just survive. But as far as bringing cultures together, I can't say. I mean, for my first album, *The Slim Shady LP,* there was a lot of me just poking fun at myself and others. On that album, I just let myself go. There was a lot of self-deprecation on that album, but that came from battling, from thinking, What is this guy going to say about me?; but before he says it, let me say it about myself. I brought that to the first album. And there was that underdog mentality, coming from the bottom and wanting to say something from my perspective. At the same time, certain songs had aggression to them, a feeling of I'm pissed off at the world, I feel the world has sh*t on me, so I'm gonna sh*t on it back. There was a bit of everything in the songs back then. But when I thought that everything was really coming together was when I started doing shows and seeing black people, white people, just people of all races in a f-ing sea of people. But also, around the time that I made "White America," I was like, now I'm in Middle America making a stink.

STOUTE: And you knew that rap had never gotten a chance before to penetrate that deep?

EMINEM: To an extent. If you look back, I want to say that Run-DMC really crossed those borders, too, with records like "Walk This

Way." The Fat Boys did early on, too. My thing, more so when I saw this happening, was realizing that what I was saying on my records was no different from any other underground MC. Man, listen, I've heard it all. I've heard so many f-ing crazy lines from my battling days and people saying such outlandish sh*t, it felt like now that I've reached this audience, now people are making a stink about it. But it wasn't that big of a deal when I was just an underground MC. These were just things that you said—and you really didn't think about it, you just thought, *Oh, that's a cool line, that's crazy.* Now people are making a fuss about it because it's on a different scale. Now I've touched a nerve.

STOUTE: What touched a nerve with you? What was the biggest creative risk you've ever taken?

EMINEM: Performing with Elton John at the Grammys.

STOUTE: The duet on "Stan"?

EMINEM: Yeah, that was probably the biggest risk. For that time, 2001/2002.

STOUTE: You were putting everything on the line, everything you'd built.

EMINEM: And him as well. He was taking a risk, too. You've got what people perceived as this homophobic rapper. And then you've got his audience and his fans and supporters and how they could have reacted—and some of mine could have been like "Yo, you're gonna go on the stage with this openly gay guy?" Now it wouldn't seem as crazy. But if you go back nine or ten years, it was.

STOUTE: Now that you mention it, hip-hop wasn't all inclusive culturally. I'm not sure that it embraced homosexuality. Maybe hop-hop culture is more open-minded now, but it wasn't ten years ago. But maybe that's because you took the risk to open up the conversation because everyone seemed to be more relaxed after the duet. I think you've been changing the mind of America from the start of your career. And on that note, I wonder what advice you would give to marketers today, going forward, in the way that they ought to be speaking to youth culture and maybe what they should be watching for as to where culture is going?

EMINEM: Well, let me start by saying, I'm not really big on business politics and saying the right things to corporate America. Some of the hip-hop influence in commercials is cool, especially when you sit back and you think how big rap has become—to the point that it's crazy how big it really is. But some of the content in commercials is corny. I watch SportsCenter and the NFL channel pretty much all day. And it sometimes irks me a little to see commercials that sound like they're written by old guys trying to be hip. But that's also the time that you can look back and appreciate how big rap has become. Some of the guys who are running the show and making the commercials probably don't even listen to rap because it's not their choice of music, but they've probably heard so many f-ing rap songs indirectly that they don't even realize how much it affects them.

STOUTE: Or how strong the influence is. But trying to sprinkle Ebonics in there or rap expressions isn't real.

EMINEM: It's not real, it's not authentic. It's culture swiping— taking from this and you don't know anything about it. Some of the marketing now is real and authentic, but I think the choices matter more—who you get to do the spot, what the spot is. You have to take it on a case-by-case basis.

STOUTE: Nuances matter now, more than ever, would you say? Anything else on this idea of tanning, of how hip-hop and artists like you helped get rid of the labels and the color lines? Anything else to add about where culture is headed next? Is there more to come for hip-hop and its influence?

EMINEM: When you just look at how big hip-hop has grown, it's almost to the point that you think, "This is it." But I remember back when I was getting started with Dre, even during the Marshall Mathers LP time, when I was getting to the height of everything and it was all moving so fast, I didn't think it could get any bigger. You look how big Jay-Z is and certain other artists are—ten years ago I didn't think it could get any bigger. Five years ago I was positive that it couldn't get any bigger. Five years later, here we are, and it's still getting bigger. You know, it just keeps growing. Like the f-ing Blob.

*

From Eminem to you, that's the power of tanning going forward, an evolving story and a hopeful one—of an economy and a cross-cultural, polyethnic world that keeps on growing like the f-ing Blob. I thanked him on behalf of the fans whose lives he has changed, and as the true artist, much more humble than you might have known or guessed, he thanked me and said, "That's dope."

ACKNOWLEDGMENTS

First, I'd like to thank Sophia—my beautiful daughter, the love of my life—for always inspiring Daddy to push further so you can be proud of him and all that he's accomplished. Every day I would wake up to write this book, and rewrite it again and again, in order to create the best legacy I could for our family to share forever. I'm grateful that I could put my heart into this book and onto these pages for you to have as a part of your life. I love you and I promise, no more excuses about how busy I am writing a book. I am so blessed to be your daddy.

Thank you to the dedicated team at Gotham Books for believing that I have a great story to tell. William Shinker, thank you for taking this leap of faith. Lauren Marino, thank you for your vision and guidance as our editor.

Mim Eichler Rivas, thank you for your patience and dedication in helping me shape my thoughts and put them to paper. Your understanding of who I am and my journey is truly why this book is a reality. Graydon Carter, throughout the years we'd see each other and you always extended yourself to me. You were always curious, and that curiosity soon developed into a friendship. The fact that twelve years later you would come forward and write the introduction to my book is just a testament to the growth and maturity of our relationship. Thank you to my agents at WME, Eric Lupfer and Jennifer Rudolph Walsh, for helping us cross the finish line in time, and to Keith Estabrook and your team for your keen insights on how to help the world understand tanning. Hanna Kim, thank you. You have endlessly been there, supporting every harebrained idea of mine. You have been the backbone of my organizations from the day you started.

Thank you to the handful of extraordinary individuals who have offered their ears, instincts, love, and friendship to me over the course of the past three years. Jay-Z, you've been a friend since our early days in the record business and never wavered despite the fact that I'm a little rough around the edges. You were there for me. You understood me and you watched me venture into the advertising business. You were one of the few people who believed in me early on and trusted me to work with you and the brand you were building as an artist. Fifteen years later you are still there for me, inspiring me with your work and providing love and support. This book pays tribute to all of the discussions we've had and the insights we've shared with each other—it captures all of that. This book is for the culture, let's keep pushing forward.

Jimmy Iovine—my mentor—the first person to show me patience, a teacher who found the time to explain the realities that exist in the world today. You've taught me so much. You took me through those critical years of twenty-eight, twenty-nine, thirty . . . guided me through all of the hurdles and pitfalls that appear when you think you already know it all. You've helped me become the man that I am today. With everything I do and accomplish in this lifetime, know that you have played an integral role in shaping that man. Thank you.

The Fark—Andrew Farkas—from the day we met in Sag Harbor, we've just been best friends. You've always been so understanding and a friend who taught me which obstacles to watch out for as I moved forward in life. Your advice has been very kind, very honest, and much appreciated. I know how much you want me to win. You and your beautiful family—Sandi, George, Arielle, and Nicole—have supported me through thick and thin. With this book, I know how proud you are that on the list of accomplishments we can now add "author." . . .

Will Smith, you had insight into the concept of tanning before anybody else did. You were on it and understood it so early on that people misunderstood your path. Your respect for your art and the innumerable things that you've selflessly done to help move our culture forward weren't acknowledged when they should have been. I've learned so much from watching you handle and work through those issues to become the most important actor and entrepreneur of our time and generation. Your work ethic and the path that you laid out before us is one of the guiding lights I have used throughout my career. I am thankful for your friendship and I will continue to keep learning from your journey.

Samuel Barnes, thank you for your friendship, your trust, and for believing in me to help manage your music career. All of the hits and time we worked together will never be forgotten. These memories are a key part of what inspired me to write this book. I remember always telling you that if we don't have another hit on the charts once a month, something is wrong. And you delivered every single time. Those are the moments I miss the most—the two of us, in the studio late at night, making . hit records. We were trying to make the industry take notice that we were doing something different, and together as a team, we were one of the best in music production. You've always been such a great friend to me, and you are a very big part of all that's transpired in my life to get me to where I am today.

To my friends who I have relied on to critique various drafts of this manuscript as we went through the dizzying stages of development, thank you. As a result of your input, *The Tanning of America* is exactly what I envisioned it would be. SLS, thanks for being there for me when I needed it the most, when gathering my thoughts to write this book needed support and clarity. Ms. Lauren Branche, thanks for keeping me focused and not letting the noise interfere with what matters most.

To the great men and women that I've interviewed during

the writing of *The Tanning of America*, thank you for your brilliance, personal anecdotes, and examples that helped enrich my narrative, and thank you for indulging my free-ranging curiosity: Russell Simmons, LL Cool J, Tommy Hilfiger, John Dempsey, Van Toffler, Ralph McDaniels, Hype Williams, Andre Harrell, Geoff Mayfield, Mitch Modell, Paul Fireman, Kim Brink, and Mike Bentley. Thank you also to those who took my phone calls just to answer a pressing question in the middle of your busy day: Lyor Cohen, Steve Berman, Darryl Cobbin, Kanye West, Sean Combs, Daymond John, and Adam Silver. Special thanks go to Fab Five Freddy for shedding light on so many turns in the tanning journey. We all owe you a debt of gratitude.

Over the years, several people I've quoted or noted in the text have been pivotal in my growth and learning with respect to my subject matter—some directly and others by inspiration and example. I'd like to express my profound (possibly belated) thanks to all of you: Tommy Mottola, Doug Morris, Bill Lamar, Pam El, Ashley Fox, Darren Orlando, Jacob Arabov, Noah Teppenberg, Don Thompson, James Lassiter, LeBron James, Maverick Carter, Larry Light, David Stern, Larry Bird, Allen Iverson, Rick Rubin, Cyndi Lauper, Beyoncé Knowles, Nas, Justin Timberlake, Bono, 50 Cent, Gwen Stefani, Eminem, Paul Rosenberg, Antonio Reid, Mariah Carey, Dr. Dre, Mark Eastmond, Sunika Sanchez, Chuck D, Ice Cube, Scarface, Timbaland, Pharrell Williams, and all the other great artists and executives who have inspired me, who believed in themselves and took their talents to an art form that was newly developing. Special thanks must also go to Roger Moore—yes, James Bond. And, of course, I must once more acknowledge Sir Sidney Poitier. You embody the power of tanning and the reality that through culture, we rise together as one. Thank you.

Many current and former clients have been extraordinarily gracious in their support of this book. That list includes the marketing teams at Reebok, GM, Estée Lauder Companies, McDonald's, Target, Hewlett-Packard, Wrigley, Tommy Hilfiger, Verizon, State Farm, Samsung, Crest, and Bing. Thank you also to the pioneers of advertising who have kept pace with tanning and been courageous enough to drop the old divisions based on color and ethnicity.

Early on, *The Tanning of America* was the beneficiary of Brett Pulley and Johnnie Roberts, who spearheaded research on my behalf—thank you. Thank you to the authors of *Can't Stop Won't Stop* (Jeff Chang), *Decoded* (Shawn Carter), and *The Big Payback* (Dan Charnas) for elevating the discussion about hip-hop culture to its rightful stature. Thanks to David Plouffe for *The Audacity to Win* and for sharing some of the iconic marketing strategies of Obama's historic 2008 presidential campaign; Larry Light and his groundbreaking writing on brand journalism; Florida State University's Spencer Overton for the analysis of the Florida vote in the 2000 election; and Christopher John Farley for the *Time* piece "Hip-Hop Nation: After 20 Years—How It's Changed America." While I didn't know it at the time, I think my book was born after I read your cover feature. I'm also grateful to the periodicals, Web sites, and blogs that cover pop culture in all respects.

There are a few different groups who truly make up my extended family. To Mary J. Blige, Madeline Nelson, and everyone at the Foundation for the Advancement of Women Now (FFAWN), I am thankful to partner with you on one of the most meaningful endeavors of my life. Mary, in such a short time I have watched the incredible unfolding of your dream to give women the means for self-empowerment and confidence whether through college scholarships, job training, or counseling. Wow! I want to also thank all of our supporters who have invested in the dream and been instrumental in giving it lift-off.

And to my other amazing partner, Lisa Price, and everyone at Carol's Daughter, I have to acknowledge all that you do to continually expand the vision of our brand while staying true to its original values. Thank you for passionately guarding the heritage while respectfully and laboriously catering to the needs of a diversity of skins that make up the tapestry of our world.

Thank you to the team at Translation, especially the guys who have been with me since day one: Charles Wright, John McBride, Lisa Musich, and Lauren Schwartz. It's been an incredible journey working with you professionals and watching us build this company brick-by-brick and client-by-client. To have this opportunity to share with the world the cultural journey I've been on and intersect that with what we've done as a team—putting our